Sufism in Britain

Also Available from Bloomsbury

South Asian Sufis: Devotion, Deviation, and Destiny, Clinton Bennett
HB: 9781441151278

Sufism, Mahdism and Nationalism: Limamou Laye and the Layennes of Senegal,
Douglas H. Thomas
HB: 9781441169075

Islam and the Veil, Theodore Gabriel and Rabiha Hannan
PB: 9781441135193
HB: 9781441187352

Sufism in Britain

Edited by

Ron Geaves

and

Theodore Gabriel

Bloomsbury Academic
An imprint of Bloomsbury Publishing Plc

B L O O M S B U R Y
LONDON • NEW DELHI • NEW YORK • SYDNEY

Bloomsbury Academic
An imprint of Bloomsbury Publishing Plc

50 Bedford Square
London
WC1B 3DP
UK

1385 Broadway
New York
NY 10018
USA

www.bloomsbury.com

BLOOMSBURY and the Diana logo are trademarks of Bloomsbury Publishing Plc

First published 2014
Paperback edition first published 2015

British Library Cataloguing-in-Publication Data
A catalogue record for this book is available from the British Library.

ISBN: HB: 978-1-44111-261-3
PB: 978-1-47423-760-4
ePUB: 978-1-44116-332-5
ePDF: 978-1-44111-487-7

Library of Congress Cataloging-in-Publication Data
Sufism in Britain/edited by Ron Geaves and Theodore Gabriel.
p. cm.
Includes bibliographical references and index.
ISBN 978-1-4411-1261-3 (hardback) – ISBN 978-1-4411-6332-5 (epub) –
ISBN 978-1-4411-1487-7 (epdf) 1. Sufi sm–Great Britain. I. Geaves, Ron.
II. Gabriel, Theodore P. C.
BP188.8.G7S84 2013
297.40941–dc23
2013029935

Typeset by Newgen Knowledge Works (P) Ltd., Chennai, India
Printed and bound by CPI Group (UK) Ltd, Croydon, CR0 4YY

Contents

Contributors

Dr. Theodore Gabriel (editor), graduated MLitt and PhD in Social Anthropology and Religious Studies at the University of Aberdeen, specializing in the Study of Islam, is Honorary Research Fellow in Theology and Religious Studies, Department of Humanities, University of Gloucestershire. His theses *Islam in Lakshadweep* and *Hindu-Muslim Relations in North Malabar* have been published. He lectured on Islam at the University of Gloucestershire from 1986 to 2000, and after retirement continues in the Department of Humanities at the university as a Honorary Research Fellow, and is also an Assistant Professor of Religious Studies at the Bader International Study Centre, Queen's University (Canada), Hailsham, England. His latest publication is *Islam and the Veil* (Continuum, 2010).

Professor Ron Geaves (editor) holds a Chair in the Comparative Study of Religion in the Theology and Religious Studies of Liverpool Hope University. His publications on contemporary Islam are numerous, in addition to student texts on the study of religion. In recent works, he has been arguing for the revival of Sufism globally (see 2007, 2008, 2009, 2009c). His most recent publications are Geaves, R. A., Markus Dressler, Gritt Klinkhammer (Eds) (2009) *Sufis in Western Society: Global Networking and Locality*, London: Routledge Sufi Series; (2010) *Islam Today*, London: Continuum and (2010) *Abdullah Quilliam: The Life and Times of a Victorian Muslim*, Leicester: Kube Press.

Dr. Sadek Hamid is a Lecturer in Islamic Studies, most recently at Liverpool Hope University, a Visiting Lecturer at the Cambridge Muslim College and former Programme Leader in Muslim Youth Work at Chester University. He is a leading researcher on issues related to British Muslim young people, co-editor of *Youth Work and Islam: A Leap of Faith for Young People* (Sense, 2011), editor of *British Muslim Youth: Rhetoric and Realities* (Ashgate, forthcoming, 2014) and author of a forthcoming book entitled *Sufis, Salafis & Islamists and the Evolution of British Islamic Activists*.

Mohammad Siddique Seddon completed his PhD in Religious Studies at Lancaster University and is Lecturer in Islamic and Religious Studies and Associate Director, Centre for Faiths and Public Policy, at the Department of

Theology and Religious Studies, University of Chester. In addition to teaching and supervising studies within the discipline, he has researched extensively on Islam and Muslim communities in Britain and has published and co-authored a number of related works, including *Muslim Youth: Challenges, Opportunities and Expectations* (2012) (with Fauzia Ahmad).

Dr. Simon Stjernholm is associated scholar at the Centre for Theology and Religious Studies, Lund University, Sweden. He defended his PhD in Islamology in 2011 at Lund University, where he is currently an associated scholar. The dissertation was entitled *Lovers of Muhammad: A Study of Naqshbandi-Haqqani Sufis in the Twenty-First Century*. Since then, he has been teaching Islamology and History of Religions at Lund University and Jönköping University. He has also been working on a study for the Swedish Media Council dealing with anti-democratic Islamist expressions on the Swedish-language web.

Dr. Sariya Cheruvallil-Contractor is a Postdoctoral fellow at the Centre for Society, Religion and Belief, University of Derby. She graduated with a BSc in Physics (University of Mumbai) and an MRes and PhD in the Sociology of Religion at the University of Gloucestershire specialising on Muslim women – their lives, feminisms and roles in pluralist British contexts. Her current work at the University of Derby focusses on two strands. First on religion and belief diversity, non-religious voices, equality and discrimination. The second strand of her research explores the formation of Muslim faith leaders in Britain and enhancing current provisions for this. She is the author of *Muslim Women in Britain: Demystifying the Muslimah* (Routledge, 2012). Her lastest publication is a co-written monograph entitled *Religion or Belief, Discrimination and Equality: Britain in Global Contexts,* published by Bloomsbury in October 2013.

Dr. Roy Jackson is Reader in Philosophy of Religion at the University of Gloucestershire. He has previously lectured in Philosophy and Religion at various universities, including Kent, Durham, and King's College London. He has a doctorate from the University of Kent and a PGCE from Roehampton University. He specialises in Philosophy of Religion, Nietzsche, and contemporary Islamic thought in relation to ethics, philosophy and politics and has written a number of books on Nietzsche, Plato, Philosophy of Religion, and Islam. More recently he has published *Fifty Key Figures in Islam* (Routledge, 2006), *Nietzsche and Islam* (Routledge 2007), *Mawdudi and Political Islam* (Routledge, 2010) and *The God of Philosophy: Second Edition* (Acumen, 2011). His latest book *What is Islamic Philosophy?* is to be published by Routledge in 2013.

Dr. Julianne Hazen is the Founding Director of the Sufi Studies Office, World Life Institute, in Medina, NY and an adjunct professor at Niagara University, Religious Studies Department, New York. She was a Visiting Scholar at Georgetown University with the Prince Alwaleed bin Talal Center for Muslim-Christian Understanding. She earned her PhD in Languages and Cultures of Near and Middle East from SOAS, University of London, specializing in Sufism in America.

M. Amer Morgahi is researcher at the Department of Social and Cultural Anthropology of VU University Amsterdam. Before this, he was a research fellow at the International Institute for the Study of Islam (ISIM), Leiden. His PhD thesis is on the comparative study of the Minhajul Quran movement in the Netherlands and the UK. Recently he published a chapter on the Minhajul Quran youth in the Netherlands in *Producing Islamic Knowledge: Transmission and Dissemination in Western Europe* by Martin Van Bruinessen and Stefano Allievi (Routledge, 2010).

Dr. Marta Dominguez Diaz is the Assistant Professor in Islamic Studies (Anthropology) at the School of Humanities and Social Sciences at the University of St Gallen, Switzerland. Marta holds an MA in Islamic Societies and Cultures and a PhD in Study of Religions (Anthropology of Islam) both from the School of Oriental and African Studies, University of London. Her work on Sufism mainly concentrates on exploring religious identities in the transnational Order Qādiriyya by looking at the ways in which religious discourses are corporeally endorsed by devotees of this Order. Her doctoral study proposed a comparative perspective between diverse Moroccan and Western European enclaves. Marta pursued post-doctoral research at the Centre for the Study of Muslim-Jewish Relations – Woolf Institute in Cambridge, comparing religious variations in attitudes towards death, dying and grief and the ways in which individuals and communities respond to death in Muslim and Jewish communities in Britain. She is currently continuing to explore her scholarly interest in contemporary Sufism and its transnational dimensions.

Dr. Yasin Dutton is Associate Professor in Arabic Studies in the School of Languages and Literatures, University of Cape Town. He gained his DPhil in Oriental Studies at the University of Oxford, specialising in early Islamic law. He taught Arabic language and the Qur'an in the Oriental Institute, Oxford (part-time, 1993–5), after which he lectured on Arabic and Islamic Studies at the University of Edinburgh (1995–2006). He is the author of *The Origins* *of Islamic Law: The Qur'an, the Muwatta' and Madinan 'Amal* (Curzon Press, 1999) and *Original Islam: Malik and the Madhhab of Madina* (Routledge, 2007), as well as several articles on early Islamic law, early Qur'anic manuscripts and the application of Islamic law in the modern world, particularly in relation to economic and environmental issues.

Dr Ian G. Williams teaches, supervises and researches in Islamic and Religious Studies at the Markfield Institute of Higher Education, Leicester / University of Gloucestershire, UK. Prior to this he has taught at the Universities of Chester, Derby and Birmingham City University. Ian's current research interests include the Fethullah Gülen Movement at doctoral level; Faith Sector education, and Sacred Spaces and Material Religion. A recent publication is: 'A Resort out of Radicalism in the World the Gülen Movement's Way of Resolution' in Sekiniz, A & Erol, M. Qasim, *The Gülen Movement in Contemporary Perspectives*, Vilnius Pedagogical University Press, 2010.

Introduction

Ron Geaves and Theodore Gabriel

This volume arises out of a renewed academic interest in contemporary Sufism, both in the Muslim world and in its formations in the West. In recent years, several collections have been published that complement completed PhDs on Sufi organizations in the West, journal articles and a handful of monographs (mostly published PhDs). Our authors have often been the source of these varied publications or contributed towards them. Thus they belong to a growing band of scholars who study contemporary Sufism and chart its trends and transformations. We constitute both practising Sufis able to reflect from within the movements and those that take a keen interest from a distance. Our work builds upon the monograph exploring Sufism in Britain published by Ron Geaves in 2000[1] and more recent works, for example, Hinnells and Malik (2006); van Bruinessen and Howell (2007); Dressler, Geaves and Klinkhammer (2009); Raudvere and Stenberg (2009).[2] The renewed interest in Sufism in the West resulted in a seminar held at the University of Gloucestershire on April 10, 2010, organized by Theodore Gabriel, entitled 'Sufism in Britain' as part of the Annual Islam Conferences held at the same venue. The editors are also indebted to the AHRC whose network funding provided the opportunity for a two-day conference entitled '*Sufis and Scholars*: The Development of *Sufism* in Britain' held at *Liverpool Hope University* on May 25 and 26, 2012. Out of these two events came the collaboration that gave birth to this volume.

In the last 50 years, Sufism in Britain has become extensively globalized as a result of mass migration and the ability of Muslim missionaries sympathetic to Sufism to engage in *dawa* (the call to Islam) activities by drawing upon international networks across the diaspora communities. Many *turuq* (Sufi movements) are both transcultural and transnational, transcending their origins in Pakistan, Bangladesh, Malaysia, Turkey, Iran, Yemen, North, West and East Africa, and it is claimed by them with some degree of persuasiveness that the Sufi brotherhoods and their supporters are enjoying a renaissance across the Muslim world and in the Muslim diasporas. However, it needs to be remembered that historically Sufis have been travellers, both in pursuit of new inspiration and in bringing Islam to new territories. Any globalization trends have to be perceived in the context of historical religious behaviour and as a continuation of the past. New developments may not so much be 'novel' but rather an opportunistic continuation of traditional religious life.

Sufism in Britain had been a significant force in counter-culture spirituality of the 1960s and 1970s, rivalling the interest in Indian religions. Those who travelled to rediscover spirituality away from traditional Christianity visited either India or North Africa. Some were to bring back Indian 'Guru' religions from India, but it was equally true that others were to be inspired by the Maghreb Sufi movements, especially the revival of the 'Alawi *tariqa*, led by shaykhs who had succeeded the Shaykh al 'Alawi who had opened his *zawiya* (Sufi lodge) in Mostaganem, Algeria. But perhaps surprisingly the 'Alawi *tariqa* was to have another significant impact on the organization of Muslim life in Britain as the number of Yemen, Somali and South Asian recruits into the British merchant fleet increased throughout the latter decades of the nineteenth century and into the middle of the twentieth century. Some of these sailors were to form dockland communities in Cardiff, Tyneside and Liverpool, politically, socially and religiously organized around the zawaya of the 'Alawi, organized through the efforts of the Yemeni Sufi, Shaykh al-Hakimi, who had received initiation directly at the hand of the Shaykh al-'Alawi.[3]

However, these early efforts to establish Islam in Britain through convert Sufis were to be submerged and lost to sight by the prolific numbers of migrant arrivals in England throughout the 1970s and the subsequent sheer numerical dominance of the South Asians in establishing a Muslim presence in Britain. Unbeknown to many, a new avenue for the construction of British Sufism had arrived transforming the inner city cultural map of England's old manufacturing cities. South Asian Islam has been dominated by Sufism since its inception in the subcontinent and many of new arrivals brought with them strong allegiances to the traditions of cultural/religious milieu of their places of origin including membership of *tariqa* (pl. *turuq*). Among the migrants, there were prominent Sufi shaykhs who began to establish Qur'an classes for children, mosques and *zawiya*, first in terraced houses, then in converted mills and finally by the 1980s purpose-built mosques of the South Asian Barelwi tradition.[4]

This presence was to be noted by Jørgen Nielsen (1992) and Pnina Werbner (1996).[5] Nielsen supplied the religious characteristics of the Barelwi movement, noting there were three that principally defined the movement, that is, the centrality of the Prophet, religious authority mediated through the descendants of the Prophet and the awliya (lit. friends of God), and a succession of popular holidays that arise out of the former two characteristics. Pnina Werbner provided the first glimpse of mawlid (the Prophet's birthday celebration) and how a Barelwi movement used public processions in the streets of Birmingham to carve out a religious space in Britain.

While the English converts inspired by the Maghreb Sufis continued their activities to generate interest in Islam among the indigenous youth of the counter-cultures in the 1970s, the first-generation South Asian Sufis operated beneath the radar of British society often in an environment of intense contestation with traditional South Asian reform movements that oppose traditional or popular Sufi beliefs and practices.[6] The Barelwi tradition, representing South Asian Sufis and its supporters, had brought with it powerful tensions between themselves and other branches of Islam located in the places of origin. Since the nineteenth century, these supporters of traditional Islam (TI) had rallied around Ahmed Reza Khan (1856–1921) to carve a common identity out of the *turuq* and the rural followers of a locality-based Islam in which the shrines of the deceased *awliya* (saints; Lit: friends of God) formed an alternative network of popular religion in alliance with more sharī`a-based Sufi movements supported by networks of sympathetic ulama. This forging of a common identity had become necessary to resist the Deobandi reformers in North India who defined themselves as a reform movement to protect a 'pure' or 'original' Islam in the context of the loss of Muslim power and the arrival of the British in India.[7] Deobandi religious reform of the Muslim communities took place with a consistent and successful critique of popular Islam and the more folk-based elements of Sufism.

In 2000, the ground-breaking text *Sufis of Britain* was published building upon the research undertaken between 1990 and 1994 when Geaves had explored aspects of the South Asian Barelwi tradition in the Midlands and West Yorkshire. He had been inspired by the work of Pnina Werbner and Jørgen Nielsen and attempted an in-depth exploration of British Sufism. In spite of some contact between the leaders of the South Asian *tariqas* and the convert Sufis, he argued that Sufism in Britain remained tightly bound up with ethnic identity, a means of maintaining traditions and customs tightly bound with localities in the place of origin that can be limited in boundary size to areas sometimes only as large as village shrine. This locality focus matched easily with the way that South Asian

Muslims were developing communities in many of Britain's manufacturing cities, with chain migration creating small areas of inner city housing that corresponded with *biraderi* (extended family) and village networks in the place of origin. Both Sylhet in Bangladesh and Azad Kashmir in Pakistan were strong regional centres for Sufi allegiance and also the main areas of migration into Britain. Sufi leaders originating from these locations formed strong centres of the tradition in respective inner city strongholds, dividing Britain into personal fiefdoms of loyalty and began to replicate familiar practices. Thus Sufism functioned not so much as a transmission of mysticism within Islam, able to cross over to a universal mysticism sought by some Western seekers, but as a boundary mechanism primarily concerned with the transmission of cultural and religious traditions.

In follow-up chapters, Geaves explored the transition of British South Asian Sufi identity from 'Barelwi' to 'Ahl as-Sunna wa Jama'at'[8] and touched upon the emergence of 'TI' as located in various prominent websites hosted by prominent British and North American converts, whose major influence had been the various offshoots of the Maghrebi Darqawi/Shadhili tariqas, most notably the 'Alawiya.[9] In these chapters, Geaves argued that throughout the late 1980 and 1990s, second-generation British Muslims sought a less boundary inhibited Islam, experimenting with Jamaat-i Islami, Ikhwan (Muslim Brotherhood) – influenced movements and Salafism. The Barelwis counter-attacked such movements as 'Wahhabi', a label used pejoratively in the milieu of South Asian contestation, but the label of 'Barelwi' itself rapidly grew to be an anachronism, unable to satisfy the youth's longing for authentic Islam. Regional labels were not able to compete with the internationalization of British Islam, as second-generation South Asian Muslims met with their peers from across the Muslim world and sought an Islamic identity freed from ethnicity.

Global forces resulting in population movements and technological narrowing of the world's geographical territoriality were not only contained within the religious and political world of the reform movements. Migrants arriving from other parts of the Muslim world, redefined the landscape of British Islam, and brought with them major *turuq* from across the Muslim world. Britain since the 1990s, as a result of these new diasporas, included several forms of Naqshbandiya, Qadiriya, Chishtiya, Alawiya, Tijaniya to name but a handful of those present. However, at that time Geaves argued that the new Sufis in Britain remained not so much adherents of new forms of Sufism but old Sufism repackaged. Yet the multinational character of British Sufism and the possibility of exchange and networking both with other British movements and also with Sufism globally would result in a transformation that would increasingly require an identity that encompassed the global range and answered the vocal critiques of opponents. South Asian Barelwis and others were to seek common identity and legitimacy under the highly contested label of Ahl as-Sunna wa Jama'at, claiming to be the authentic traditional practices of Muslims worldwide and back through history.

A number of factors were to contribute to the revival of Sufi-led Islam under the banner of Ahl-as Sunna wa-jamaat in Britain. Prominent among these is the common desire of the South Asian origin Barelwi Muslims to win the loyalty of their children in order to secure the future of their tradition. In order to achieve this, they realized that they had to match the efforts of the reform movements in the arena of education. Even more important is the need to counteract the criticisms made against traditional belief and practice and reclaim the position of Muslim orthodoxy based on the Qur'an and Sunna. To this end the efforts of erudite shaykhs such as Muhammad Hisham Kabbani and Muhammad Tahirul-Qadiri were essential.[10] In addition, the *turuq* were learning from their critics how to successfully use tracts, publications and, more recently, websites to promote their message. Ironically, the multinational and multiethnic nature of the British Muslim community is also serving to overcome the reformist critique of the Barelwis as Hindu-influenced superstition. Efforts by some *turuq*, especially the Haqqani Naqshbandis, to promote conferences that bring together traditional Muslims from many parts of the world had undermined the criticism that Sufi beliefs and practices result from contact with non-Muslims in the Indian subcontinent. Such conferences have enabled traditional Muslims with Sufi allegiance to perceive the unity of belief and practice that extends across the Muslim world in spite of minor regional differences. In Britain, the shaykhs are beginning to successfully argue that it is their *aqida* (belief and practice) which is the norm of Islam, and it is the Wahhabi/Salafi critique that is the aberration from traditional belief and practice.

Certainly by the 1990s, the signs were there that Sufism in Britain was beginning to go transglobal and escape the confines of ethnicity and locality. Ahmad Riza Khan had argued that the followers of TI should assert themselves to be Ahl-as Sunna wa-jamaat rather than Barelwis. This label had provided the possibility of claiming to be the legitimate form of Sunni Islam as practised by the vast majority of Muslims throughout the world rather than a sect or school of thought confined to the subcontinent. By claiming to be the true orthodoxy of Islam, the tables could be turned and the various reform movements could be accused of being a sectarian innovation bundled together in a polemic narrative as 'Wahhabi' or 'Salafi'. There remained huge hurdles to overcome before the

Ahl-as Sunna wa-jamaat could successfully compete with the reform movements' ability to organize themselves, promote their message and recruit from British-born Muslims. The reform movements focused on doctrine and the universal *umma* and the Sufi-based claim to be Ahl-as Sunna wa-jamaat needed to provide its own scriptural claim to legitimacy.

From Ahl as-Sunna wa Jama'at to Traditional Islam (TI)

The arrival of the World Wide Web was to provide another arena for Islamic contestation, one that escaped the confines of geographic territoriality and further broke down the borders of ethnic and convert Sufis. A number of prominent websites placed by significant North American and British convert Sufis began to challenge the hegemony of the Salafi scripturalist claim to be the authentic Islam, but this time the banner of Sufi counterattack was to be 'TI' rather than 'Ahl-as Sunna wa-jamaat'. Sadek Hamid's work seems to suggest that TI was transforming into a coherent movement able to bring together various strands of Sufi allegiance.[11] It would appear that the TI claim that Sufism's packaging as the legitimate and authentic voice of Islamic normative values was a transglobal phenomenon able to link Britain with Sufis throughout the world, and not only in South Asia. Yemen, Syria and Mauretania would become important locations for British Sufis seeking the authentic spiritual traditions of Islam.

The World Wide Web is an essential aspect of this globalization but the online presence of traditional Muslim *tasawwuf* does not advertise itself as Sufism but rather prefers to speak of itself as representing TI and the teachings of the four schools of law. The answers to online questions posed by enquirers provide erudite explanations based on classical *fiqh* but most of the websites are owned by educated young Western Muslim converts with an allegiance to 'TI' and Sufism and skilled in the traditional Islamic sciences.[12] The new label of 'TI' has advantages over *Ahl-as Sunna wa-jamaat* in that (i) the latter category is also claimed by the revivalist reform movements and leads to contestation over ownership; (ii) 'TI' offers the use of the English language to British Muslims less and less familiar with Arabic or Urdu terminology. The shift to TI completes the process of moving away from labels that can be accused of representing either a sectarian innovation or an ethnic corruption of the universal religious truths of Islam.

Epitomizing the rebranded Sufism are websites such as www.masud.co.uk and www.deenport.com, but Muslims who have an allegiance to Sufism are easily recognized with a discerning eye. They will emphasize *tawhid* (God's unity and uniqueness), *istikhlaf* (viceregence), *dhikr* (remembrance), *taqwa* (God-consciousness) and *rabbaniyah* (relationship with God) which form the core of Sunni Muslim spirituality but combine this with an elevated sense of the Prophet and his place in Muslim cosmology. Muhammad is perceived as more than the bringer of revelation and exemplar. The Prophet of Islam is regarded as the ultimate mystic and unique in creation, the first manifestation of God's light. In addition, they will look to a hierarchy of the dead and living *awliya* able to mediate between Allah and human beings.[13]

The websites originate in Spain, Britain and North America and address themselves specifically to Muslims in the West. There is an implicit but not explicit critique of Wahhabism and Salafism. For example, Imam Zaid Shakir, born in Berkeley, California states on his website 'it is our desire to see Muslims, especially here in the West, avoid the historical tendencies that have resulted in fragmentation and the loss of influence of our *Umma* by benefiting from our wealthy heritage'.[14] The site is advertised as 'able to present you with a wealth of information mined from classical sources of our enduring tradition'.[15] The key to interpreting the allegiance of the site lies in the acknowledgement of tradition as an oblique critique of the Wahhabis and Salafis who are often critical of *isnad* and *ijaza*, preferring direct interpretation of original sacred sources. Tradition refers to the four founders of the schools of law, Al-Ghazali and various other 'sober' Sufis acceptable to the wider Muslim world.

A common feature of the websites is the emphasis on *fiqh*. This 'fiqhization' echoes and competes with the scripturalist approach used so successfully by the Wahhabi and Salafi groups and manifests a more gentle but nonetheless equally conviction-orientated version of Islamicization that avoids politicization.[16] In other respects, the websites demonstrate a continuity with the earlier strategies adopted by the traditional *tariqas* and their supporters. The websites demonstrate common themes in Sufi polemical writing aimed towards traditional opponents but the articles also function as pedagogical material for young supporters of *tasawwuf* and recruitment devices for the uncommitted. The websites provide a means for the traditional supporters of Sufi-orientated Islam to narrow the gap on their rivals who have been previously able to more effectively mobilize in Britain and elsewhere in the Muslim diaspora spaces, but more significantly they demonstrate the international or global identity now attached to the supporters of such forms of Muslim tradition.[17] The online *shaykhs* are not guardians of tomb-shrines, successors to hereditary lineages descended from long-deceased *awliya*, first-generation *pirs* and *shaykhs* who have formed bastions of support around mosques built in various British cities and commandeered as territory, nor are they those that visit from places of origin to preach, collect funds and return home. Although commanding support of young British Muslims attracted to their teachings and seeking both tradition and spirituality, such support transcends regional or ethnic loyalties. Most of the online shaykhs are trained and educated in the Middle-East, especially Damascus and are unlikely to have connections with Pakistan, Bangladesh or the cultures of places from which the families of British Muslims originate.

The influential presence of the online shaykhs may well be part of an emergence of a transglobal Sufism that will differ from historic precedents in that it will not be *tariqa*-dominated around the influence of one significant charismatic figure but rather will find *tariqa* and *shaykh/murid* relations sublimated to serve the cause of 'TI'.[18]

Aftab Malik argues, in his popular text *The Broken Chain*, that the term 'TI is elastic in its usage:

> . . . means different things to different people depending on the context. The usage implied throughout the book is the legacy of the juristic, theological and spiritual interpretive communities that form around the third century and continues to develop and be codified onto tenth century *hijri*. These interpretive communities developed a particular set of paradigms, symbolism, and linguistic specificity that constitute what we now call, orthodoxy, 'mainstream' Islam, otherwise known as the Ahl al-Sunna wa al-Jama'a. Characteristically of all traditionalist scholars is the *isnad* that links him or her with scholars of a prior generation and so on until this chain links back to the time of the Salaf and ultimately to the Prophet of mercy himself. (2002: 8)[19]

Sufism appears to be enjoying new popularity among the Muslim communities in Britain where it was already a significant part of the South Asian presence in the country. Both young South Asian origin seekers of authentic Islamic experience and the Western converts to Islam are able to come together to forge a powerful narrative under the banner of 'TI' and the centres of British forms of Sufism appear to be moving away from South Asian-centred manifestations to seek knowledge in Syria, Yemen, Egypt and even Mauretania. This new emergence results from a combination of conscious strategies of already existent Sufi groups to regroup against radical reform movements in the struggle to maintain the loyalty of the younger generations and the realization among the leaders of Sufi movements that they can use the government's search for allies in the war against religious extremism to reposition themselves as the historic voice of moderate Islam. However, it should be noted that adherents of 'TI' claim that it is not only in the West that Sufism is enjoying a renaissance but that the revival of Islam across the Muslim world does not only relate to Islamist radical movements but has also witnessed a regeneration of TI which includes the devotional piety of Sufism.

In attempting to present an overview of transformations in British Sufism, it is also necessary to examine a number of theoretical positions taken up by the small band of scholars of Sufism in this country, in so far, as they provide us with an understanding of the growth and development of the tradition. Significant among these would be Geaves' categorization of Sufism in relation to ethnicity (2000); Werbner's thesis of growth and decline, 'waxing and waning' that provides a variation of the classical Weberian notions of charisma and institutionalization; contested notion of 'popular Islam' and orthodoxy; the relationship between local and global; theories of Islam and modernity.[20]

Perhaps, most significantly, it is hoped that the volume will challenge notions of Sufi decline under the dual onslaught of modernist and Islamist critique. Carl Ernst had noted that the Sufi *turuq* have been criticized by both Muslim modernists and the nineteenth-century revivalist movements, and this criticism has been continued by the various movements usually defined as 'fundamentalist' in the twentieth century. He states that Sufism is perceived by them as an 'enemy of Islam only slightly less threatening than Western secularism'[21] in spite of the fact that these revivalist movements and their sympathisers consist of only around 20 per cent of any given Muslim population.[22] Even when Trimmingham wrote back in 1971, he argued that the Sufi *turuq* were in decline and danger of disappearing altogether under the dual threat of modernization and the Wahhabi/Salafi critique heavily supported by propaganda materials funded by the superior wealth of the Saudi regime. In particular, he shared the concerns of the *turuq* that they would lose the loyalty of their secular educated children.[23] However, this does not appear to have materialized as during the decades of the 1980s and the 1990s, the *turuq* have revived themselves as they have begun to fight back against the Wahhabi/Salafi critique and the twenty-first-century dawns with battle lines drawn up between these two conflicting groups within the world of Sunni Islam.

Joffe argues that this rigid separation of the two traditions into competing and antagonistic movements is something new. He suggests that in the past, the competing beliefs were defended by individual scholars such as Ibn Taimiyya, but there was 'an integrated and graduated spectrum of belief between the two extremes of religious practice'.[24] Joffe agrees with Gellner's distinction between rural Muslims, whose Islam relies on a multiplicity of ritual and mystical practices and devotion to charismatic personalities, and urban Muslims, who stress strict monotheism, Puritanism and scriptural revelation[25] and argues that the increasing divide between rural and urban Muslims is helping to create ideological differences drawn along class lines where middle-class professionals and educated elites are more likely to be attracted towards the reform movements. Increasingly, Muslims loyal to the *turuq* have become concerned that the combination of urban environments, Western education and the secular ethos will provide the conditions in which they will lose their children either to the attractions of the pursuit of material pleasures or to recruitment by the better organized reform movements.

The editors and contributors to this volume hope that in exploring various manifestations of Sufism in Britain they will have something to say about these various theorizations of Sufism and its place in the Islamic spectrum of belief and practice. Most significantly we hope to say something not only about Sufism in Britain but also its place in an increasingly globalized religious terrain in which legitimacy and authenticity are highly contested in increasingly public domains.

In this collection of chapters on Sufism in Britain, we have commenced our volume with one that appears to be an anomaly. It draws upon Theodore Gabriel's research on Sufis of the Lakshadweep Islands in the Indian Ocean. The purpose of this chapter is to reveal something of how Sufism appears in a relatively isolated and traditional environment and to provide a contrast with Sufism in Britain, with its interconnectedness caused through international travel and global communication systems. The chapter provides some insights into the classic theorization of Sufis as ideal type mystics and shows how, in practice, Sufi missionaries were able to integrate classic Islamic spirituality with local cultures. A comparison is made between Lakshadweep Sufism's compromises with Hindu-based caste and family networks and the typical South Asian Sufi networks in Britain drawing upon Geaves' (2000) analysis of Sufism and ethnicity.[26] The intention is to raise questions concerning the uniqueness or commonality of British Sufism and to provide a comparison that can make readers consider whether the British scene provides us with a British Sufism or merely the transplantation of Sufis into Britain. A third possibility is the blending of both into a unique form that is still developing and finding its identity as part of the Muslim presence in this country.

Chapter 2 continues with an in-depth analysis of transformations and trends within British Sufism, exploring the presence of Sufism in Britain from the nineteenth century to the far more complex multinational and transglobal community of the twenty-first century. Ron Geaves attempts to place Sufism in Britain within the context of various theorizations of Sufism and ask the question whether Sufism can be considered to be reviving and, if so, what are the causes of the revival.

Chapters 3–5 provide important historical case studies of the Sufi presence in Britain. Chapter 3 attempts to find out the relationship between Sufism as universal mysticism and Islam. Drawing upon personal encounters, Roy Jackson takes the reader into the various offshoots of the Sufi Movement founded by the Indian musician and Sufi, Hazrat Inayat Khan in the early twentieth century. With fascinating insights the chapter explores how cultured middle class members of British society embraced Sufism and appropriated it from Islam to form a syncretic blend of mysticism promoted as a perennialist common origin of all religion. However, in Chapter 4, the reader is made to realize that even while this was taking place, more conventional Islamic forms of Sufism were entering Britain. Muhammad Seddon explores the significance of the Yemeni Shaykh al-Hakimi and his attempts to organize the Lascars of Yemeni origin and their British wives and children into coherent communities in various English and Welsh seaports based around the teachings and practices of the 'Alawiya *tariqa*. His insights show us how these first efforts to organize a Muslim migrant community extended into the British cities of Manchester and Birmingham as a second wave of Yemenis entered Britain after WWII. In Chapter 5, Yasin Dutton provides us with a profile of the influential convert to Islam, Ian Dallas, who also through the inspiration of the 'Alawiya and other Maghrebi *turuq,* went onto become the internationally renowned Shaykh 'Abdulqadir as-Sufi, inspiring a number of British counterculture converts in the 1960s and 1970s to establish a community in Norwich, and to promote Sufism worldwide in South America, South Africa and Spain. The influence of the Norwich community remains relatively unexplored but was an important ingredient in the transition of British Sufism away from both perennialism among converts and ethnic loyalties among South Asian Barelwis to the transglobal versions of TI it claims to be today. In the profile of Shaykh 'Abdulqadir as-Sufi, we see the contours of Islamic conservatism and tradition taking shape in an influential individual.

In the following chapters, there are a number of case studies that focus on individual tariqa that demonstrate some of the variety of the British Sufi scene. Marta Dominguez Diaz and Julianne Hazen present two lesser known presences that have been able to attract converts as well as various other Muslim constituencies. Chapter 6 explores the British Budshishiyya, originating in

Morocco, Marta Dominguez Diaz examines the history of the *tariqa* and shows how the various constituencies among Berber tribesmen, middle-class urban North Africans, migrant and convert communities in Mediterranean Europe compare with the South Asian youth that have been attracted to the *tariqa* in Britain. She argues that contrary to a generally taken view that when religions turn global they develop 'universal' identities, the Budhishiyya develops and encourages distinct patterns of development in local milieu. In Chapter 7, Julianne Hazen sensitively explores her own convert experience to the Alami *tariqa*, originating in the Balkans, through interviews with other British converts to Sufism. She attempts to categorize conversion in the *tariqa* and allied shaykhs, adding to our knowledge of conversion processes to Islam and the role of Sufism in this process.

Chapter 8 gives a very different view of conversion and reversion processes in the midst of growing up as a young British Muslim with the challenges of secularization, consumerism, Islamicization, Islamic contestation, all embedded in the processes of growing up in contemporary urban Britain. Sariya Cheruvallil-Contractor explores through a number of case studies how young British Muslims explore issues close to their intimate lives within a framework of asking ancient 'truth' questions pertinent to the spiritual life of Muslim personhood. Through the exploration of one Sufi-orientated website, she demonstrates how young British Muslims use virtual space as a safe haven to address difficult questions that may be deemed 'dangerous in real locations'.

In the final four chapters, the collection presents case studies of some influential players on the British Muslim scene that demonstrate the changes that are emerging within the Sufi context. In Chapter 9, Sadek Hamid provides an in-depth exploration of 'TI' showing its birth and emergence on the global and British terrains. The chapter reveals the key players and the main identifiers of TI and shows how it builds upon previous attempts to create a unified space for Sufism as authentic Islam. Chapter 10–12 give insights into particular *tariqa* or global Sufi-influenced movements that reformulate Sufism within the context of both modernity and contestation over what constitutes orthodoxy in Islam. Simon Stjernholm explores the well-known Naqshbandi Haqqani *tariqa* in order to provide a typology of Sufism, within the context of transnational flows of people and information and the politics of identity formation. The Naqshbandi Haqqani have been key players in promoting a Sufi brand as 'TI' in opposition to Wahhabi and Salafi trends. However, the author agrees with Marta Dominguez Diaz that transglobal *turuq* manifest differently in different places, showing diversity even within one location, that is the Naqshbandi Haqqani centre in North London.

Chapters 11 and 12 focus on two international movements that have modified the traditional Sufi focus on *shaykh/murid* relations within a traditional *tariqa* formation. Amer Morgahi explores the rise of Minajul Quran and their founder Shaykh Tahirul Qadri. The chapter notes the challenges of repositioning the traditional Barelwi formations to fit a world in which Islamic movements strive for legitimacy and authenticity where the old paradigms of structural organization and *shaykh/murid* relations may not fit or meet the challenges. However, old traditions die hard and the author shows how ritual can be redefined to provide authenticity to new structures. In our final chapter, Ian Williams examines the rise of the Fethullah Gülen movement, originating in Turkey. Although formed in the unique environment of Turkish secularism and Islamism, attitudes to Sufism and traditional Islamic identity, has forged these into a unique reformulation of Sufism drawing upon tradition, modernity, exegesis of Islamic sacred texts to provide a European model of Sufi-orientated Islam that may fit well in the British context as ethnicity becomes less of a factor in the identity of British Muslims.

It should be remembered that Sufism was the brand of Islam successful in propagating Islam in the non-Arab world. With its flexibility, tolerance and readiness to absorb cultural elements from non-Islamic contexts Sufism was able to make Islam acceptable, and eventually as in the case of large tracts of the Indian Subcontinent and South East Asia make Islam the dominant faith. The more Arab-orientated and literalist, legalist and strict form of Islam now advocated by Salafist movements originating in the Middle East could not have made such rapid progress in non-Arabian milieus of the world. Perhaps in the West also eventually Sufism may be the form of Islam, *mutatis mutandis*, likely to make headway. This volume has examined and presented the various ways in which Sufism has countered opposing movements and adapted and even transformed to suit local conditions. This has always been the strength of Sufism. It can transcend regional and cultural barriers and allegations of lax orthodoxy and orthopraxy to achieve success and strength.

All in all, we hope that the dynamism, fluidity, and diversity of the British Sufi scene will be revealed to the reader, demonstrating both the significance of the Sufi option for expressing contemporary spirituality within a traditional format and the complexity of Sufi responses to the highly charged world of Islamic diversity.

Notes

1   R. Geaves (2000) *Sufis of Britain: An Exploration of Muslim Identity*. Cardiff: Cardiff Academic Press.

2   J. Malik and J. R. Hinnells (Eds) (2006) *Sufism in the West*. New York: Routledge; M. van Bruinessen and J. Day Howell (Eds) (2007) *Sufism and the 'Modern' in Islam*. London: IB Tauris; M. Dressler, R. Geaves and G. Klinkhammer (Eds) (2009) *Sufis in Western Society: Global Networking and Locality*. London: Routledge; C. Raudvere and L. Stenberg (Eds) (2009) *Sufism Today: Heritage and Tradition in the Global Community*. London: IB Tauris.

3   See Seddon in this work and F. Halliday (1992) *Arabs in Exile: Yemeni Migrants in Urban Britain*. London: IB Tauris.

4   For a detailed examination of this process see R. Geaves (1996) 'Cult, Charisma, Community: The Arrival of Sufi Pirs and Their Impact on Muslims in Britain', *Journal for the Institute of Muslim Minority Affairs, Institute of Muslim Minority Affairs*, 16, 2, Saudi Arabia, pp. 169–92.

5   J. S. Nielsen (1992 1st edition) *Muslims in Western Europe. New Edinburgh Islamic Surveys*. Edinburgh: Edinburgh University Press; and Werbner (1994) 'Stamping the Earth with the Name of Allah: Zikr and the Sacralising of Space among British Muslims', *Cultural Anthropology*, 11,3, pp. 309–338.

6   See A. Shaw (2000) *Kinship and Continuity: Pakistani Families in Britain*. London: Routledge.

7   See R. Geaves (2005) 'Tradition, Innovation, and Authentication: Replicating the Ahl-as Sunna Wa Jamaat in Britain', *Journal of Comparative Islamic Studies*, 1, 1, pp. 1–20.

8   R. Geaves (2009) 'A Case of Cultural Binary Fission or Transglobal Sufism? The Transmigration of Sufism to Britain' in R. A. Geaves, M. Dressler, Gritt Klinkhammer (Eds) (2007) *Global Networking and Locality: Sufis in Western Society*. London: Routledge.

9   Sadek Hamid in this volume and R. A. Geaves (2006) 'Learning the Lessons from the Neo-revivalist and Wahhabi Movements: The Counterattack of New Sufi Movements in the UK' in *Sufism in the West*. Jamal Malik and John Hinnells (Eds). London: Routledge.

10   See Simon Stjernholm and Amer Morgahi in this volume also Geaves (2006).

11   See Sadek Hamid's contribution in this volume.

12   See Sariya Sariya Cheruvallil-Contractor and Ian Draper in this volume and Ron Geaves, Op. cit., (2009).

13   Geaves, op. cit., 2009: 108.

14   Ibid., p. 108.

15   Ibid., p. 108.

16 Ibid., p. 109.

17 R. A. Geaves (2012) 'The Transformation and Development of South Asian Sufis in Britain' in *South Asian Sufis: Devotion, Deviation and Destiny*. Clinton Bennett and Charles Ramsey (Eds). London: Continuum, pp. 188–9.

18 Ibid., p. 190.

19 A. Malik (2002) *The Broken Chain: Reflections on the Neglect of Tradition*. Amal Press, p. 8.

20 V. John (2007) 'Contemporary Sufism and Current Social Theory' in *Sufism and the Modern in Islam*, M. van Bruinessen and J. D. Howell (Eds). London: IB Tauris, pp. 281–98.

21 C. Ernst (1997) *Sufism: An Essential Introduction to the Philosophy and Practice of the Mystical Tradition of Islam*. Boston: Shambhala, p. 200.

22 p. 212.

23 J. S. Trimmingham (1971) *The Sufi Orders of Islam*. Oxford: Oxford University Press.

24 J. George (1998) 'Maghribi Islam and Islam in the Maghrib: the Eternal Dichotomy' in *African Islam and Islam in Africa*, D. Westerlund and E. Rosnander (Eds). London: Hurst & Co., p. 56.

25 E. Gellner (1968) 'The Pendulum Swing Theory of Islam' in *Sociology of Religion*, R. Robertson (Ed.). Harmondsworth: Penguin, pp. 130–6.

26 See Geaves (2000).

Part One

Theory

1

Expressions of Spirituality in Islam: Unity and Diversity in Sufi Thought and Practice

Theodore Gabriel and Ron Geaves

This chapter is not specific to Sufism in Britain and lays out some remarks and analysis of Sufism in general. It provides a historical and theoretical background to the more specific studies in subsequent sections. It also draws upon some examples from Sufi practice in the Lakshadweep Islands of India and the nearby region of Kerala and makes some comparisons with Sufism in Britain. The intention is to illustrate the diversity of Sufi practice and even syncretism with other religions and illuminate issues of orthodoxy and heterodoxy in Islam. Although the commencing sections provide the reader with examples of Sufis that support the ideal-type classification of Sufism as 'Islamic mysticism', the later section shows that Islamic Sufism is able to develop practices that can creatively absorb local cultures and fuse them into a seamless Muslim holistic environment in which religion and culture combine. In the Lakshadweep Islands, Theodore Gabriel has shown the complex interweaving of Sufi practices and pre-existing caste and extended family networks.[1] Ron Geaves compares this with his own studies undertaken in 2000 that reveal the complex association of Sufi loyalty with ethnic identities of South Asian origin Muslims in Britain.[2] The chapter ends with an attempt to categorize Sufi loyalties through showing how allegiance is constructed through circles of belonging around the shaykh.[3]

The origins of Sufism

There has been much speculation about the origins of Sufism, including those by Western scholars who have looked outside Islam to the influence of other religions and cultures on the expanding Arab empire in the early centuries of Islam.[4] Others have sought for a glimpse of an eternal essence of religion found in a primordial mystical experience of union with God.[5] It is possible to speculate that the initial preoccupation of Islam might have been with the law. As a fledgling community in Medina, regulations and details of rituals were important to sustain and create an orderly basis for the new religion and a fledgling but growing community of believers. Later on, in the early centuries, the creation and expansion of empire, the concern for law to bind the various parts into a whole, might have led to the ulama becoming more pedantic, and there was the ever-present danger of the religion becoming a dry legalistic and ritualistic affair losing the early fervour of the first generations of Muslims.

But Sufis are inclined to believe that even in the earliest stages of Islam concern for spiritual development or *tasawwuf* (lit. purification) existed in parallel with other concerns. The Prophet himself was a highly spiritual person as evinced by his meditation in Mount Hira and elsewhere, his visions and the mystical journey of the Miraj and his love for God. The Prophet did not advocate celibacy or asceticism but nevertheless sought to find ways of spiritual expression. The Qur'an contains a current which stressed the need for mystical inspiration, elevation and encounter with God, and which sought to oppose the lapsing of Islam into blind obedience or political advantage. The Hadith demonstrate the wisdom, compassion and intimacy of the Prophet with the divine Being. There is also mention in the Hadith of a group of Muslims whom the Prophet permitted to gather on the front of the entrance to his home and who were called the people of the porch (*ahl al suffa*), a label to which some attribute the origins of the term Sufism. The Qur'an also refers to them and approves of and recommends their God-centeredness and detachment from the opulence and concerns of the world. The passage states

> And keep yourself patient [by being] with those who call upon their Lord in the morning and the evening, seeking His countenance. And let not your eyes pass beyond them, desiring adornments of the worldly life, and do not obey one whose heart We have made heedless of Our remembrance and who follows his desire and whose affair is ever [in] neglect.[6]

Thus we see that even though generally it is believed that the relationship of the human to God is one of *Ibadah* (servanthood), the Qur'an is not without indications that a closer and more intimate relationship is possible. The preamble to every surah *Bismillahi al Rahman al Rahim* (In the name of God, merciful and compassionate) indicates the love of God for the human being and the verse

Sura 15:16 declared that God is closer to you than the vein in your neck and hears the innermost whisperings of your heart (*Wa hua aqrabu ilaykum min habl al-wareed*). Also the Qur'an states, 'He is with you wherever you are' (*Wa hua ma..akum ayna ma kuntum*).

These verses speak of at least a God who is in close proximity to human affairs, if not actually immanent in the person, and definitely not a God who is wholly transcendent. This has led the Islamic scholar R. A. Nicholson to declare Sufism as:

> The transformation of the One transcendent God of Islam into
>
> One real Being who dwells and works everywhere, and whose throne
>
> is not less, but more, in the human heart than in the heavens of heaven.[7]

Indeed the life of a Sufi is one that seeks to be God-permeated. Everything is done in the name of God. Dhikr, the remembrance of God, is the central feature of life and activities should be carried out maintaining God-consciousness. The name of God is constantly on their lips – whether the *takbir*, or the words *inshallah, al andulilah, Mashallah, Bismillah*.[8] A life absorbed in adoration of God is the purpose of the Sufi quest and *adab* is the essential hallmark of a Sufi. The ultimate objective of the Sufi is intimacy with God, even a mystical union in which the veil is lifted between God and His creation.

The paths for *Tasawwuf* can be diverse. In Islam, the individual expressions of spirituality on the path to purification can take many forms. A striking example is Rabia al Adawiyya (d. 801). Born in Basra in Iraq she is noted for her altruistic love of God. Wholly devoted to her Lord, she spurned offers of marriage even though the social pressures for a woman to marry in Muslim cultures is very high. She is claimed to have said

> The contract of marriage is for those who have a phenomenal existence.
>
> Here in my case existence has ceased and I have passed out of self.
>
> My existence is in Him and I am wholly His. The marriage contract must be asked for from Him, not from me.[9]

Rabi'a is regarded as someone whose love for God was not born out of fear of hell or desire for heavenly joys. In a famous incident, she was seen carrying a torch in one hand and a bucket of water in the other. When asked about her strange behaviour she is said to have, remarked 'I wish to set fire to heaven and douse the fires of hell!' Rabi'a is believed to have followed her life of poverty and self-denial meticulously to the end.

Rabi'a seems to be self-confident and even assertive in her behaviour. This contrasts with the story of Jahanara (1614–81), a well-known female mystic of India. She was the daughter of the Mughal emperor Shah Jehan (1592–1666), and she desired to live the life of a Sufi, hard to achieve in those times for any woman, especially for a princess living in opulence. She was willing to give up all her luxuries and study under the famous teacher Mullah Shah. Her several missives to the Sufi teacher were not answered until finally, impressed by her determination and perseverance, Mullah Shah consented to accept her as a novice. Under the direction of her famous brother Dara Shikoh (1615–59), she was initiated into reciting the dhikr according to the formulae of the Quadiriyya and of the Order of Mullah Shah. Returning to the palace *masjid* she prayed and meditated where upon she is said to have had a vision of the Prophet and the awliya. Under the direction of Mullah Shah Jahanara became a true mystic and gained the admiration of her famous teacher to the extent he acknowledged that she could act as his deputy.[10]

In complete contrast to what we have heard of Rabia al Adawiyya, one of the earliest phases of Sufism was characterized by despondency and fear. The emphasis for these ascetics was on the wickedness of the world and God's judgement and punishment. A notable exponent of this school was Hasan al Basri (d. 728). He was the teacher of Wasl ibn Atta, founder of the Mutazilite school.[11] He is reported to have said

> God has created nothing more hateful to him than this world, and from the day he created it he has not looked on it; so much he hates it.[12]

Hasan al-Basri would claim that fear of God is the basis of morality, and sadness the characteristic of religion as life is only a pilgrimage on route to the Hereafter, and physical comfort must be denied to subdue the passions. Al Fudayl (d. 187 AH) was another of these sad and fearful Sufis. He is said to have smiled only once, that is when his son died: He is said to have remarked 'When God loves his servant He afflicts him and when He loves him very much He takes hold of him and leaves him neither family nor wealth'.[13] Also, 'When God loves a servant He increases his pain, and when He hates a servant He makes this world wide for him'.[14] Fudayl also said, 'If the whole of this world were spread before me and I was not accountable for what I did with it, I would still shun it, just as one of you shuns the gutter when you pass by it, lest it soil your clothes'.[15] Such was Fudayl's condition that Ibn al-Mubarak remarked, 'When Fudayl bin Iyad died, sadness passed out of this world'.[16] It is likely that these ascetic Sufis with their emphasis on fear and sadness arose out of the conditions of the Umayyad dynasty (661–750 CE) when some pious Muslims feared that the true Islam of the Prophet and his companions had been lost to the luxuries of Empire. In trepidation for their afterlife in the face of corruption, they left the cities of the Empire and retired back to Medina, the city of the Prophet, to protect their piety in ascetic mode.

Sobriety and intoxication

In addition to the distinction between the fearful ascetics and the proponents of divine love, scholars have also divided Sufis between those who are deemed to be sober and those who were considered to be intoxicated. The dichotomy does not refer to drunkenness but to their inner state. Those known as the sober mystics were very restrained and reflective in their practices. They insisted on the need for mental introspection – to know the self and to thoroughly examine motives in order to guard oneself from error. These sober Sufis were, on the whole, more inclined to stay within the confines of the shari'a than those intoxicated on ecstatic union. A prominent example is al Junayd (d. 910 CE). Al Junayd talked of the original unity of humanity, a belief based on Qur'an 7:172:

> And (remember) when thy Lord brought forth from the Children of Adam, from their loins, their seed, and made them testify of themselves, (saying): Am I not your Lord ? They said: Yea, verily. We testify. (That was) lest ye should say at the Day of Resurrection: Lo! Of this we were unaware.

This speaks of the submission of the whole of humanity to God, while in the loins of Adam. Al Junayd wished to regain this primordial unity and harmony, so he analysed the ecstatic experiences of devotion to God, and sought to avoid the dangers of the theories which assert either that there is only one God and all creation is one with him (monism) or that there is God in every object (pantheism) that had attracted other Sufis.

Al Junayd emphasized renunciation and *fana* – extinction as the ultimate objective. He said,

> To relinquish natural desires, to wipe out human attributes, to discard selfish motives, to cultivate spiritual qualities, to devote oneself to true knowledge, to do what is best in the context of eternity, to wish good for the entire community, to be truly faithful to God, and to follow the Prophet in the matters of the Shari'a.[17]

He suggested that the key is (1) the passing away from one's attributes through the effort of constantly opposing one's ego-self (*nafs*); (2) passing away from one's sense of accomplishment, that is, passing away from 'one's share of the sweet deserts and pleasures of obedience'; and (3) passing away from the vision of the reality 'of your ecstasies as the sign of the real overpowers you'. All these stages help one to achieve fana.[18]

In contrast, other Sufis have been labelled as the 'intoxicated' school of Sufism when they displayed highly ecstatic states when meditating on God and praising him. They are perceived to abandon themselves wildly and without restraint to the expressions of their adoration of the Divine. The Mevlevi *tariqa* originating in Turkey is seen as an instance of these charismatic Sufis. This order derives its name from the title of Mevlana/Maulana given to Jalal al din al Rumi (1207–73) who founded the order. His transition from the sober path to 'intoxication' came about from his association with Shams al Din of Tabriz (1185–1248) who impressed upon Rumi the need to abandon himself to God and throw his scholarly output into a river. These more exuberant Sufis were prone to identifying themselves with God in their experience of Unity. Well known is Mansur al Hallaj's (858–922) statement *ana al haqq* (I am the Truth) which may have cost him his life. Abu Yazid Bastami of Iran (d. 874 CE) also appears to have such an identification when he uttered, 'Glory be to me how great is my Majesty!'[19] or 'I sloughed off myself as a serpent sloughs off its skin, then I considered my essence and behold I was He'.[20]

It may be down to Bastami that 'intoxication' became associated with such ecstasy as he used the term *wajd* (drunkenness) to describe his state. Equating himself to God or even greater than God, he is supposed to have stated 'Thy obedience to me is greater than my obedience to Thee'. This invited criticism from the orthodox and even other Sufis.[21] However, Bastami may only have been describing the final stage of Sufi intimacy in which a level of closeness is achieved in the degree to which Allah serves his beloved, pouring down divine benevolence on a life sublimated and harmonized with the Divine Will. Rumi also challenged orthodox doctrine and ritual practice in one of the many stories told in his masterpiece, the *Mathnawi*, known as the Persian Qur'an. In the tale, a pilgrim meets with a Sufi on his way to the Hajj. The Sufi asks the pilgrim how much he had saved to afford the journey to Makkah. On being revealed the cost of the pilgrimage, the Sufi replies that it would have been more beneficial to give the money to him and circumambulate his person seven times.[22]

It is evident that such narratives of immanence would offend those whose view of Allah was rooted in transcendence and the primary relationship of divine law as the bond between man and God. Immanence ultimately poses questions of religious authority and undermines the authority of the *ulama* whose link to both the populace and the rulers was based on their control of the shari'a. Sufis were able to command the loyalty of the people based upon their charismatic authority rooted in an inner direct experience. On the other hand, even the ulama had to acknowledge the deep commitment of the Sufis and their piety. Indeed not all Sufis were so arbitrary in their obedience to the outer forms of Islam and many would live traditional Islamic lives. The Sufi's claim to experience of divine oneness would divide the orthodox.

Shuhud and Wujud

One final dichotomy needs to be explored before we proceed to look at some examples of contemporary Sufi experience. The examples given above of mystical experiences would raise the question of the authenticity of claims to be one with God. The conservatives among the ulama were caught in the horns of a dilemma. On the one hand, the Sufi claims to intimacy and unity would seem to contradict the nature of the revelation and the need for outward compliance to Islam's divinely revealed law. Yet there could be no denial of the piety manifested by the exponents of mysticism. In India most Sufis would accept the doctrine of Unity of Being (Wajdat al-Wujud) as propounded by Ibn al-Arabi (d. 1240) in which there is no being other than God's and mystical unity is the awareness of that condition. Others were more cautious of such intimacy and advocated that those who proclaimed mystical union were in a condition of Wahdat al-Shuhud (unity of perception or appearance). For example, Ahmed Sirhindi (1564–1624) declared that the experience of unity between God and creation to be subjective and only existing in the mind of the believers.

The lived religious experience of Sufis

In reality, most Sufis do not live in the sublime heights of mystical oneness and, to a great extent, the focus on Sufism as Islamic mysticism has distracted from the presence of Sufism in varying degrees across the Muslim world, where it is much more likely to be associated with traditional Islamic practice or certain 'folk traditions' which can be described as an holistic milieu of Muslim vernacular religion. Until recent times such studies have been the domain of the anthropologist, and it is only in very recent times that scholars of religion and Islamic studies scholars have moved away from the texts of classical Sufi works to exploring the everyday lives of those that claim allegiance to the traditions of Sufism. Such studies are likely to reveal a diversity and flexibility of practice that permits divergence and syncretism. It is this very ability to create fluid forms of lived Muslim religious experience that draws down upon Sufis, the wrath of the orthodox Islamists, and even divides Sufis themselves. To explore this phenomena of lived Sufism, the remainder of the chapter explores some aspects of Sufism in the Lakshadweep Islands and compares with the British experience.

Lakshadweep Islands

Two striking instances of Sufi practice drawn from South India are illustrative of the diversity of Sufism and perhaps show some vestiges of the sober/intoxicated dichotomy within Sufism. This diversity in Sufi practice is apparent even in such a small area as the Lakshadweep Islands. All the islands together come to only ten square miles, even though it is the most densely populated region in India. Above all, they demonstrate the permeability to other religions and cultures, in particular, in these examples, to the forms of Hinduism practised in South India. Field work carried out on the Lakshadweep Islands reveals two dominant *turuq*. The Qadiriya tariqa local to the islands have a rather quiet and even staid dhikr, in which the proponents stand in orderly lines tapping their daff (tambourines) gently, bowing up and down slowly in rhythm to the beat. The tempo of chanting and drumming does increase as time goes on and seem to terminate only when the dhikr reaches a certain speed. The use of only a drum to maintain the tempo, with otherwise only the unaccompanied human voice shows an awareness of more orthodox views on the use of music in the repetition of God's names. There are no thaumaturgical acts in the Qadiriya dhikr.

On the other hand, The Rif'ai dhikr on the islands is dramatic and striking. The Sufis carrying out the Rif'ai dhikr do not stand in orderly lines and seem to sway from side to side as though drunk, their movements suggesting a wild ecstasy. Their awls, knives and swords are repeatedly used to stab and cut themselves. They move to the shaykh or Tangal who has initially blessed these weapons, and he touches their bodies gently, leading, it seems to immediate healing of what would appear to be quite traumatic injuries. These Sufis seem to reach altered states of consciousness where they become oblivious of pain and seem to transcend the natural conditions of feeling. Unlike the Qadiriya, the drumming and chanting in this ritual rises to a rapid crescendo when the dancers stabbed and cut themselves with apparent impunity. It is believed that not even a scar will remain from these self-inflicted wounds.

Veneration of saints

This is an indispensable part of most popular Sufi practice in South Asia and elsewhere. Circumambulation of a Sufi's' *mazar* (tomb), intercessionary prayer to the awliya and holding of celebrations with dances, music, processions and even fireworks are seen in the Sufi ritual complex associated with veneration of Sufi shaykhs. On the Islands, the urs of Ubaid Allah of Lakshadweep is a grand affair, and in the dinner accompanying the festivities every individual in Androth Island and visitors from outside are fed. A huge procession traverses the entire length of the island and culminates at the saint's tomb.

The veneration and adoration of Tangals (shaykhs) is a phenomenon observed in both Lakshadweep and neighboring Muslim communities of Kerala in the Indian mainland. In Kerala the famous Mambram Tangal, Sayyid Alawi Ibn Muhammad (1749–1843), a shaykh from the Hadramaut, was so highly venerated that the Muslims of Kerala used to collect the dust from the places where he walked. This saint was known as a wonder worker and inspired the Muslims in their altercations with the British colonial government. After his death his son was suspected of involvement in the Mappila Rebellion of 1921 and deported to Yemen by the British. The Mambram Tangal established most of the mosques seen in Malappuram District, the headquarters of Islam in Kerala. 'By the foot of the Mambram Tangal' is a commonly articulated oath in this district.

An interesting variant is the leadership of Muhammad Shah Tangal, a Persian shaykh who arrived from Mumbai and settled down in Kondotti, near Calicut. He is well known for miracles such as healing a blind woman. The Zawiya he established at Kondotti still stands. His descendants have documents in Persian, and his tomb has a distinctive Middle Eastern touch in contrast to the Keralan architecture of most mosques and mausoleums there. He may be said to have introduced a Shi'i element into the Sufi praxis there.

Sufism and caste

Another remarkable aspect of Sufism on the Lakshadweep Islands is the association of the *turuq* with social classes. Muslims pride themselves on the egalitarianism of Islam, but in Lakshadweep there are caste-like divisions in the Muslim community. This can be attributed to the pre-Islamic caste configurations of the population who are all supposed to have converted en masse to Islam from Hinduism owing to the charisma of a famed Muslim missionary from the Middle East, none other than Ubaid Allah, a grandson of Abu Bakr, the first Caliph, who is believed to have been shipwrecked on the islands where he performed astounding miracles and with these demonstrations of his spiritual prowess converted the local inhabitants to Islam. He later on married and settled down in the territory. His tomb still stands in Androth Island, the venue of a great annual *urs* celebration in his honour and remembrance. It is more likely that conversion took place at a more moderate rate, even though the influence of these Arab traders in the first century of Islam was profound. However, the story reveals that these devout and intrepid Muslims were willing to marry local women and risk the consequent merging of Lakshadweep culture with Islamic and Arab norms.

Muhammad Qasim, also an Arab and claimed to be a *sayyid* (descendent of the Prophet), is said to have introduced Sufism into the islands. Local hagiography asserts that he healed a woman named Ayesha who was suffering from leprosy and later sought her hand in marriage. His descendants in Androth have many shaykhs among their number who are well known in South and Southeast Asia and who proceed on religious journeys overseas known as *Safar* in the islands.

The identification of Sufi allegiance to both *turuq* is with two castes, the Koya and the Melacceri. The Koya are landlords, and the Melacceri are landless laborers whose main occupation is plucking coconuts from trees belonging to the Koya and performing other menial duties for their upper caste overlords. Caste interdictions such as deferential behavior, restrictions in wearing of clothes and foot wear, use of music and processions in celebration of weddings and caste endogamy are as rigorous as those of the Hindus elsewhere in South India. However, interestingly, the Melacceri have sought to obtain religious freedom by aligning themselves to the Rif'ai *tariqa* rather than the Qadiriya favoured by their masters. Shaykh Muhammad Qasim had apparently first initiated *murids* into and established the Qadiriya order, but it seems that the lower castes affiliated themselves with and established the Rif'ai order. This may be because the Rif'ai is an Arab tariqa and would permit the low-caste Melacceri to link themselves to original Arab settlers in South India and thus raise their caste profile. On the other hand, the Rif'ai religious practices may have borne more similarity to the thaumaturgical acts well known in South Indian Hinduism.[23] Yet the shaykhs of both orders claim to be descendants of the lineage of Shaykh

Muhammad Qasim but in the matrilineal family system anomalously followed by the Muslims of Lakshadweep, the respective shaykhs belong to two separate high-caste families, the Aranikkat and Ekkarpally tarwads of Kavaratti Island, the capital of Lakshadweep.

Strangely enough these leaders do not belong to the Melacceri lower caste, since as Sayyids they are considered as from the upper echelons of Lakshadweep society. But the two castes remain fiercely loyal to these shaykhs and to their respective traditions.

Thus we find that the Melacceris conduct their dhikr ceremonies separately and in the mode favoured by the Rif'ai Sufis. During festive days, such as Eid al Fitr and Eid al Adha, there is considerable rivalry between the two castes in the conduct of their *dhikr*. Therefore the police do not allow these to be conducted on the same day in case of public disorder. It may also be that the greater fervour and self-mortification of the Rif'ai ritual is symptomatic of the suffering and oppression suffered by the lower castes in Lakshadweep.

As noted the shaykhs or Tangals of the Sufi orders are from the upper echelons of Lakshadweep society and are therefore considered to be Koya rather than Melacceri. Initially when the Melacceris started practicing the *dhikr* there was opposition from the Koya and the matter was referred to the Tangals. They, however, sided with the lower caste and decided that any Muslim could observe *dhikr* and it was not possible to exclude the lower castes from this spiritual practice. So we see that the practice of Sufism and the caste system run parallel on the Islands, and the two castes have different mosques at which the *dhikr* is conducted. Nevertheless Islamic egalitarian religious norms return on Fridays when all gather together in the same *juma masjid*.

Some remarks

Sufism in both Lakshadweep and Kerala manifest syncretism with Hinduism, the majority religion of India. The Hindu antecedents of Muslims may account for this. In Lakshadweep, the social institution of caste and matrilinear extended families, both not common in Islamic societies is a vestige of their Hindu antecedents. So also is the use of a sacred multi-wicked oil lamp in mosques and the presence of a tank near every mosque, a feature of all Hindu temples in South India but not normally a characteristic elsewhere in the case of Islam. The higher castes often term their houses 'illam', a term which is common among the Nambudiri Brahmins of nearby Kerala. In Kerala, the nercca or mowlids at the mausoleums of Sheikhs also manifest Hindu influence. The festivities are in the pattern of Hindu Velas or Poorams, festivals in the region. The use of processions, dances, feasts, elephants and even fireworks are ample testimony to this. The efforts of more conservative Islamic movements to purge Islamic practice of these elements along with other Sufi practices have not been very successful. These syncretistic features testify that Sufism is a less rigid, more flexible and open form of Islamic ideology and praxis, ready to absorb from the cultural traits of other religions, without compromising the essential tenets of Islam. Sufism thus lends itself to more diversity and perhaps this accounts for the success of Islam in South and Southeast Asia and how long it has existed harmoniously side by side with other religious traditions in the area.

Sufism and ethnicity in Britain

Gabriel's field work in Lakshadweep reminds us that Sufism is not only about individual mystics gathering around themselves circles of disciples all seeking the objective of union with God. It is also about complex belongings linked to caste and family networks. In the British context, this is more likely to be connected to ethnicity. Most of the post-WWII Muslims with Sufi allegiance also originated from South Asia. Even though dominantly from North India, they also brought links to extended family networks. Most of the first generation migrants hailed from a few defined areas of South Asia. The vast majority came from rural areas in Mirpur in Southern Kashmir or Sylhet in Bangladesh. Sufism was strong in these areas. Although allegiance to Sufism is part and parcel of Islam's offer of the possibility of intimacy with God, there was also the possibility of Sufism being a repository of religious beliefs and cultural practices given significance through their association with life in the place of origin. In 1996, Geaves wrote that the typical mosque with loyalty to the Barelwi tradition in Britain's Northern cities would serve a community living in the streets around it. Through the process of chain migration, often these Muslims originate from relatively small areas in South Asia and often the imam would originate from the same area. The community would have its innermost loyalty to biraderi (extended family networks), both settled in Britain and in the place of origin. Through these networks of kin marriages would be arranged, religion celebrated in home and elsewhere, and all held together by a complex arrangement of mutual gifts and caste allegiance linked to families that extended back through time to sacred ancestors in the form of the founding saint. All of this would be sacralized by chains of spiritual lineage (*silsila*) that would always link back to the Prophet. However, set against this ethnicizing of religion is a counterflow that renews the original religious impulse of Sufi allegiance. In Britain, there is an urgent need to maintain Islam in the face of a secular, non-Muslim environment, which on one hand offers the freedom to practise one's religion, but, on the other hand may appear hostile. Loyalty to locality and extended family may not be enough to preserve South Asian Sufism in Britain unless wider, more powerful transglobal identities are sought through the original Islamic impulse to seek guidance to discover purity.

In this respect Britain will differ from the Lakshadweep Islands, but there may be some commonality in the diversity in Sufi membership. To some degree this will be in thought and practice. Closeness with God remains as an overriding grand narrative as the ultimate objective of all Sufis, even though the paths to this are variations of a theme. Immanence is more likely to vie with the transcendence that characterizes much of the Islamic approach to God in the popular imagination. The *awliya* remain the goal with their God permeated lives providing wondrous tales that show the power of the divine world over the troublesome forces of nature. Followers are unlikely to distinguish ecstatic, loving or sober Sufis who renounced worldly pleasures and devoted themselves wholly to spirituality, but remain confined to loyalties that primarily focus on their own shaykhs and their ancestors.

The fieldwork carried out in the Lakshadweep Islands and in Britain calls out for a classification of Sufi allegiance. Figure 1.1 provides a possible way of demonstrating allegiance that acknowledges that such belongings may well be substantively different with regard to degrees of varying loyalties and motivations.

Only the shaykh and his *murids*, including *khalifa* and family members, would belong to the tariqa as defined by oaths of allegiance *(bai'a)* and *silsila*. The two outermost circles (4 and 5) would form large amorphous allegiances based on status, emotional loyalty or pragmatic need. The two innermost circles would indicate a primary loyalty based on spiritual guidance, although this would need to be reassessed in the case of family members. All the circles would be united by the common characteristics identified by Nielsen and listed above. However, it is important to factor into the equation changing relations with wider global circles of allegiance. There is also evidence that the relationship of young South Asian Sufi-orientated youth in Britain has changed in recent decades, with many moving away from the outer circle allegiances which form constituents of ethnic loyalty to discover new ways of expressing inner circle loyalties.[24] Recent globalization makes the reality of Sufi allegiance more complex. Figure 1.2 shows the complexity.

Figure 1.1 Patterns of Sufi Allegiance

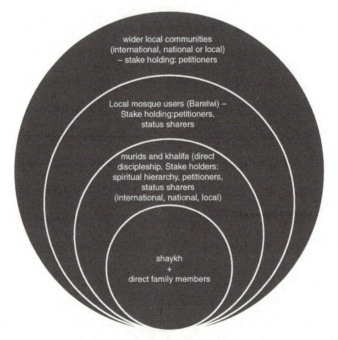

Figure 1.2 Layers of Traditional Sufi Allegiance in Britain

Notes

1   T. Gabriel (2001) *Lakshadweep, History, Religion and Society*. New Delhi: Books and Books.

2   R. Geaves (2000) *Sufis of Britain: An Exploration of Muslim Identity*. Cardiff: Cardiff Academic Press, pp. 85–101.

3   Ibid., p. 76.

4   A number of prominent orientalists including Adalbert Merx (1838–1909), Ignaz Goldziher (1850–1921), Theodore Noeldeke (1836–1930), Miguel Asin Palacios (1871–1944), Tor Andrae (1885–1947) and Reynold Nicholson (1868–1945) have all suggested that Sufism emerged out of Islamic contact with Eastern Christianity's traditions of asceticism. If some were to see Sufi practices demonstrating links with Christian monasticism, others such as E. H. Whinfield (1835–1922), E. G. Browne (1862–1926) and Louis Massignon (1883–1962) sought the origins of Sufi theosophy in the neo-Platonic writings of Plotinus, Gnostic and Dionysian cults encountered in Egypt and through translation of Greek philosophy into Arabic in the eighth and ninth centuries. One of the earliest European writers on Sufism, Friedrich Thöluck (1799–1877), claimed that Sufism had emerged from the Magian or Zoroastrian religion in ancient Persia.

5   The German orientialist Paul Klappstein wrote in 1919 in the preface to his translation of Sufi texts that Sufism was a form of universal mysticism and should be understood as a 'psychic predisposition' in all human beings. This understanding of Sufism was to fascinate orientalists such as Massignon, Nicholson and scholars of comparative religion in Britain. For example, Walter Stace (1960), Geoffrey Parrinder (1976) and Ninian Smart (1978) all argue that the mystical experience has enough common features, in spite of the obvious differences arising from a multiplicity of religious traditions in which they occur, to be defined as universal.

6   *The Qur'an*, Al-Kahf, 18:28.

7   R. A. Nicholson (1989 3rd edition) *The Mystics of Islam*. Harmondsworth: Arkana, p. 8.

8   Takbir – the words *Allahu Akbar* (God is the greatest), *Inshallah* (if God wills), *al Andulilah* (praise be to God), *Mashalla* (what God has willed), *Bismillah* (in the name of God).

9   A. J. Arberry (1968) *Sufism*. London: Allan and Unwin, p. 42.

10 S. Margaret (2001) *Muslim Women Mystics*. Oxford: One World Pubns, p. 184.

11 Arberry, Op. Cit., p. 34.

12 p. 42.

13 p. 42.

14 http://privat.bahnhof.se/wb042294Texter/bionotes/bio_fudayl_b_3iyad. htmlaccessed 21/01/2013

15 Ibid.

16 Ibid.

17 Ibid.

18 Arberry, Op. Cit., p. 54.

19 Ibid., p. 54.

20 Ibid.

21 S. Annemarie (1975) *Mystical Dimensions of Islam*, University of North Carolina Press, p. 50.

22 Mathnawi.

23 See R. A. Geaves (2007) *Śaivism in the Diaspora: Contemporary Forms of Skanda Worship*. London: Equinox for a detailed study of South Indian thaumaturgical rituals in diaspora and Tamil Nadu.

24 See Geaves in this volume and (2012) 'The Transformation and Development of South Asian Sufis in Britain' in *South Asian Sufis: Devotion, Deviation and Destiny*. C. Bennett and C. Ramsey (Eds). London: Continuum.

2

Transformation and Trends among British Sufis

Ron Geaves

In defining Sufism in Britain I have avoided Nicolson's understanding of Sufism as 'the transformation of the One transcendent God of Islam into one real Being who dwells and works everywhere, and whose throne is not less, but more, in the human heart than in the heaven of heavens'.[1] Equally I have resisted al-Hujwiri's quoting of the tenth century al-Fushanji as having said 'Today Sufism is a name without a reality; but formerly it was a reality without a name'.[2] Both have their attractions but the former relies too much on the earlier Orientalists' understanding of Sufism as something exceptional in the world of religion, a privileging of the mystical, but as Gai Eaton reminds us, many Sufis are not mystics. The second presents us with problems of authenticity both within the world of eleventh century Indian Sufis and the wider world of Muslim contestation. The etymological denotations of Sufism are many, but I return to Al-Hujwiri who cites a prophetic tradition to define a Sufi as the one who adopts *safa* (purity) and gives up *kadar* (impurity). The definition is broad and works well with Hoffman-Ladd's interpretation of Sufism as 'purification of the heart, sincerity of worship, and renunciation of fleshly passions'.[3] The two definitions combine to produce an emic and etic harmony that is able to reflect the ethnographic insider testimonies that insist upon naming Sufism, 'practical Islam'[4] and are broad enough to encompass the everyday realities of the various manifestations of Sufism in Britain.

Early development

Between 1890 and 1908, the English convert to Islam, William Abdullah Quilliam established a mosque in Liverpool in which a community of converts, lascars, Muslim university students and rich Muslim travellers arriving on the steamships in Liverpool worked together to establish the first organized Muslim presence in Britain.[5] There is no evidence that Britain's only Shaikh al-Islam was a Sufi in the sense of *tariqa* membership or having accepted *bai'a* (oath of allegiance) from a legitimate Sufi shaikh (teacher). However, Abdullah Quilliam celebrated *mawlid* (the Prophet's birthday) at the mosque every year in Liverpool, decorated the mosque in the traditional mode of the Ottomans and published *dhikr* (formulaic remembrance of Allah)and other Muslim creedal formulae known to Sufi adherents as part of his instruction to the new converts. Quilliam was a renowned Ottomanist and learned his Islam in Morocco and Turkey and never questioned the traditional Islam he observed and had no objections to Muslim visits to the shrines of the Sufis as long as their behaviour was appropriately restrained. In 1916, he translated the poetry of a Turkish Sufi after an extended stay in Istanbul, entitled *Sheikh Haroun Abdullah: A Turkish Poet and his Poetry*. He was fully aware of the Wahhabi movement but considered it to be a rebellion against the legitimate Sunni Caliphate and its customs and traditions. He welcomed the defeat which prevented them from extending into the Ottoman empire. Quilliam admired the mystical tradition of Islam and defined himself as an Ottoman Hanafi with an allegiance to traditional Islam. In exploring trends in British Sufism, we will need to return to his terminology used to position himself within the world of Islam.

Abdullah Quilliam was raised in Liverpool at a time when Yemeni, Somali and Indian Muslims began to appear in the dock areas of the city. He worked closely with the sailors, functioning as their imam while they were in the city waiting for a ship to return to their ports of origin, he performed their funerals, marriages and provided hospitality, accommodation and a place of prayer, but it was not until later that the Yemeni lascars were able to organize their own community building in Cardiff, Tyneside and Liverpool between the two world wars. These were created around religious centres (*zawiya*) led by North African Alawi Sufis (see Chapter 4). The Yemeni sailors formed shifting dockyard settlements, many of them originating from Hadramaut where there was a tradition among Hadramis to leave their homeland and supplement their incomes. The region is a significant Sufi stronghold especially the Bani Alawi, whose shaikhs have contributed significantly to Hadrami settlement and religious life. However, the largest group of Yemeni migrants were Shamiris from around Aden who had little connection with the Bani Alawi and the earlier migrants from Hadramaut. It is these communities around the seaports that remain significant in the history of British Sufis and the organization of religious life for British Muslims. Their seaport settlements, however, were not organized under the leadership of the Bani Alawi, but through the efforts of Shaykh Abdullah Ali al-Hakimi of the Alawi Shadhilli, a tariqa that remains significant in the development of British Sufism in other contexts as this chapter demonstrates.[6]

Sheikh Abdullah Ali al-Hakimi remained leader of the Yemeni communities in Britain in the late 1930s and 1940s until he returned to Aden in the early 1950s to become president of the Yemeni Union. He appears to have met his spiritual guide, Shaykh Ahmad ibn Mustafa al-'Alawi al-Mustaghanimi, more commonly known as Shaykh al-'Alawi, in Morocco in the late 1920s and to have been appointed a muqadam (teacher assisting the Shaikh) within his branch of the Alawi tariqa. In the years before the Second World War, the Alawi had extended their missionary activities beyond North Africa and had won many disciples among Yemeni seamen in European ports. Sheikh Abdullah had lived and worked in France and Holland before arriving in Britain in 1936. He founded what was known as the 'Zaouia Islamia, Allawouia Religious Society in the United Kingdom' establishing zawiyas in Cardiff, South Shields, Hull and Liverpool.

Religious life was regularized and customary rituals and practices were introduced with colourful processions through the streets organized to mark the major Muslim festivals. In addition to celebrating the Eid al-Fitr, Eid al-Adha and mawlid, a fourth festival was introduced to commemorate the death of the founder of the Alawi tariqa who had died in 1934. On these occasions many of the seamen discarded their European clothing for Yemeni dress or the Arab dress of North Africa. Special attention was given to the religious instruction of children born to seamen and their Welsh and English wives. Classes in Quranic studies were organized for both boys and girls and also for those wives who had converted to Islam.

Sheikh Abdullah cultivated contacts with local government officials in both Cardiff and South Shields. Throughout the 1930s, unemployment among Arab seamen at British ports remained acute and many were destitute. Support for Sheikh Abdullah's efforts to strengthen the religious organization of these communities were welcomed as far as the British authorities were concerned. At a dinner hosted by Sheikh Abdullah in Cardiff in July 1950, attended by the

Deputy Lord Mayor and other leading citizens, the Assistant Chief Constable paid tribute to the law-abiding behaviour of the Muslim community under the Shaikh's leadership. This organization of a migrant community around the leadership of a Sufi pre-shadowed the much larger post-war migration of South Asians in which Barelwi Sufi leaders from Pakistan and India were to play a major role until the present day.

Before coming to an analysis of this dominant South Asian presence and its impact on British Muslim life, it is important to note that the Shaikh Alawi was to influence trends in British Sufism in other significant ways. Frithjof Schuon (1907–98) is known as the inspiration of the Traditionalists and an exponent of the perennialist school of mysticism. His search for the Absolute would lead him on a journey through the world's sacred texts, including the *Upanishads* and the *Bhagavad Gita*. He discovered the works of René Guénon and was influenced by his metaphysical position. He studied Arabic in Paris at the local mosque school and travelled to Algeria in 1932 where he also met the Shaykh Ahmad al-'Alawi and accepted initiation, taking the name 'Isa Nur al-Din Ahmad'. In 1935, he visited Algeria and Morocco; and in 1938 and 1939, Egypt where he finally met Guénon after correspondence with him for nearly 30 years.

Schuon's meeting with Shaykh Ahmad al-'Alawi in Algeria would be instrumental in shaping Sufism in Europe and North America, and was especially influential in Britain. The Darqawiya was a Moroccan branch of the Shadhiliya founded in the last decades of the eighteenth century by Muhammad al-Arabi al-Darqawi (1760–1823). As stated the 'Alawiya branch of the Darqawiya was founded by Ahmad ibn Mustafa al-'Alawi al-Mustaghanimi, popularly known as Shaykh al-'Alawi, and one of the greatest renewers of Sufism in the Muslim world in the twentieth century.[7] After his time with the Shaykh al-'Alawi in Algeria, Schuon returned to the West to found the Maryamiya branch of the Shadhiliya Order in Europe and North America where he promoted the teachings of the Shaykh. Sedgwick claims that of all the 'neo-Sufi' groups, the Maryamiyya was the closest to Sufism as found in the Muslim world. However, he points out some key differences. He affirms that it was almost identical with other Shadhili branches with regard to practices, but it was far more relaxed in its approach to the Shari'a. He also notes that Schuon's version of the Traditionalist philosophy of René Guénon was taught alongside Sufism and included Guénon's anti-modernist philosophy of history which was in part influenced by Theosophy.

Schuon's first book *The Transcendent Unity of Religions* expresses fully his perennial stance, but later he wrote several texts on Islam, including *Understanding Islam*, *Dimensions of Islam* and *Sufism: Veil and Quintessence*. However, it is the people that he attracted to his 'Traditionalist' stance, often introducing them to the teachings of the Shaykh al-'Alawi that were to be most influential. Some of his most eminent students include Seyyed Hossein Nasr, Titus Burckhardt (1908–84) and Martin Lings (1909–2005). Lings would publish the biography of the Shaykh al-'Alawi under the title *A Sufi Saint of the Twentieth Century,* which remains one of the most influential books on Sufism published in the Western world. He would also write the acclaimed *Muhammad: His Life Based on the Earliest Sources.*

Schuon's syncretic mix of traditional Islamic *tassawuf* and European or North American esotericism would combine with a British interest in Sufism as a form of esotericism that had been growing under the influence of Gurdjieff (1877–1949), Ouspensky (1878–1947) and Idries Shah (1924–96), peaking in the 1960s and 1970s search for perennial wisdom in the alternative counter-culture milieux when young British men and women would travel to India or North Africa.

Half-a-century earlier, paralleling Abdullah Quilliam's and the Woking Mosque's efforts to establish Islam in Britain, the Chishti Sufi Hazrat Inayat Khan arrived in England in 1910. Inayat Khan was versed in a style of truth-seeking unique to a certain kind of North Indian cultural/religious milieu in which Sufism and Yoga merged into a syncretic claim to a universal truth embodied in the *Upanishads*, the *Qur'an* and the poetry of Sufi and Sant mystics. Immersed in this eclectic background from childhood, he taught a form of Sufism that was uprooted from shari'a and transcended the borders of discrete world religions. Hazrat Khan's vision of an inner essence of religion achieved by direct experience echoed with the message of the Theosophists and the Gurdjiefian oriental esotericism and consequently attracted the same kind of seeker. Conversion to Islam was never part of his message of eclectic spirituality with an emphasis on the universal aspects of mystical experience.

Sedgwick is convinced that all these 'neo-Sufi' trends, as he labels them, are rooted in Western spirituality, with an emphasis on the individual spiritual search that he argues has no equivalent in the Muslim world. He also notes that although some eastern Sufis may have displayed a more ecumenical spirit with regard to other forms of spirituality that they encountered, the Traditionalist's version of perennialism that perceived Sufism as an outer manifestation of a universal and essential mysticism was not the Islamic interpretation of the tradition.[8] The relationship between the Perennials and the Muslim world is succinctly described by Sedgwick who may have over-emphasized the distinction between the Traditionalist's brand of Western Sufism and Islam. I would argue that the borders between these two had always been fluid and the degree to which the shari'a was followed, although problematic, is not a definitive test of allegiance to Islam. Shari'a compliance is often used to critique Sufis in the arena of contestation between Islamic forms of religiosity among Muslims and Muslim Sufis have ranged considerably in their interpretations of shari'a. The trajectory of individual transformation achieved by contact with Sufis in North Africa or the Middle East would appear to be in a number of cases drifting towards a gradual Islamicization. Evidence exists in Britain that the two phenomena were not disassociated from each other. The first migrants from India and Pakistan were arriving in Britain at around the same time as counter-culture individuals were following in the footsteps of the Traditionalists. Little is known of contacts between them but anecdotal evidence seems to suggest that the two groups were interconnected or, at least, fleetingly aware of the presence of each other.

The first counter-culture contact with Sufism in the second half of the twentieth century appeared to occur through rediscovery of the Alawi sheikhs who had succeeded the Sheikh al-'Alawi in Mostaganem, Algeria. Robert Irwin has courageously presented his story of conversion to Islam and visits to Mostaganem while a Merton College undergraduate between 1965 and 1967 in his recently published *Memoirs of a Dervish*.[9] In his memoirs, the young Oxford undergraduate recounts arriving at the *zawiya* where he gained entry by producing a copy of Martin Ling's biography of the great Sufi revivalist of the twentieth century. The *fuqarā'* were amazed to discover their founder's photograph on the cover. Robert Irwin left his copy at *the zawiya* as a gift, and this resulted in the French translation of the book.

Martin Lings (also known as Abu Bakr Siraj Ad-Din) (1909–2005) had also been an Oxford undergraduate at Magdelan College where he discovered the writings of René Guénon, a French metaphysician and Muslim convert, and those of Frithjof Schuon, the German perennialist. In 1938, Lings went to Basle to make Schuon's acquaintance. After a spell in Egypt, he returned to the United Kingdom achieving a BA in Arabic and a PhD from the School of Oriental and African Studies (SOAS). His most famous work was a biography of Muhammad, written in 1983, which earned him acclaim in the Muslim world and prizes from the governments of Pakistan and Egypt.

Robert Irwin mentions in his memoirs that on arrival in Mostaganem, he was informed that he had just missed Sidi Ahmed, described as majdhub (a holy fool, one crazed by God). Sidi Ahmed was an earlier English convert and a mature student at Merton during the same period. Irwin attributes his conversion to Islam to meeting a fellow undergraduate Sidi Ahmed who had travelled to Algeria earlier before returning to study Arabic at Merton College. Like Martin

Lings, whose Sufi group he would later attend, Sidi Ahmed had been drawn to the writings of Guenon and Schuon. Born Harvey Mellor in Yorkshire, he was something of a prodigal. At the age of fourteen, he had decided that Islam was the true religion after exploring the doctrines of the world's major faiths. His challenge was to become a Muslim in the Britain of the 1950s. As a fifteen year old he hitchhiked to Sheffield where someone had told him there were Muslims working in the steel works. The fifteen year old found himself confronted with a group of Pakistani night shift workers with little knowledge of English and attempted to explain that he wanted witnesses to his *shahadah*. He explained to me recently that he was never sure that it had been done correctly and two years later he reaffirmed his allegiance to Islam in Woking Mosque. Sidi Ahmed, Robert Irwin and Martin Lings are significant in that they converted to Islam and practised Sufism as Muslims. Sidi Ahmed's story of his conversion is also significant as his encounter with Pakistani night shift workers in Sheffield and his maintenance of daily Muslim life in Oxford involved praying in the basement of the city's first curry house owned by East Pakistanis (linking converts and migrants).

The proximity of North Africa, compared with India, would attract a continuous flow of counter-culture seekers of the oriental experience from Western Europe. Contact with the Shadhili or Darqawi *tariqas* was therefore inevitable. Both of these orders had been rejuvenated from time to time by charismatic shaykhs, most notably, as we have seen, the Shaykh al-'Alawi. Most significant among European contacts with the *tariqa* is the Mirabitun movement, founded in Britain by Ian Dallas around 1976. Dallas, a writer and actor, had travelled to Morocco in 1967 where he was initiated into the Darqawiya and took the name Abd al-Qadir. Somewhere around 1976, a group of British and North American followers gathered around Shaykh Abd al-Qadir in a row of derelict houses in London. Little study has been carried out on the group and its activities but Köse notes that they numbered between twenty and thirty and were all former members of 1960s counter-culture and had taken drugs prior to contact with Sufism.[10] Although the group dressed in green turbans and traditional Moroccan dress, conversion to Islam was seen as secondary to acquiring Sufism. Yet, like the earlier Traditionalists and the Oxford undergraduates, many would embrace Islam as a feature of Sufi lifestyle. Shaykh al-Qadir would become more overtly Muslim throughout 1976. He insisted that followers withdraw from a Western lifestyle, even to the extent of removing children from mainstream schools. He initiated public prayer meetings in Hyde Park, and his writings began to be translated into Arabic. After visiting Libya, he announced himself as a unifying shaykh of the Shadhili and Darqawiya. At the end of 1976, he moved his community to near Norwich in Norfolk, with the intention of establishing a fully self-sufficient village of believers. The community purchased Wood Daling Hall, a mansion with extensive grounds. At its peak, the community numbered around two hundred families, forming the Darqawi Institute. Shaykh al-Qadir would travel extensively throughout the Muslim world achieving fame internationally as a scholar. For a variety of reasons, the community fragmented. Shaykh al-Qadir moved to Andalucia and in 1994, a new offshoot of the movement was founded in Scotland. The original community remains in Norwich and is still active in promoting Islam in Britain.[11]

The Darqawi Institute is important for a number of reasons. Köse notes that the movement had two distinct phases. In the first, Abd al-Qadir attracted new followers through promoting himself as a Sufi who emphasized the esoteric teachings of the tradition. In the second, he shifted to an emphasis on the outer practices of Islam and shari'a compliance. Although Sufism was perceived as the authentic version of Islamic practice, and embedded in Sunni traditionalism, the promotion of Islam in the West became the primary objective of the movement. This is significant as it confirms the fluid borders between Sufism encountered as an esoteric but universal mysticism and Islamic allegiance. Perhaps more significantly for the development of Sufism in the West, the movement would produce a number of individuals who would have an impact today, bridging the borders between convert Sufis and the British children of South Asian migrants with a pre-existing Sufi familial allegiance. Shaykh Yasin Dutton remembers that such contacts were already taking place in the 1970s when the Sufis of the Norwich community would travel around England in order to meet with South Asian shaykhs who were beginning to teach in the inner cities where Muslims migrants had recently settled. This re-emerging Maghrebi influence on Sufi allegiance in Britain links back to the the Yemeni dominated seaport communities in Cardiff, Liverpool, Hull and Tyneside that had their origins in the expansion of the British merchant fleet and the consequent mass employment of Asian sailors, who owed their religious and social organization to the spiritual descendents of the Shaykh al-'Alawi. They remind us that before the influx of the post-war South Asian migrants, the dominant force in British Sufism originated in the Maghreb. It has never disappeared and is now re-emerging as one of the major points of contact for British-born children of the South Asian migrants who wish to divest themselves of the ethnic dimension in their parent's and grandparent's Sufism.

The South Asian migrations

These early encounters between British Sufi converts to Islam and the newly arriving South Asian migrants were to be drowned out by the prolific numbers of arrivals in England throughout the 1970s and sheer numerical dominance of the South Asians in establishing a Muslim presence in Britain. But unbeknown to many, a new avenue for the construction of British Sufism had arrived transforming the inner city cultural map of England's old manufacturing cities. South Asian Islam has been dominated by Sufism, since its inception in the subcontinent and many of new arrivals brought with them strong allegiances to the traditions of cultural/religious milieu of their places of origin including membership of *tariqas*. Among the migrants, there were even prominent Sufi shaikhs who began to establish Qur'an classes for children, mosques and zawiya, first in terraced houses, then in converted mills and finally by the 1980s purpose-built mosques loyal to the Barelwi tradition of South Asia. If Sidi Ahmed had travelled further south to Birmingham he might have found the Pakistani factory nightshift where Sufi Abdullah of the Naqshbandiya laboured at night while teaching Qur'an to the children of the migrant workers during the day, slowly building up powerful Sufi institutions for the Pakistanis in the city. Similarly other Sufis from the Subcontinent had established strongholds in Bradford, Coventry and Manchester. Mosques declared their loyalty to the Barelwis even when no Sufi was in residence, with imported ulema whose allegiance was to the tradition.

Sufis in the West

Klinkhammer has pointed out that any assessment of the Sufi presence in European nations must take into account patterns of immigration and the different situations in the countries of origin of Muslim migrants in the twentieth and twenty-first centuries, for example, 80 per cent of Muslim migrants in Germany originate from Turkey where Sufism is not widely represented or, at least, not publicly visible. The ban on Sufi Orders in Turkey in 1925 strongly limited the public practice of Sufism and would have significance for the public representation of Sufism among Muslim migrants in Germany and elsewhere.[12] In Britain, where the great majority of Muslims originate from rural Pakistan, India and Bangladesh, Sufism is practised as a popular religion in the villages and towns. This is duplicated in the strongholds of South Asian migrant presence in British cities. In France, where the majority of migrants are from North Africa, Sufism, although once dominant is less so due to the changing formations of Algerian Islam after the struggle for independence. Other factors influencing the development of Sufism are critical mass of migration, class and ethnicity of the migrants and the presence of individual Sufi leaders among the migrants.

Initially the appropriation of Sufism by Western orientalists and successive generations of seekers of a 'mystical truth' hid the vibrant reality of millions of traditional Muslims in the Muslim world who practised the core disciplines of Sufism as an integral part of Islam firmly based on the teachings of the Qur'an and Hadith. Until the arrival of migrant populations in post-World War II Western Europe, the articulate Sufi intellectuals hid the everyday life of traditional Muslims and the role of the *tariqas* and the shrines of deceased Sufis in Muslim religious life. Sufism in the West was an elitist presence with fluid links to Islamic religiosity. The everyday religious life of traditional Muslims would not have a significant impact on Sufism in the West until the 1960s when some nations in Western Europe began to be transformed by the arrival of various Muslim populations, in the case of Britain predominantly from Pakistan and Bangladesh and also from Malaysia, Turkish Cyprus, Iran, Yemen, North, West and East Africa. These are all places where, either historically or as a living faith tradition, Sufism is significant.

Although slow to organize themselves in the British Muslim diaspora, the last 20 years have seen the transplantation of several prominent Sufi *tariqas* including various offshoots of the Naqshbandis, Chishtis, Qadiris, Mevlevis, Alawis, Shadhilis and Tijanis. This pattern repeats itself in other nations of Western Europe, Scandinavia and North America. This significant presence of Sufis or Sufi-influenced Muslims has done much to offset the appropriation of Sufism by Western orientalists and has to a significant degree restored the awareness of the Sufi path at the heart of traditional Islam. However, it could be argued that even with the establishment of the *tariqas,* wherever Muslim populations have settled in Western Europe and North America, Sufism remains relatively invisible both to academics and the general public as other aspects of Muslim religious life have dominated the agenda for political and security reasons.

The dominance of Muslims of South Asian origin in the British context has perpetuated custom-laden Sufism with its roots in the subcontinent and continued historic rivalries between *tariqas* and with other Islamic movements that have been historical competitors in the highly contested religious environment of colonial India. The subcontinent Sufis, with their custom-laden version of Islam focused on the intercession of saints and the Prophet, shrines, *baraka* (the power to bless), powers, miracles and the performance of *dhikr* maintained within the *shaykh/murid* relationship, had never successfully organized themselves nationally in Britain in spite of their apparent numerical superiority. Even so, the arrival of a number of charismatic Sufi *pirs* and *shaykhs* from the subcontinent provided the impetus for greater cohesion as they formed powerful groups of Sufis able to construct mosques and produce promotional literature to counter the modern reformist movements. The traditional loyalty of each group of *murids* to their own *shaykh* however undermined this push towards a stronger and more assertive national identity.

Moreover, the establishment of these *tariqas* has provided a series of organizational structures to Sufi adherents and capitalized on the strong empathy with the teachings of traditional Islam among British Muslim populations. The term 'traditional Islam' is used in this context to distinguish a brand of Islam that acknowledges 1,400 years of tradition as authoritative alongside the teachings of Qur'an and Sunna and recognizes the contribution of Sufi spirituality, the legal interpretations of the *ulama* and the four schools of law. This label of traditional Islam has been harnessed by Sufis and Sufi sympathizers in opposition to neo-orthodoxies which have vociferously criticized Sufism, accusing it of introducing *bida* (innovation) into the Muslim religious arena.

Thus, in recent years, the representatives of the *tariqas* have provided a unifying Islamic discourse based on practice and belief and drawing upon the traditional loyalty of the above populations to the leadership of *pirs* and *shaykhs* rather than the *ulama*. They have also discovered a successful discourse that is able to recruit from the younger generations of British Muslims. However, unlike the USA, Sufism has made less impact on the original non-migrant non-Muslim population, and with the exception of the Haqqani Naqshbandis, led by the charismatic Shaykh Nazim, very few outside the Muslim migrant communities have been attracted. The main contributory reason for this difference, at least, up to the end of the twentieth century was that Sufism in Britain, in particular, remained associated with ethnic identity and communication in Urdu, a means of maintaining traditions and customs tightly bound with localities in the place of origin. Thus Sufism has functioned not so much as a transmission of mysticism within Islam, able to cross over to a universal mysticism sought by Western seekers, but as a boundary mechanism primarily concerned with the transmission of cultural and religious traditions. However, this is only part of the story.

In recent years, there are signs of significant change. The British Sufi scene now demonstrates marked attempts to carve out a new cultural and religious space that creatively interacts with the new environment of Britain.[13] The *tariqas* have become more aware of the need to draw upon the transnational and transcultural nature of globalized memberships and to articulate the narratives of *tasawwuf* and traditional Islamic sciences in an intellectual environment, addressing both Muslims and non-Muslims in the lingua franca. The World Wide Web is an essential aspect of this globalization. The online presence of traditional Muslim *tasawwuf* does not advertise itself as Sufism or even rally behind the epithet of *Ahl as-Sunna wa Jamaʿat*, but rather prefers to speak of itself as representing traditional Islam and the teachings of the four *madhhabs*. The websites originate in Spain, Britain and North America and address themselves specifically to Muslims in the West.

Influential converts, notably Shaikh Nur Ha Nim Keller and Shaikh Abdul-Hakim Murad, are able to communicate fluently in English and are often members of academia. They are not exponents of an Islam imbedded in local tradition and are often fluent in their understanding and use of *fiqh*. These Western Sufis are as scriptural as their Salafi adversaries, able to utilize Qurʾan and Hadith to great effect to put across their message on the issues that matter to them. Ethnicity is transcended to discover common cause in either a universal consciousness of *umma* or the ideological belonging to traditional Islam. For young British Muslims of South Asian origin, inspiration is more likely to come from such figures as it is from the South Asian elders in the *tariqas* who are still perceived to pull up drawbridges of isolation in their respective spiritual fiefdoms of Coventry, Birmingham, Bradford or Manchester. *Tasawwuf* in Britain, North America and Western Europe is beginning to go trans-global and escape the confines of ethnicity and locality. Marcia Hermansen comments on this drawing together of 'theirs' and 'ours' and argues that mobility, rapid dissemination of information and encounters of Eastern (Muslim) and Western individuals has brought about the creation of trans-global networks that to some extent override the old orientalist discrepancies of power described by Said. She asserts that '"theirs" and "ours" ultimately converge in an age of globalism'.[14] The re-emergence of the North African influenced Western converts operating on a global scale, but above all, able to position themselves prominently in the struggle for Islamic authenticity and attract the British and North American children of the migrants whose forefathers belonged to traditional *tariqas* in their places of origin begs a reassessment of Sedgwick's differentiation of Sufism and neo-Sufism. Sedgwick's argument that Western Sufism always emphasizes the individual spiritual search as distinguished from the Eastern approach of a guided journey may need to be reassessed as the allegiance of young European and North American children of migrants reassess their parents' and grandparents' Sufism in the light of their in-between status in Western society.

The re-emergence of Sufism

Writing in 2005, I had concluded that recent developments suggested that the multitude of movements and mosques that represent traditional Islam, as embodied in the beliefs and practices that they declared to be normative of the *Ahl-as Sunna wa-jamaat,* were beginning to respond to the challenges presented to them by the reformist Wahhabi/Salafist critique.[15] There is no doubt that the efforts to promote the revivalist message of a pure and universal Islam among young British-born Muslims anxious to define their identity has borne dividends for the revivalist movements. The *turuq* and mosques claiming allegiance to the *Ahl-as Sunna wa-jamaat* banner had often been perceived as centres to maintain loyalties and relationships established in the country of origin and important to the older generation of migrants. They were also seen to be fragmented and obsessed with maintaining ancient feuds and divisions within the *umma*. Evidence for the 'insider' Sufi narrative that claims a counter revival of the *tariqas* and their supporters, not in Western esotericism or the immanentist mysticism of Ibn'l Arabi, nor, as in Britain, the popular ritual practices common with the South Asian *pirs* and the shrines associated with their ancestors, but in a well-developed narrative of traditional Islam rooted in the Qur'an, Sunna and the legitimate traditions of the four schools of law is not easy to demonstrate. This article has used the case study of Sufis in Britain to show that a number of high-profile Western converts and Levant and Maghreb Shaykhs have begun to emerge as a major influence on second and third generation South Asian origin British Muslims, drawing upon global networks and significant use of the World Wide Web.[16] These voices are able to articulate already existing discursive narratives of the South Asian *shaykhs* that arrived through migration, but perceived to be devoid of the cultural baggage that was so successfully used by the reformist opponents of the South Asian *turuq* as they attempted to carve out a space for their particular version of Islam within British Muslim identity politics. Whereas the British Salafi, Wahhabi, Jamaat-i Islami and Muslim Brotherhood reformists were able to recreate the Islamic paradigm of the global *umma* to develop international links, challenge local cultural forms of Islam, promote a narrative of 'British Islam' and politicize under the banner of religion, entering even into mainstream politics, the Sufis learned to counter with an understanding of *umma* that was more than a collectivity extending across geographical Muslim space and also back across the generations, linked by *isnad* and *silsila* (chains of transmission) to the Prophet himself.

International comparisons might be helpful to determine if there is global revival of Sufism across the Muslim world. There is no doubt that some Sufis have tried to reposition themselves as the moderate or peace-loving representatives of mainstream Sunni Islam, but the success of such strategies are hard to gauge. Itzchak Weismann has claimed that since the 1980s, as Muslim governments struggled against the radical upsurge, and with the general increase of interest in 'Oriental' mysticism in the Western world, there has been a significant revival in Sufi activities.[17] According to Weismann this re-emergence occurred after a period of losing ground throughout the twentieth century to both the forces of modernity and Islamic reformist movements. This pattern identified by Weisman is paralleled to some degree in the British context.

Weismann also reminds us that the criticisms of popular Sufism are not the sole prerogative of modern reformist movements, or even the earlier thirteenth and fourteenth-century critique by the Hanbali theologian Ahmad ibn Taymiyya and continued by the influential eighteenth- and nineteenth-century Wahhabi movements but that Sufism was capable of rigorous self-examination. He points out that the reform and revival of Islam even in these earlier centuries was more likely to come from Sufis than the 'ultra orthodox Wahhabiyya' or their predecessors.[18] He considers that is precisely these reforming Sufi brotherhoods originating in the pre-modern era which have proved resilient in the modern circumstances. This would appear to be borne out by developments in Britain where Naqshbandis and other Sufi orders maintain traditional forms of Islamic religious life that co-exist with the disciplines of the tariqa.

Hamid argues that 'Traditional Islam' can be compared with 'neo-Sufism' as defined by Fazlur Rahman (d. 1988). Rahman uses the term to refer to the reformist branches of Sufism described by Weissman, that is, an impulse to maintain Sufism within the orthodox features of Islam through auto-reforming impulses by conservative traditionalists among the Sufi orders of the eighteenth and nineteenth centuries. According to Hamid, the 'Traditional Islam' network is able to demonstrate both 'continuity with history and change in relation to the impact of modernity' and, in the British context, 're-invent and distinguish their religiosity from other Sufi currents and activist Islamic groups'.[19]

Hamid's study of 'Traditional Islam' among Muslim activists in Britain and Weissman's longitudinal perspective of Muslims in Palestine raise the question of 'newness' in the revival of Sufism rebranded as traditional Muslim orthodoxy. The revival would seem to challenge Werbner's anthropological studies of Pakistani Sufism that posit a pattern of 'waxing and waning' of Sufi movements based upon the classic Weberian theory of charisma and institutionalization. Werbner argues that Sufism is revived through the charisma of the living 'saint' but the revival of the late twentieth century seems to suggest a more diffused charisma than that held in the person of shaykh and is rather an integral part of Islamicization processes across the Muslim world.[20] Increasingly Sufism is being repackaged not so much as a 'network of disciples' but rather as a set of beliefs and practices that constitute normative Islam.[21]

On the other hand, John Voll is uneasy with analyses of these trends as either reactions against modernity or secularism as represented by West-influenced Muslim elites or even a searching for Islamic commitment that offers a more acceptable choice than the discredited jihadists and their allies. He argues that we need to understand the popularity of Sufism in the Muslim world in the light of a growing literature on 'post-materialist values in late- or post-modern societies'.[22] He draws upon Inglehart's theorizing of 'post-modernization' replacing modernization and reflecting a shift of 'what people really want out of life'.[23] However, such processes have to be seen in the context of changes to Western spirituality in the late twentieth and twenty-first century, described by Inglehart as a failure of confidence in 'organized religion' but where spirituality remains secure as a repository for a 'cross-national tendency for people to spend more time thinking about the meaning and purpose of life'.[24] This view is echoed by studies undertaken of contemporary British religious life by Paul Heelas and Linda Woodhead in which they argue that 'religion might be in decline, but spirituality – perceived to be less dogmatic, more tolerant and flexible, and better suited to the pursuit of personal inner quests is waxing'.[25] Yet there is little evidence of the separation of religion and spirituality in Muslim societies or other societies where the religious worldview remains the dominant paradigm for understanding reality. Such theories to explain the revival of Sufism would need to take account of second and third generation Muslims and also provide homes for converts in Western Europe and North America, let alone the attraction of Sufism to Muslim intellectuals, shopkeepers, taxi drivers and the *ulama.* The theories of a post-modern separation of religion and spirituality can be applicable for middle-class elites in the Muslim world but would need to be explored as only one factor in the complex mix of motivations that require offering allegiance to Sufism as an Islamic option.

The return to 'Traditional Islam' with its powerful discourse of authentic traditions verified by unbroken chains of transmission to the foundational figures of Islam, and its emphasis on allegiance to the four schools of law combined with sober piety, would seem to be a trend that reversed the emphasis on universalism and eclecticism that can be found in more ecstatic forms of Sufism that could meet and accommodate new spiritualities in Western Europe and North America. Returning to Voll's unease, it is clear from analyses of the content of the websites loyal to 'Traditional Islam' that their discursive oppositional apologetic remains largely targeted at Salafi and Wahhabi reformist positions and that contemporary Sufis and their supporters are not adverse from repositioning themselves as the voice of moderate Islam, and thus 'discrediting jihadists'. In addition, the Muslim converts who dominate the discourses on the websites were often influenced at some point on their journeys by the Traditionalists, especially Frithjof Schuon and Seyyed Hossein Nasr. The Traditionalists were also passionate critics of modernism because it denied the ancient and absolute truths of a perennial wisdom that is part of the collective inheritance of revelation and inspiration. The critique of contemporary values is heard in Schuon's warnings.

> Because one no longer admits. . .the supersensible dimensions. . . one seeks the solution to the cosmogonic problem on the sensory plane and one replaces true causes with imaginary ones which, in appearance at least, conform with the possibilities of the corporeal world . . . In doing this, one forgets what man is, and one forgets also that a purely physical science, when it reaches vast proportions, can only lead to catastrophe . . .[26]

or

> That which is lacking in the present world is a profound
> knowledge of the nature of things; the fundamental truths are
> always there, but they do not impose themselves because they
> cannot impose themselves on those unwilling to listen.[27]

Arguably such sentiments are not peculiar to criticisms of contemporary society but would have found a sympathetic ear with the philosophers and mystics who developed Sufi understandings of the human condition in the early centuries of

Islam. Yet is clear that any understanding of the revival of Sufism in its varied forms needs to detach itself from theoretical frameworks that Sufi traditionalism appeals to conservative voices who remain attracted to the old ways and resist modernization. It is apparent, that neither in Muslim majority nations nor in Britain's Muslim enclaves, does Sufism represent any longer a vehicle for expressing rural piety. It is at least as urban as the Islamic movements are often claimed to be. Globalization plays a part, not only through migration and physical travel but also through new technologies as a means of communication of ideas. As to whether 'Traditional Islam' is an emergent trend in the history of Muslim contestation, Zaman reminds us that: 'appeals to tradition are not necessarily a way of opposing change but can equally facilitate change; that what passes for tradition is, not infrequently of quite recent vintage; and that definition of what constitutes tradition are often the product of bitter and continuing conflicts within a culture'.[28]

Notes

1　R. Nicholson (1989 3rd edition) *The Mystics of Islam*. Harmondsworth: Arkana.

2　Cited from M. Lings (1993) *A Sufi Saint of the Twentieth Century*. Cambridge: Islamic Texts Society, p. 34.

3　V. Hoffman-Ladd (1992) 'Devotion to the Prophet and His Family in Egyptian Sufism', *International Journal of Middle-Eastern Studies*, 24, 4, p. 616.

4　R. Geaves (2000) *The Sufis of Britain*. Cardiff: Cardiff Academic Press.

5　R. Geaves (2010) *Islam in Victorian Britain: The Life and Times of Abdullah Quilliam*. Markfield: Kube Press.

6　See Geaves (2000), p. 65. The story of these Arab port communities has been told in detail by Fred Halliday (1992), *Arabs in Exile*. London: IB Tauris and more recently in Humayun Ansari (2004) *The Infidel Within*. London: Hurst. Mohammad Sedden is also researching al-Hakimi contributing a chapter to this collection entitled 'Shaykh Abdullah Ali al-Hakimi, The Alawi Tariqah and British Yemenis'.

7　See Martin Ling (1993) for a detailed biography.

8　M. Sedgwick (2009) 'The Reception of Sufi and neo-Sufi Literature' in *Sufis in Western Society*. R. Geaves, M. Dressler and G. Klinkhammer (Eds), London: Routledge, p. 184.

9　R. Irwin (2011) *Memoirs of a Dervish*. London: Profile Books.

10　A. Köse (1996) *Conversion to Islam*. London: Kegan Paul, p. 176.

11　Geaves (2000), pp. 142–4.

12 G. Klinkhammer (2009) 'The Emergence of Transethnic Sufism in Germany: From Mysticism to Authenticity' in *Sufis in Western Society*. R. Geaves, M. Dressler and G. Klinkhammer (Eds). London: Routledge, p. 144.

13 For detailed study of these developments, see a series of articles written by the author. R. A. Geaves (2005) 'Tradition, Innovation, and Authentication: Replicating the Ahl-as Sunna Wa Jamaat in Britain'. *Journal of Comparative Islamic Studies*, 1:1, 1–20; (2006) 'Learning the lessons from the neo-Revivalist and Wahhabi Movements: the Counterattack of New Sufi Movements in the UK' in *Sufism in the West*. J. Malik and J. Hinnells (Eds), London: Routledge; (2009) 'A Case of Cultural Binary Fission or Transglobal Sufism? The Transmigration of Sufism to Britain' in *Global Networking and Locality: Sufis in Western Society*. R. A. Geaves, M. Dressler and G. Klinkhammer (Eds), London: Routledge.

14 M. Hermansen (2009) 'Global Sufism: Theirs and Ours' in *Sufis in Western Society*. R. Geaves, M. Dressler and G. Klinkhammer (Eds), London: Routledge, p. 26.

15 Geaves (2005), 1–20.

16 R. Catharina and S. Leif (2009) 'Translocal Mobility and Traditional Authority' in *Sufism Today*, C. Raudvere and L. Stenberg (Eds). London: IB Tauris, pp. 1–12, p. 1.

17 W. Itzchak (2004) 'Sufi Brotherhoods in Syria and Israel: A Contemporary Overview', *History of Religions*, 43, 303–18, p. 303.

18 W. Itschak (2007) The *Naqshbandiyya: Orthodoxy and Activism in a Worldwide Sufi Tradition*. London: Routledge, p. 8.

19 H. Sadek (2012) *Convergent and Divergent Trends in British Islamic Youth Activism*, PhD Thesis, University of Chester.

20 P. Werbner, (2003) *Pilgrims of Love*. London: Hurst.

21 H. Paul, (2009) 'The Politics of Sufism' in *Sufism Today*. Raudvere, Catharina and Stenberg, Leif. London: IB Tauris, pp. 12–29, p. 15.

22 V. John (2007) 'Contemporary Sufism and Current Social Theory' in *Sufism and the Modern in Islam*. M. van Bruinessen and J. D. Howell (Eds). London: IB Tauris, pp. 281–98, pp. 296–8.

23 I. Ronald (2003) *Modernization and Post-Modernization: Cultural, Economic and Political Change in 43 Societies*. Princeton: Princeton University Press, p. 328.

24 p. 328.

25 W. Linda, H. Paul and D. Grace (2003) 'Introduction' in *Predicting Religion*. W. Linda, H. Paul and D. Grace (Eds), Aldershot: Ashgate, p. 2.

26 F. Schuon (1969) 'No Activity Without Truth', *Studies in Comparative Religion*, 3, 4, Autumn, 67.

27 p. 28.

28 Z. Muhammad Qasim (2007) *The Ulama in Contemporary Islam*. Princeton University Press, p. 3.

3

Universal Sufis in the UK: Sufism for Everyone?

Roy Jackson

While visiting a colleague who I have known for many years and to have an interest in matters philosophical and religious, he declared to me that he had 'become a Sufi'. Knowing my colleague as I do, though 'philosophical' in temperament and extremely interested in all things religious and, dare I say, 'spiritual', he had not previously subscribed to any particular religious tradition and had often been critical of institutional religions, Islam especially. Digging a little deeper on this declaration that he had chosen the Sufi path, it turned out that he had not become affiliated to the Sufi groups that I was familiar with in my own studies within the Islamic tradition, but with what he called the Sufi Way whereby, it seemed, one could declare oneself to be a 'Sufi' without adhering to the strictures and demands of that ascetic tradition as I understood them. This resulted in some further research on my part.

Sufi Order, Sufi Way, Sufi Movement

My research has taken me in many different directions, but what was extremely enlightening for me was a visit I paid to Professor Peter Sharif Hawkins.[1] Peter Hawkins is part-time Professor of Leadership at Henley Business School as well as Visiting Professor at the Universities of Bath and Oxford Brookes. His main research concerns, then, are in the field of next-generation leadership and organizational transformation, and he is the author of such works as *Leadership Team Coaching*,[2] and *The Wise Fool's Guide to Leadership*.[3] Hawkins may, therefore, seem like an unlikely candidate for my research into Sufism, in the same way my friend seems an unlikely candidate for being a Sufi. However, it is not so much Hawkins' research into leadership skills as such that is of interest here, but that his research is informed by the fact that he is a senior member of The Sufi Way. I had come across Peter's name during a series of lectures he gave on Sufism (more specifically three lectures on Rumi, Hafiz and Ibn al Arabi, respectively) at the Bath Royal Literary and Scientific Society and which also included music and readings. Peter kindly invited me to his home, so that I might find out more about his association with Sufism.

His home is actually a grand property called Barrow Castle, which he also uses as a venue for retreats and Sufi meetings. This castle is certainly in very pleasant surroundings, with views of the surrounding fields of Bath, and I found Professor Hawkins to be friendly, welcoming and intelligent company. The rest of this chapter is based on a series of questions I asked Professor Hawkins as the initial impetus for further research. There is, however, a specific focus to this chapter and it goes back to my conversations with my friend, for my main interest here is to examine the extent to which the use of the term 'Sufism', when applied to The Sufi Way (and, as we shall see, not *only* The Sufi Way), can be understood as having any correlation to Sufism in the Islamic tradition. I came to the interview with a largely open mind, but, I confess, with a degree of scepticism concerning the 'Islamic-ness' of The Sufi Way as well as some related groups in the United Kingdom and the West that come under the broad umbrella term of 'Universal Sufism'.[4] During my interview, Peter Hawkins provided me with an account of not only the Sufi Way (or, more formally known as the Sufi Way International) but also another related group called the International Sufi Movement, and, indeed, a third group called the Sufi Order International. What all three groups have in common is that they trace their lineage back to Hazrat Inayat Khan, the founder of the International Sufi Movement, and it is this charismatic and influential figure that is worthy of more exploration later on in this chapter.

The beliefs and practices of 'Traditional' Sufism

First of all, however, just how hard is it to be a Sufi? More specifically, what engagement with the rigours and discipline of aesthetic practice is required and how much religious conviction in the tenets of Islam are expected in order to qualify oneself as a Sufi? I ask this question simply because the response is not an easy one and it is dependent on a number of factors: what Sufi Orders are we referring to? Are these Sufi groups as practiced in the United Kingdom really

Sufism at all? By that, I mean to bring into question how the term 'Sufism' can be rightly applied to certain Sufi groups in the United Kingdom which, of course, also begs the question as to whether or not there is a right or wrong when using such a term or whether in fact we simply need to be more broad minded in its usage. Does it really *matter* if certain groups refer to themselves as 'Sufi' but see no connection between that term and the Islamic tradition? While accepting that Sufism, like any 'ism' one may come across, can never be treated in a monolithic sense, there needs to be a reason, one might argue, why Sufism is what it is and what it is that distinguishes it from other 'isms'. The central features of Sufism may well be inevitably broad, but an essence of some sort should be achievable, otherwise one is compelled to retort that there is no such thing as Sufism, which would be a nonsense.

What, then, are the defining features of Sufism? First, Sufism is *traditionally* considered to be firmly rooted within the Islamic tradition. While 'mystical', it is, nonetheless, not inimical to what is referred to as 'traditional' Islam (which, of course, is as pluralistic in form as Sufism). That is to say, Sufis who are also Muslims closely identify their tradition as part of the interpretation of Islam's holy text, the Qur'an, and that the final Prophet, Muhammad, is *insan al-kamil*, the 'Perfect Man', for which Sufis set out to emulate. Muhammad, in this sense, is the first Sufi and the Master of all Sufis. Aside from the holy text and the Prophet, Sufis also desire to have contact with the One and Only God. In these respects, Sufism is 'traditional': a holy text, belief in prophecy and monotheistic.

The path, however, may well differ, adopting as it does more 'mystical' practices although, again, Sufis would argue that the Prophet Muhammad would not have received the revelations of the Qur'an if he had not also been a mystic. Sufis perceive mysticism as central to religious engagement, not on the periphery, despite the suspicions of some of the more orthodox elements in Islam. These suspicions in some cases are rooted in the belief that Sufi mystics have a tendency to bypass *shari'a* in their efforts to be good Muslims. The perceived antagonism between *shari'a* and *tariqa* is not so clear cut, of course, and it has been strongly argued that Sufis are quite in line with *shari'a*, while giving Islamic law an extra mystical and poetic dimension that complements it.[5] What is evident is that any attempt to draw a line between 'traditional Islam' and 'traditional Sufism' is destined to fail; there is considerable overlap between the two. In fact, one can be both a Sufi and a traditional Muslim.

As is often the case with 'isms', we must be extremely wary of falling into an orientalist approach to stereotype what is such a diverse and sometimes contradictory phenomena, yet it is also the case that within Islamic tradition itself attempts have been made to classify the mystical tradition. The question of whether certain Sufi orders in the United Kingdom are really 'Sufism' at all really depends upon how precious one wants to be about Sufism. For example, in Trimingham's excellent *The Sufi Orders of Islam*, on the very first page he says the following,

> 'I define the word sufi in wide terms by applying it to anyone who believes that it
> is possible to have direct experience of God and who is prepared to go out of his
> way to put himself in a state whereby he may be enabled to do this.'[6]

Trimingham then immediately adds, 'Many will not be happy with this definition, but I find it the only possible way to embrace all the varieties of people involved in the orders.'[7]

One can understand why many may not be happy with this, as the definition he provides omits any mention of Islam as being part of the tradition. The emphasis on God, at least, may narrow things down to the monotheistic traditions (although, of course, not necessarily) but, essentially, this definition can be suitably applied to any form of mysticism. However, it should be pointed out that Trimingham does make a distinction between 'sufi' and 'Sufism'; the latter he defines as, 'those tendencies in Islam which aim at direct communion between God and man.'[8] Here it is clear that Sufism is firmly within the Islamic tradition, running, ideally, parallel with the Islamic sciences, although perhaps inevitably coming into conflict with them due to the former's more personal relationship with God.

In the traditional sense, a Sufi belongs to a named order, a *tariqa*. The diversity of *tariqas* makes the task of determining any essential characteristic for all of them a hard one indeed. Certainly in terms of command structures this is so different from one order to the next; some being considerably more egalitarian than others. Similarly, while they all strive towards Allah, these paths, *warifas*, also differ from one order to the next. In practice, Sufi orders have a central focus upon a saint (living or dead) as *ta'ifas*[9] (regional cults). Each of these cults would have a sacred centre and a lodge which is founded by a living saint. It has branches that recognize affiliation to it and participate in its annual festivals. The saint has emissaries, his khalifas and disciples, who can settle anywhere. These are just some of the distinguishing features of traditional Sufism and so it is interesting to consider whether the Sufi Way and its correlates possesses any or all of these.

The chaordic nature of universal Sufism

A very important question here is whether Sufi orders *have* to be 'Islamic' or even necessarily religious. Pnina Werbner has written of the 'chaordic nature' of Sufi orders.[10] The term 'chaordic' has its origins with Dee Hock, the founder and CEO, Emeritus of VISA USA and VISA International, but it is not just restricted to the world of business. Hock's definition is

> By Chaord, I mean any self-organizing, adaptive, non-linear, complex system, whether physical, biological, or social, the behaviour of which exhibits characteristics of both order and chaos or, loosely translated to business terminology, cooperation and competition.[11]

Hock cites VISA as an example of an organization that lies between chaos and order (hence Cha-ord): it has no centralized command structure and no one owns it; it has no value or shareholders; it is not your typical multi-national company, yet it 'exists' in almost every part of the world. Visa companies sprout, in an organic manner, independently – 'chaotically' – while depending upon a set of rules and agreements for its continued existence – the 'Order' element. Another example may well be the internet. Relevance of Chaord here, however, is that Sufi orders operate in a seemingly not dissimilar manner; a diaspora of orders that are independent and even competitive.[12] Despite having distinctive identities, there are nonetheless various features that lead them to come under the umbrella identity of 'Sufi'.

Most Sufi orders that have migrated to Britain, while transforming from their origins in certain ways, nonetheless maintain an identity with their traditions through recognition of sacred genealogical links to the orders from their geographical origins. For example, the various branches of the Naqshbandi Order. This is a very good example of Chaord; the chaos element is that the Order in, for example, Turkey does not have the same tradition of dissenting against the political authorities as, say, the branches of the Order in Pakistan which – being very strict in terms of adherence of shari'a – is often critical of the not-so shari'a-minded politicians. In Britain, some branches of the Naqshbandi are more traditional than others. However, what does unite these groups is that its dominant forms are almost exclusively Pakistani Muslim.[13] Whether more or less traditional in their outlook, there is no dispute that these groups are 'Muslim'.

The origins of universal Sufism

What first attracted Western people to Sufism was largely a result of Christians who converted to Islam as a result of Sufi practices, or remained Christian while finding Sufism – as part of a wider mystical tradition – particularly appealing. It was this universal aspect of Islam, an Islam without the seeming need for shari'a or, for that matter, commitment to much in the way of the standard rituals and practices of Islam.

What is interesting is the extent to which this notion of Sufism as 'universal' is more of a Western creation than an inherently Islamic one. The 'discovery' of Sufism by Western scholars resulted in it being presented as an esoteric practice based primarily on neo-Platonic and neo-Zoroastrian beliefs, rather than having any particularly strong connection with Islam, yet previous to this there does not seem to be any evidence that Muslims themselves saw Sufism as distinct from Islam. This Orientalist approach saw Sufism as anti-dogmatic and monistic or pantheistic and therefore having little concern for shari'a and transcending the borders of Islam.[14] This allowed non-Muslims a way into at least one form of Islam, given a distrust and dislike for Islam per se. As Uzdavinys notes, the attitude of Westerners to Islam was 'mostly negative, based on the pre-judicious stereotypes and current Islamophobia which required to exclude Muslims from Western civilization altogether'.[15]

Sufism originally reached the West in two ways: through texts translated into Western languages and, secondly, through actual Sufis who travelled to Europe and the United States. Andrew Rawlinson provides a useful outline of the origins of Sufism in the West. He points out that one need only go back a century for there to be no Western 'gurus', as in Westerners who were Hindu swamis, Zen roshis, or Sufi sheikhs, whereas now there are many hundreds. The proliferation of these Western gurus has led to a presentation of a view of the human condition which is new to the West. This, according to Rawlinson, can be narrowed down to four principles:

1. Human beings are best understood in terms of consciousness and its modifications.
2. Consciousness can be transformed by spiritual practice.
3. There are gurus/masters/teachers who have done this.
4. They can help others to do the same through their guidance.[16]

The first significant Sufi individual to have brought this new kind of Sufism to the West is Hazrat Pir-o-Murshid Inayat Khan (1882–1927), which now brings us to the Sufi Way and its correlates, beginning historically with the International Sufi Movement.

The links with Hazrat Pir-o-Murshid Inayat Khan

Beginning first, then, with the International Sufi Movement, Hazrat Inayat Khan died quite young (late 40s) so lineage first went to his brother Shaikh-ul-Mashaikh Maheboob Khan, and then to his cousin Pir-o-Murshid Ali Khan in 1948. In 1956, leadership passed to his youngest brother Pir-o-Murshid Musharaff Khan and then to his grandson Pir-o-Murshid Fazal Inayat-Khan in 1968. Fazal, who was only 26 when he became Pir, got married at 16, and, according to Peter Hawkins, was considered quite a wild member of the family. He took over the Movement, which had become very strong in Europe, particularly in Holland, Germany, United Kingdom, South Africa, parts of United States, but was considered by some, including Fazal himself, as conservative in its teachings and practice. The current Pir of the International Sufi Movement is Murshid Hidayat Inayat-Khan.

Fazal went on to found a new movement called the Sufi Way International, in 1985. Fazal was succeeded by the first woman pir of the Order, Pir-o-Murshida Sitara Brutnell. After her death in 2004, her successor, and current Pir, is Pir-o-Murshid Elias Amidon. Elias received his initiation in 1969 and he was a student of Fazal's. He also studied with Qadiri Sufis in Morocco, Theravada Buddhists in Thailand, Native American teachers of the Assemblies of the Morning Star, Christian monks in Syria and Zen masters of the White Plum Sangha.[17] Meanwhile, Inayat's eldest son, Vilayat (1916–2004) had set up the Sufi Order International as he saw himself as his father's natural successor and might well have been had his father died older. The current Pir of the Sufi Order International is Hazrat Pir Zia Inayat Khan, son of Vilayat. As Fazal himself states

'It is interesting to note that the differences between The Sufi Movement and the Order are quite comparable with the variations of the Orthodox and Catholic wings of the Christian faith, or the Sunni and Shia divergence in Islam and scores of other divisions, schisms and resurgences which one finds where human beings are deeply committed and involved with purposive and/or idealistic actualisation.'[18]

On the Home Page of the Sufi Order UK website – which is the UK branch of the Sufi Order International – the quote below is from Hazrat Inayat Khan and it sums up succinctly how all three of these movements see themselves:

> Sufism is not a religion or a philosophy, it is neither deism nor atheism, nor is it a moral, nor a special kind of mysticism, being free from the usual religious sectarianism. If ever it could be called a religion, it would only be as a religion of love, harmony, and beauty.[19]

This form of Sufism is, therefore, both a religion and not a religion. Presumably this is synonymous with saying that its adherents are in some way devoted to love, harmony and beauty, if that is what is to be understood by 'religion' in this sense. Whatever the case, Hazrat Inayat Khan is deliberately distancing this Universal Sufism from the conventional understanding of religion.

According to the UK website of the Sufi Order, Pir-O Murshid Hazrat Inayat Khan 'came to the West – from his perspective we might call it "the mysterious West" – in 1910. He brought with him the traditions of the Sufi schools of India and Central Asia.' Inayat was born into a 'family of musicians'[20] in 1882, and it seems he was brought up in an enlightened environment surrounded by visiting musicians, poets, thinkers and mystics. Inayat himself began as a musician, skilled in playing the Veena,[21] but he also began to see 'a very spiritual bearded man'[22] in his dreams and, one day in Hyderabad, this same man appeared in his room and became his teacher. The man of his visions was Shaykh al-Mashaykh Sayed Muhammed Abu Hashim Madani, who was a member of the Chishti Order.

Therefore, we have here two essential features of Sufism: a *silsala* and a *murshid*. Inayat was initiated, then, into the Chishti order and maintained a close link with his *murshid* until the latter's death after four years. His Pir, on his deathbed, told Inayat to 'Go to the Western world my son and unite East and West through the magic of your music'.[23] This Inayat did two years later, setting sail for the United States. For ten years he travelled, performing his music and lecturing, across America and Europe. In 1920, he took up residence near Paris in Suresnes where he held 'summer schools' to engage in more intensive teaching. In this teaching, Inayat laid emphasis on the oneness of all religions:

> It was at Suresnes that Inayat developed the Universal Worship service that is now associated with the "Sufi Order in the West". The ritual consists of an invocation, a reading from one of the holy books of the world's major religions, and the lighting of a candle for each tradition. A candle is also lit for all those

individuals or religious systems (unknown or forgotten) that have inspired mankind. The ritual continues with a discourse, and ends with a blessing. One goal of the Universal Worship service is to show people from different cultures the many common elements they share in their religious traditions, and to create a sense of unity among people from different cultures by teaching them to read each other's scriptures and 'pray each other's prayers'.[24]

If Inayat's murshid was Hashim Madani, what then was the *silsila* of Hashim Madani? Fortunately the Universal Sufi Order's websites has a page that displays its *silsila*, with Madani just above Inayat. This is the standard Chishti *silsila*, and so below is a digested lineage, which sets out to highlight how the Sufi Order – with slight variations more recently for the Movement and the Way – maintains links with traditional Sufism:

Hazrat Khwaja Abu Ishaq Shami
Hazrat Khwaja Mu'inuddin Hasan Sanjari-Ajmiri
Hazrat Khwaja Qutbuddin Mas'ud Bakhtiyar Kaki
Hazrat Khwaja Fariduddin Ganj-i Shakar Ajhodani
Hazrat Khwaja Nizamuddin Mahbub-i Ilahi Badauni
Hazrat Khwaja Nasiruddin Chiragh Dihlavi
Hazrat Shaykh al-Masha'ikh Kamaluddin 'Allama
Hazrat Shaykh al-Masha'ikh Shah Kalim Allah Jahanabadi
Hazrat Shaykh al-Masha'ikh Muhammad Hasan Jili Kalimi
Hazrat Shaykh al-Masha'ikh Muhammad Abu Hashim Madani
Hazrat Pir-o-Murshid 'Inayat Khan
Hazrat Pir Vilayat 'Inayat Khan

From the above list, links are being made with the Chishti Order, hence Hazrat Khwaja Abu Ishaq Shami (d. 941 AD) who initially brought Sufism to the town of Chishti in what is today Afghanistan. Also in the silsila above is Hazrat Khwaja Mu'inuddin Hasan Sanjari-Ajmiri (d. 1229) who, with his disciples, introduced the Chishtiyya to the Indian Subcontinent. Then his successor, Hazrat Khwaja Qutbuddin Mas'ud Bakhtiyar Kaki, who reportedly died in 1235 after a mystical couplet sent him into ecstasy. Next in line here is Hazrat Khwaja Fariduddin Ganj-i Shakar Ajhodani (d. 1265) whose verses are contained within the Sikh holy text Guru Granth Sahib. Chishti Sufism spread throughout the Indian subcontinent with Hazrat Khwaja Nizamuddin Mahbub-i Ilahi ('Beloved of God') Badauni (d. 1325). The Chistiyya has a number of splinter groups, such as the Sabiriyya (from Khwaja 'Ala al-Din 'Ali

Sabir) and the Nizamiyya (from Khwaja Nizam al-Din), but the Sufi Order follows from Hazrat Khwaja Nasiruddin Chiragh Dihlavi and his nephew Hazrat Shaykh al-Masha'ikh Kamaluddin 'Allama (d. 1355), including the significant figure of Hazrat Shaykh al-Masha'ikh Shah Kalim Allah Jahanabadi (d. 1729) who came from the family of architects who designed the Taj Mahal, composed the meditation manual *Kashkul-i Kalimi* and also established a school in Delhi that flourished until its demise as a result of the Indian Rebellion of 1857 which effectively saw the end of the Mughal Empire. Just before the Rebellion, the story goes that Hazrat Shaykh al-Masha'ikh Muhammad Hasan Jili Kalimi received a premonition that he should take his family to Hyderabad. He was followed by Hazrat Shaykh al-Masha'ikh Muhammad Abu Hashim Madani who then became the teacher (Murshid) of Hazrat Inayat Khan. The rest, as they say, is history. Hazrat Inayat Khan recounts his first meeting with his teacher in his *Confessions*:

> After a time of suspense the Pir-o-Murshid entered, bringing with him a very great sense of light. As all those present greeted him, bowing down in their humility, it seemed to me all at once that I had seen him before, but where I could not recall. At last, after gazing at him earnestly, I remembered that his was the face which so persistently haunted me during my silence. The proof of this was manifested as soon as his eyes fell on me.
>
> He turned to his host, saying, 'O Mawlana, tell me who this young man may be? He appeals intensely to my spirit'.
>
> Mawlana Khayr al-Mubin answered, 'Your holiness, this young man is a genius in music, and he desires greatly to submit himself to your inspiring guidance'.
>
> Then the Master smiled and granted the request, initiating me into Sufism there and then.[25]

In a video entitled *Murshid as I Remember Him*, the narrator, Pir Vilayat (the eldest son of Inayat Khan), recalls

> Murshid in the first years was using the word 'Sufi' a lot. In fact, in the early days, of course, the teaching was very much similar on the pattern of the classical tradition of Sufi teachings, Sufi schools, but later on Murshid used the term 'Sufi' less and less and he used the word 'Message' more and more and he made it clear that the esoteric school was just a school of training for those who were spreading the Message and, of course, then naturally people would ask Murshid what do you mean by the Message? . . . He said the Message is the awakening of humanity to the divinity in man.[26]

On the website, it states that the Sufi Order is a religious philosophy that emphasized no particular religion more than any other, but it nonetheless has what is called a 'philosophical container' which 'could accommodate the diversity of peoples and faiths found in both the East and West'.[27] This consists of the 'Ten Sufi Thoughts'. The first of these states the following: 'There is One God, the Eternal, the Only Being; none exists save He'. It then goes on to say that

> the God of the Sufi is the God of every creed, and the God of all. Names make no difference to him. Allah, God, Gott, Dieu, Brahma, or Bhagwan, all these names and more are the names of his God; and yet to him God is beyond the limitation of name. He sees his God in the sun, in the fire, in the idol which diverse sects worship; and he recognizes Him in all the forms of the universe, yet knowing Him to be beyond all form: God in all, and all in God, He being the Seen and the Unseen, the Only Being. God to the Sufi is not only a religious belief, but also the highest ideal the human mind can conceive.

We are presented here with an extremely vague God, that defies any attempt to adhere to specific attributes and is almost Platonic or neo-Platonic. The second Sufi Thought states that, 'there is One Master (Murshid), the Guiding Spirit of all Souls, Who constantly leads his followers towards the light'. While God is acknowledged as the source of all knowledge, inspiration and guidance, man is the 'medium through which God chooses to impart his knowledge to the world'. Reference is made to previous masters, which does include the Prophet Muhammad, but also Shiva, Buddha, Rama, Krishna, Jesus, Abraham and so on.

Space does not allow us to explore the other 'thoughts', but there is a pattern here. The third Sufi thought is 'one Holy Book', the fourth is 'one Religion', the fifth is 'one Law' and so on, but when the researcher pursues the specifics here, one is left with an unclear account. The Holy Book is in fact 'the sacred manuscript of nature', and the 'one Religion' is 'the right direction towards the ideal'. Perhaps it is my analytic mind that is betraying me here, but these 'thoughts' seem imprecise in the extreme.

The dances of universal peace UK (DUPIK)

Aside from these three main groupings, another group is worth a mention to demonstrate the kind of diversity that exists, despite the familiar silsila and the importance of Hazrat Inayat Khan, and this is the Dances of Universal Peace, established by Sam Lewis (1869–1971). Although the Dances of Universal

Peace is an entirely separate order, its founder credits Hazrat Inayat Khan as his inspiration for the movement. In 1923, West met Hazrat Inayat Khan and received initiation from him. On their UK website, the quote from its founder is 'Words are not peace. Thoughts are not peace. Peace is fundamental to all faiths, all religions, all spirituality'.[28] It goes on to introduce Murshid Samuel West: 'He became the spiritual leader of the hippies, by teaching them how to get 'high' without drugs. His simple plan for achieving peace within and without was to 'Eat, Dance and Pray together'. His father, Jacob Lewis, was vice president of the Levi Strauss Company, and his mother was Harriet Rothschild. Despite this privileged background, or perhaps because of it, he turned to spiritual concerns in his early twenties, delving into theosophy and Zen teachings. After his initiation into Sufism by Hazrat Inayat Khan, West went on to write essays on spiritual topics and, in 1956, he travelled to Asia where, according to the website, 'he was widely accepted as an awakened being and a Zen-shi or teacher of Zen Buddhism, a teacher of Bhakti yoga by Swami Papa Ramdas, of Christian mysticism and of the Hebrew Kaballah'.[29] In the late 1960s, he started to incorporate dance as part of spiritual apprenticeship, inspired by Ruth St. Denis (1878–1968). The pictures of her on the website presents a glamorous, aesthetic woman. She was a pioneer of contemporary dance in the United States by introducing Eastern ideas.[30] In her unpublished book *The Divine Dance* (1933), Ruth St. Denis wrote of her vision of a future dance for life and peace:

> 'The dance of the future will no longer be concerned with meaningless dexterities of the body . . . Remembering that man is indeed the microcosm, the universe in miniature, the Divine Dance of the future should be able to convey with its slightest gestures some significance of the universe . . . As we rise higher in the understanding of ourselves, the national and racial dissonances will be forgotten in the universal rhythms of Truth and Love. We shall sense our unity with all peoples who are moving to that exalted rhythm.'[31]

In 1983, the Dances of Universal Peace was established and is now known as the Dances of Universal Peace International with branches in twenty-two countries, including the Dances of Universal Peace United Kingdom, which was established in 1990. Sam West also founded the Sufi Ruhaniat International to broaden the scope and mission of the movement. The current spiritual guide for Sufi Ruhaniat International is Pir Shabda Khan. In June 2011, he paid a visit to the Sheldon Centre in Devon. This one-hour interview is significant in terms of this chapter because he addresses the question of the relationship between the Sufi path and Ruhaniat International. Shabda quotes Hazrat here, again with no reference to Islam, but rather adopting a universal understanding as mysticism rather than belonging to any specific religion: 'Our Sufi lineage certainly is not a religion'.

Conclusion

It is this difficulty in determining what The Sufi Way and these other related groups essentially believes in that makes it frustrating for me, and perhaps appealing for those who do not wish to be constricted by something so troubling as 'belief'. As I was leaving Peter Hawkins' picturesque castle, he handed me a small booklet with the typically esoteric title *Fresh Rain*. The author was the Pir of the Sufi Way International, Elias Amidon, and it was subtitled *An Introduction to The Sufi Way*. This was a quick read, and its final pages stood out for me in terms of the following:

> . . . A sufi, after all, is simply a human being, not a "Sufi". There is actually no such thing as a "Sufi," and the essence of Sufism recognises this. In fact, there is no such thing as "Sufism." Despite what you may read in some accounts, there are no dogmas, doctrines, or essential beliefs involved in Sufism. There is no "ism" at all. Sufism is simply an openness of heart.[32]

This in many respects sums up the dichotomy between 'Sufism' (in Islam) and 'Sufism' (in its 'universal' sense), between an Islamic tradition that is complex and rich in doctrine and essential beliefs, and one that defies definition and is vague when it comes to academic scrutiny. These Western sufi orders often come across as forms of contemporary spirituality, and I subscribe to the view of Jeremy Carrette and Richard King that 'There are perhaps few words in the modern English language as vague and woolly as the notion of 'spirituality'.[33] Adherence to *genuine* religious belief is not meant to be easy, as Kierkegaard so succinctly noted, and much of modern spirituality seems little more than pick-and-mix spiritual shopping and a way of avoiding conviction and existential concerns. As Dr. David Webster states in *Dispirited*:

> If we truly step beyond a world of spirituality, have the real courage of our convictions, we step into a landscape which might seem featureless, bleak and devoid of the potential for happiness. But this nihilistic dawn is not what it seems. It is what we choose it to be. We are so locked into essentialist accounts

of human spirit, of it as a source of value and morals – that even the atheist lives a little in fear of the consequences of their beliefs'.[34]

As Pir Murshid Fazal Inayat Khan states, 'Western Sufism is non-Islamic as seen from the perspective of orthodox Muslim thought'.[35] However, he goes on to add,

If one traces Sufism historically to the ancient Pythagorean orders, it becomes clear that Sufism is a spiritual cultural force throughout civilised history. Interestingly, one can conclude in historical perspective that the cause of Sufism's resurgent, adaptive and changing permanency as a feature of human, spiritual thought and practice, is its ability to decentralise and evolve its body of thought among a great variety of leaders. So it remains continuously in a flux of spiritual searching, responding to the present human condition at any particular time. I therefore define Sufism as remaining ever the same by always changing'.[36]

This emphasis on the flexibility and evolving nature of Sufism is certainly one of its attractions, but there is a concern that the results can seem somewhat vacuous for the scholar who is concerned with more intellectual rigour and commitment. In the case of those I have spoken to at various meetings, of which some would profess to be Sufis, they admit to having an interest in 'spiritual issues' but possess little knowledge of Islam or traditional Islamic Sufism, and would be unwilling to subscribe (or have knowledge of) to the strictures that some of the members of Islamic Sufi orders are subject to. Repeating the quote above from Fazal Inayat Khan, 'I therefore define Sufism as remaining ever the same by always changing[37]', and being quite prepared to acknowledge that the groups of western Sufism considered here are not Islamic, then there is certainly no reason to criticize these groups for calling themselves 'sufi' in this respect, for they are not making claims to be more than what they are. From a scholarly point of view, however, the attempt to determine the teachings of many of these groups can leave one frustrated.

Nonetheless, the three main schools considered in this chapter do maintain certain characteristics that would not be unfamiliar to traditional Sufism. Fazal himself notes the existence of other western Sufi groups in the West, 'such as Sufism Reoriented, and the various North American dancing dervish groups, etc. I do not consider these groups as part of Western Sufism today, because their silsilae (chain of spiritual succession) is not clearly defined and/or they no longer follow a succinct initiatic tradition'.[38]

This is interesting because of the emphasis on the importance of silsila. This is echoed by Hazrat Inayat Khan, who, while affirming the universalist message of Western Sufism, is also stressing the importance of the Islamic heritage through, especially, the *Mazhab-e Ishq*, the 'Path of Love' in Sufism which is closely associated by traditional Sufi figures as Bayazid Bistami, Rumi, Ibn al-Arabi and Suhrawardi. Khan has also demonstrated a keen knowledge of Chishti silsala tradition (something not always the case with his followers) and displays a familiarity with Chishti Sufi manuals.[39]

There is, therefore, a tension that exists between these high ideals of maintaining an association within the Islamic tradition and the needs of many of the followers of these Western Sufi Orders who embrace its more universal qualities.

Notes

1 The interview took place on May 1, 2012.

2 Hawkins (2011) *Leadership Team Coaching*. London: Kegan.

3 H. Peter (2005) *The Wise Fool's Guide to Leadership*. Alresford, Hants: O Books.

4 See Geaves 2000 and 2011 for an analysis of the term 'universal Sufism'. There are other labels used for this religious tradition but I argue that 'universal Sufism' has advantages over the others.

5 See especially Baldick (2000 2nd edition) *Mystical Islam: An Introduction to Sufism*. IB Tauris & Co..

6 Trimingham (1971), *The Sufi Orders of Islam*. Oxford: OUP, p. 1.

7 Ibid.

8 Ibid.

9 For excellent studies of ta'if I would recommend Trimingham (1971). For regional cults see Richard Werbner (1977, 1989).

10 P. Werbner (2002), 'The Place Which is Diaspora: Citizenship, Religion and Gender in the Making of Chaordic Transnationalism', *Journal of Ethnic and Migration Studies*, 28, 1, 119–34.

11 D. W. Hock (1995) 'The Chaordic Organization: Out of Control and Into Order', *World Business Academy Perspectives*, 9, 1.

12 Sufi disciples will, for example, 'shop around' by attending festivals of different Sufi orders.

13 P. Werbner (2006) 'Seekers on the Path: Different Ways of Being Sufi in Britain' in *Sufism in the West*, J. Malik and J. Hinnells (Eds), London and New York: Routledge, p. 130. In some cases they are British born, but of Pakistani origin.

14 U. Algis (2005) 'Sufism in the Light of Orientalism', *Acta Orientalia Vilnensia*, 6, 2, pp. 114–25.

15 Ibid.

16 Rawlinson, A. (1993) 'A History of Western Sufism' in DISKUS Vol. 1. No.1, pp. 45–83.

17 Amidon (2011) *Fresh Rain: An Introduction to the Sufi Way*. Boulder, Colorado: Open Path Publishing, p. 43.

18 Ibid.

19 http://sufiorder.uk.org.

20 http://om-guru.com/html/saints/khan.html.

21 'The Veena is the oldest instrument in the world – not, of course, in its present form, but in its original form. It is the mother instrument of all instruments in the East, and it is chiefly used for concentration and meditation.' Quote from Hazrat Inayat Khan: http://sufimessage.com/music/vina.html.

22 Ibid.

23 Ibid.

24 http://om-guru.com/html/saints/khan.html.

25 Bloch (1915), pp. 38–42.

26 http://wahiduddin.net/hik/hik_dvd.htm.

27 http://sufiorderuk.org/our-roots.php.

28 http://dancesofuniversalpeace.org.uk.

29 Ibid.

30 You can see snippets of her performances on YouTube, such as the East Indian Nautch Dance (1932) at http://youtube.com/watch?v=j8XvHX1FKsY, A documentary *On the Trail of Ruth St. Denis* came out in 2011. Directed, produced and co-written by Kuwait-based Talal Al-Muhanna, it is a historical dance documentary where the camera follows British-Australian dance artist Liz Lea as she retraces the 'footsteps of one of the twentieth century's greatest artistic innovators'. See the trailer at: https://vimeo.com/45029153.

31 http://dancesofuniversalpeace.org.uk.

32 Amidon (2011) *Fresh Rain: An Introduction to the Sufi Way*. Boulder, Colorado: Open Path Publishing, p. 32.

33 J. Carrette and R. King (2005) *Selling Spirituality*. London: Routledge, p. 30.

34 Webster (2012) *Dispirited: How Contemporary Spirituality Makes Us Stupid, Selfish and Unhappy*. Alresford, Hants: Zero Books, p. 71

35 Pir-o-Murshid Fazal Inayat Khan, *Western Sufism: The Sufi Movement, the Sufi Order International, and the Sufi Way*. http://sufiway.org/history/texts/western_sufism.ph.

36 Ibid.
37 Ibid.
38 Ibid.
39 For example, the Wujud al-Ashekin of Gizu Daraz and the Kashkul-i-Kalimi of Kalim Allah Jahanabadi.

Bibliography

Amidon, E. (2011) *Fresh Rain: An Introduction to The Sufi Way*, Boulder, Colorado: London: Open Path Publishing.

Baldick, J. (2000) *Mystical Islam: An Introduction to Sufism*, Second Edition, IB Tauris & Co.

Bloch, R. M. (1915) *The Confessions of Inayat Khan*, London: The Sufi Publishing Company Ltd.

Carrette J and King R. (2005) *Selling Spirituality*, London: Routledge.

Dances of Universal Peace UK, http://dancesofuniversalpeace.org.uk (accessed May 5, 2012).

Hawkins, P. (2011) *Leadership Team Coaching*, London: Kegan.

— (2005) *The Wise Fool's Guide to Leadership*, Alresford, Hants: O Books.

Hock, Dee W. (1995) The Chaordic Organization: Out of Control and Into Order, *World Business Academy Perspectives*, 9(1).

Khan, Pir Vilayat Inayat, *Murshid as I Remember Him*. http://wahiduddin.net/hik/hik_dvd.htm (accessed July 5, 2012).

Om-Guru: Saints, Teachers and Seekers in the Indian Tradition http://om-guru.com/html/saints/khan.html (accessed September 6, 2012).

On the Trail of Ruth St. Denis (4 min trailer), https://vimeo.com/45029153 (accessed September 12, 2012).

Pir-o-Murshid Fazal Inayat Khan (March 10, 1987) *Western Sufism: The Sufi Movement, The Sufi Order International, and the Sufi Way* http://sufiway.org/history/texts/western_sufism.php (accessed September 9, 2012).

Ruth St Denis in the 'East Indian Nautch Dance' (1932) http://youtube.com/watch?v=j8XvHX1FKsY (accessed September 12, 2012).

The Sufi Order UK, http://sufiorderuk.org (accessed July 9, 2012).

Trimingham, J. S. (1971) *The Sufi Orders of Islam*, Oxford: OUP.

Uzdavinys, A. (2005) Sufism in the Light of Orientalism, *Acta Orientalia Vilnensia*, 6(2), 114–25.

The Vina: http://sufimessage.com/music/vina.html.

Webster, D. (2012) *Dispirited: How Contemporary Spirituality Makes Us Stupid, Selfish and Unhappy*, Alresford, Hants: Zero Books.

Werbner, P. (2002) 'The Place Which is Diaspora: Citizenship, Religion and Gender in the Making of Chaordic Transnationalism', *Journal of Ethnic and Migration Studies*, 28(1), 119–34.

— (2006) Seekers on the Path: Different Ways of Being Sufi in Britain'. In: Malik, Jamal and John Hinnells (Eds). *Sufism in the West*. London and New York: Routledge.

Werbner, R. (1977) 'Introduction'. In: Werbner, R. (Ed.). *Regional Cults*. London and New York: Academic Press.

Werbner, R. (1989) *Ritual Passage, Sacred Journey: The Process and Organisation of Religious Movements*, Washington DC: Smithsonian Institution Press.

Part Two

History

4

Shaykh Abdullah Ali al-Hakimi, the 'Alawi Tariqa and British-Yemenis

Mohammad S. Seddon

Al iman al Yaman wa al- hikmatul Yamaniyah
'Faith is of the Yemen and wisdom is of the Yemenis.'[1]

Introduction

By the end of the First World War, British-Yemeni communities had been established across a number of port cities in the United Kingdom including South Shields, Cardiff and Liverpool for almost a generation. In South Shields, Yemenis numbered around 4,500 most of whom were single-males catered for by some 60 'Arab only' boarding houses. These apparently exclusive lodging places were not set up out of a sense of isolation but, were rather, a response to the prohibition of 'black and coloured' sailors from the boarding houses in which white and indigenous sailors lodged, a form of racial discrimination which did not change in the United Kingdom until the early 1960s when South Asian single male migrants experienced something similar. Racial discrimination soon took the form of legislation when in March 1925, the Home Office implemented a Special Restriction Order, under Article 11 of the Aliens Order 1920, which required the registration of all 'coloured seamen' in the United Kingdom at local police stations. Ironically, many 'coloured' sailors, particularly Yemenis, were actually British citizens. The plight of the Yemeni, Somali and Indian Lascars (Oriental sailors) in Britain caused much consternation among Christian charities and missions in the latter part of the nineteenth century when their acute destitution and deprivation was recorded in the two works of the Reverend Joseph Salter.[2]

By 1919, the *Western Islamic Association*, based in London, and the *Islamic Society*, affiliated to the *Woking Muslim Mission,* had both made representations on behalf of the Yemenis of South Shields to the local City Council and the Port Authority after increasing race disturbances and employment discrimination which deliberately targeted the Yemenis. Because the Yemenis were largely a transient community, there was, at that time, no permanent religious centre such as a mosque, where the Yemenis could collectively offer their prayers. However, after the docklands disturbances, Dr Khalid Sheldrake, an English convert to Islam and a representative of the *Western Islamic Association*, made efforts in August 1929 to establish a purpose-built mosque for the South Shields Yemeni Muslim community. He collected some donations from the Aga Khan and the wealthy Nizam of Hyderabad, India, and purchased a plot of land in the city, but the scheme never came to fruition.[3] It was not until the appearance of Shaykh Abdullah Ali al-Hakimi, one of British Islam's most important figures, that British-Yemenis were able to establish themselves firmly, through his unique brand of Sufism, on to the United Kingdom's religious landscape, as the oldest settled Muslim community in Britain.

Shaykh Abdullah Ali al-Hakimi

In the 1930s Shaykh Abdullah Ali al-Hakimi, a Yemeni religious scholar and merchant from al-Hakim, a *dhubhani* village near Tai'zz, and an adherent of the North African 'Alawi *tariqa,* a branch of the Shadhili *Sufi* order, was given permission by his Shaykh, Abul 'Abbas Ahmad ibn Mustafa al-'Alawi (1869–1934), to begin a Muslim mission among the Yemenis in Britain. As a part of his Sufi proselytizing, he established a number of *zawaya* (Sufi centres)[4] throughout the Muslim communities in Britain.[5] Al-Hakimi met Shaykh Ahmad Mustafa al-'Alawi in the early 1920s, most probably in Morocco and then later studied Sufism with the Shaykh at Mustaganem, a Mediterranean port on the coast of Algeria where the centre of the *tariqa* was located. After initially becoming a *faqir* ('initiate') al-Hakimi was eventually appointed a *muqaddam* (a representative of the *tariqa* under the Shaykh) of the 'Alawi *tariqa* before moving first to Marseilles and then later Rotterdam to establish *zawaya* in both locales among the migrant Yemeni sailors. In 1936, al-Hakimi obtained the Shaykh's *ijaza* (permission) to begin his mission among the Yemeni communities in Cardiff, South Shields, Hull and Liverpool. Yemeni communities had been established in the port cities of Cardiff and South Shields since the mid-eighteenth century. Under al-

Hakimi's guidance, these Yemeni communities underwent a dramatic religious revival, introducing new rituals and practices in accordance with the teachings of the 'Alawi *tariqa*. As a result, the communities became highly visible where previously they had been practically ignored.

Religious processions were held regularly through the city streets of Cardiff and South Shields on the occasions of Eid ul-Fitr and Eid ul-Adha in which Yemenis would don the apparel, not of their native Yemen – the *fowta, shawal* and *jambiyyah*, but rather, the adopted dress of North African Arabs and Berbers, in respect of their Algerian Grand Shaykh, Ahmad Mustafa al-'Alawi. Other processions were held to celebrate the birthdays of the Prophet Muhammad (*mawlid*) and the Grand Shaykh in which the indigenous English and Welsh convert wives and their mixed-race children all paraded in their oriental Islamic garbs. Al-Hakimi's work among the Muslim convert spouses and progeny of Yemeni sailors was particularly developed, establishing Qur'anic and Islamic instruction classes along with Arabic language studies for mothers and children alike. In fact, al-Hakimi published a number of Arabic books including, *al-As'ilato wal Ajwibato Bayin al-Masihayyato wal-Islam* ('Questions and answers concerning Christianity and Islam'), to aid Arab husbands concerning theological questions regarding Christianity and Islam that they might be asked by their wives, children or native British acquaintances. In another book, *Din Allahi Wahid* ('The Religion of God is One'), al-Hakimi emphatically states

> 'In it [his book], to the best of my knowledge, I endeavour to bring closer together the religious Moslems and Christians, and others, but as regards Religion, God's religion is one. For those of the past age and those of this present age, and on the tongues of all the Prophets, was one religion and no other.'[6]

Richard Lawless' work further informs us of the importance placed on the Shaykh's Sufi missionary work among the indigenous wives by offering the following quote,

> 'Before the Shaykh came, we felt we were only Arab's wives, but after we felt differently. We felt better, we had our own religion and priest [sic] and we were proud of it.'[7]

Conversely, Fred Halliday asserts that al-Hakimi faced fierce opposition to his pro-women stance from a number of Yemeni and Somali men who perhaps felt threatened by his reformist religious empowerment of their converted Muslim wives. Halliday even suggests that al-Hakimi's move from South Shields to

Cardiff was precipitated by the controversy and dispute over the women being given a space to pray and hold religious activities within the recently established *zawiya*.[8] However, the British authorities appeared to be pleased with the Shaykh's religious activities and he was also able to forge good local political contacts in both Cardiff and South Shields. Furthermore, at the international level he also developed close relations with senior British officials in Aden, including Sir Bernard Riley the then Governor of Aden and Tom Hickinbotham who later became the Governor of Aden in 1951.[9] In the United Kingdom, al-Hakimi was able to spiritually channel the physical abuse and discrimination that many Yemenis faced as a result of the employment struggles and unrest experienced across the maritime communities throughout the British docklands after the First World War. The claim levelled at the Arab seamen was that they were taking the jobs of white indigenous sailors by working for less pay. However, legislation introduced in 1920 under the Aliens Order had already restricted the movement of Arab sailors by enforced registration with the local port authorities and the police. Further, by the 1930s, the National Union of Seamen (NUS) was employing wholesale discrimination against the Lascars, as the Asian seamen were known, which eventually forced a punitive rota system on Arab seamen operating from the ports of Cardiff, South Shields and Hull. Effectively, the rota system limited the number of coloured and Arab seamen registering on individual vessels sailing from British ports. In response a number of violent demonstrations and riots between Arab and white sailors across British ports ensued. Al-Hakimi's religious activities seemed to steer the Yemeni sailors away from radical trade unionism and communist politics, focusing instead on spiritual self-reform. This point was later publicly acknowledged by both the Chief Constable and the Deputy Lord Mayor of Cardiff during a dinner given by Shaykh al-Hakimi in the city in July 1950. However, al-Hakimi was not himself devoid of political activism and he eventually went on to become a fiery and outspoken critic of the ruling Zaydi Imam Yahya of Yemen, and in the subsequent developing anti-Imamate struggles, he became one of the leaders of the Free Yemen Movement.

His activities included the publication of Britain's first Arabic periodical, *Al-Salam,* which printed the Free Yemen Movement's manifesto that called for political and material reforms including an end to the Yemen's isolationist policy and the building of roads, schools and hospitals across the Yemen. When al-Hakimi visited the Yemen in 1943, travelling through the northern mountain city of Ta'izz in that summer, he was arrested and duly deported by the then Crown Prince Ahmad, probably for his involvement with the promotion of the

Free Yemen Movement throughout the diaspora Yemeni communities in Britain and Europe. Al-Hakimi eventually established a centre for his political activities based at the Nur ul-Islam Mosque at 16 Peel Street, Cardiff. He had originally established the 'Zaouia Allawi Friendship Society' from a house in Bute Street, Cardiff, that had previously been used as a small *zawiya* by his former deputy, Shaykh Hassan Ismail.[10] The Shaykh continued with his political activities as President of the Yemen Union Organization by announcing the formation of the Grand Yemeni Association (GYA) in Aden, January 1946, and by publishing a book, *Da'wat al-Ahrar* ('A Call to Freedom'). By November of the same year al-Hakimi formed the Committee for the Defence of Yemen which pledged its support of the GYA and sent representatives to diaspora Yemeni communities in Europe, USA and Africa to

> 'Set up a permanent delegation to visit Arabs and Islamic capitals so that the leaders of the Arabs and Muslims will understand the need to solve the Yemeni problem.'[11]

The Committee for the Defence of Yemen continued to function for a number of years gaining support from Yemenis in Cardiff, Liverpool, South Shields and Hull. Al-Hakimi stepped up the anti-Imamate political pressure by writing to Ernest Bevin, the then British Foreign Secretary, claiming to speak for the whole Yemeni nation via the auspices of the GYA. His letter graphically spelled out the gross atrocities committed against the Yemeni people by the Imam, stating that it was time to 'Smash the bonds of tyranny and injustice which has burdened her [Yemen] for the last 30 years.'[12] Shaykh Abdullah urged the British Government to support the Aden-based GYA against the Imam, concluding that if Yemenis could not live under the rule of a democratic government then they would, 'face a glorious death for the sake of justice.'[13] By December 1948, al-Hakimi began his publication of *Al-Salam* from the Nur ul-Islam Mosque in Cardiff. Although produced in Britain, the majority of the magazines were posted overseas to North Africa and the Middle East with a small number of copies even smuggled into the Yemen. Al-Hakimi used *Al-Salam* to publicize an international Islamic conference held in Cardiff in 1949 and attended by delegates from eleven Muslim countries. The conference discussed key issues facing the Muslim *umma* which would have presumably included the independence struggles of the then colonized Arab and Muslim world.

In February 1948, Imam Yahya was assassinated and succeeded by his son, Ahmad, who was a fierce enemy of al-Hakimi and the Free Yemen Movement. Lawless claims that in 1950 the new Imam found copies of *Al-Salam* mysteriously placed in his bedroom accompanied by a note pinned to his pillow simply saying, *'Alayhis-Salaam'* ('upon him be peace'), a posthumous prayer recited over the deceased.[14] Imam Ahmad was convinced that al-Hakimi was supported and sponsored by the British Government, and he rapidly set about funding a pro-Imamate movement within the British-Yemeni communities. In Cardiff, this pro-Imamate movement was ironically led by another 'Alawi *tariqa* Shaykh, Hassan Ismail. Ismail had previously been al-Hakimi's deputy for many years but both became bitter rivals in the late 1940s and early 1950s resulting in a few disturbances between opposing factions across the British-Yemeni communities. However, the overall outcome was that the majority of British-Yemenis were eventually won over to the pro-Imamate movement led by Shaykh Hassan Ismail. This move had perhaps less to do with the *realpolitik* of the Yemen and more to do with the transnational tribal loyalties and allegiances ever-present within the global diaspora Yemeni communities. In May 1952, al-Hakimi closed down his *Al-Salam* publication and announced he was returning to Yemen where he intended to publish the periodical from the British Protectorate of Aden. However, once there the British authorities refused to permit him a licence to print the magazine. This decision was probably as a result of their unwillingness to offend the ruling Imam of North Yemen. Furthermore, when al-Hakimi arrived in Aden in January 1953, where he was welcomed by thousands of Free Yemen Movement supporters and activists, he was arrested just a few days later and charged with smuggling arms and ammunition into Aden. The Cardiff police had allegedly informed the British port officials in Aden of the alleged smuggled cargo and as a result the Shaykh was sentenced to a year's imprisonment. There is little doubt that the arms had been planted in the Shaykh's luggage but, whether that was done by the British authorities or supporters of the Imam is difficult to substantiate. However, after a hearing at the court of appeal al-Hakimi was released in October 1953. Thereafter, he was elected President of the Yemen Union, an Aden-based democratic political party that sought both political reunification and an end to Imamate-rule. Unfortunately, within the same year, the Shaykh fell seriously ill and was eventually admitted to hospital with a kidney infection in August 1954. When I met with al-Hakimi's elderly grandsons in Sana'a in 2005, they both confirmed that they believed the Shaykh had been poisoned by an agent of the Imam while in hospital in 1954. No official confirmation of this claim has ever been issued, but it seems the most likely event, cutting short the life of a man who may have perhaps gone on to become the first president of an independent South Yemen after the withdrawal of the British in 1967.

The 'Alawi *Tariqa*

The Grand Shaykh of the 'Alawi *tariqa*, Abu 'l-Abbas Ahmad Ibn Mustafa al-'Alawi, was born in the coastal town of Mustaganem, near Oran in Algeria in 1869. The town was quite conservative in that it had barely been affected by French colonialism. His great-great-great-grandfather was given the title 'al-Hajj' (denoting someone who has made pilgrimage to Makkah) and his name, al-Hajj 'Ali lent itself to the diminutive, 'bin al-'Alawi' – the name given to his descendants.[15] Although his ancestors were local notables and his great-grandfather, Ahmad, was a renowned Islamic scholar, the Shaykh was born into a poor family as the only son with two sibling sisters. He received no formal education apart from learning the Qur'an from his father and memorizing nine-tenths of its contents. As a young man, he appears to have drifted through a number of different trades before becoming a cobbler. At the age of 16, his father died and he took up trading and opened up a small shop in partnership with a close friend. At this relatively young age, the Shaykh was already frequently visiting *majaalis al-dhikr* (remembrance circles of Sufi orders) and initially his mother was resistant to him leaving the house to attend such gatherings in the evenings but she eventually gave her blessings as she continued to live with the Shaykh until her death in 1914. As the Shaykh became more involved in his spiritual path, aided by frequent home visits by a local Islamic scholar, his wife became so perplexed that she filed for a divorce on the grounds that the Shaykh was not giving her conjugal rights. However, she was dissuaded when the Shaykh reluctantly abandoned his home tuitions.

Al-'Alawi founded his *tariqa* in 1918 after he was granted *ijaza* (permission) from his Shakyh, al-Buzidi, leader of the Shadhili *tariqa*, to establish his own order as a result of displaying extraordinary spiritual prowess. Thereafter, he soon established a *zawiya* in his hometown where after his demise the Shaykh was then buried. His *tariqa* quickly spread across North Africa and the Middle East and, perhaps aided by Muslim sailors, there were also a small number of adherents in France and Holland. In his biography of the Shaykh published in 1961, Martin Lings opens his preface stating, 'The sheikh al-'Alawi is almost entirely unknown outside the precincts of Islamic mysticism'. But, Lings also acknowledges the Shaykh's scholarly contribution to Islam through his publications and travels. Lings also mentions that the Shaykh was briefly celebrated among contemporary French Orientalists such as Dermengham and Massignon, with the former noting that al-'Alawi was, 'one of the most celebrated mystic Shaykhs of our time'.[16] However, beyond these passing references, it is not really until Lings' own biography, published some 30 years after the death of the Shaykh, that any serious academic study of his life and work becomes noted by Western scholars. In terms of his spiritual path, al-'Alawi first became an adherent of the 'Isawi *tariqa*, a Shadhili branch of Sufism which appears to have been a form of cultic-charismatic Sufism from which the Shaykh soon disassociated himself in preference for litanies and invocations based on the Qur'an and hadith. Although, al-'Alawi recounts how he slowly withdrew from the *tariqa*, he admits to continuing the practice of snake charming, a particular speciality of the 'Isawi *tariqa*, until he eventually met with Shaykh Sidi Muhammad al-Buzidi. Shaykh al-Buzidi had established a local reputation as a saintly scholar but as one who did not seek to gather initiates to his order. However, after the Shaykh had made many frequent visits to al-'Alawi's shop, during which many profound discussions concerning faith had taken place, both al-'Alawi and his business partner, Sidi al-Hajj bin 'Awdah, took *bay'ah* (allegiance) with Shaykh al-Buzidi. As a *faqir* of al-Buzidi, al-'Alawi was carefully guided by his master who instructed him to abandon his informal studies in Islamic theology in preference of his Sufi litanies (*dhikr*). Al-'Alawi admits to conceding to his Shaykh's request with some considerable reluctance. Cited at length in Lings' biography, al-'Alawi gives a wonderful detailed account of the step-by-step initiations (*muqamaat*) he was guided through by his Shaykh. Once he had reached a certain *muqaam* (spiritual station), he was then instructed to re-start his theological classes. In the ensuing studies, al-'Alawi began to understand the literal texts of Islamic theology through the prism of his intense meditation and the spiritual teachings of his Shaykh. The resultant effect was a flurry of esoteric philosophical writings which included, *Miftah al-Shuhuud* ('The Keys of Perception'), a book on astronomy that sought to explain the cosmological phenomenon through a spiritual understanding of the Divine.[17]

As al-'Alawi reached higher levels of spirituality, he was eventually taken to Morocco to aid his Shaykh in proselytizing the *tariqa* among the masses. He remained in Morocco for some 15 years and it is most probably during this time that Shaykh 'Abdullah 'Ali al-Hakimi first came into contact with al-'Alawi. After the death of Shaykh al-Buzidi, al-'Alawi returned to Mustaganem after first stopping off at Tlemcen, where he had previously sent his wife to stay with her parents. Unfortunately, within a few days of his arrival, his wife, who had been seriously ill for some time, passed away. On his eventual return to Mustaganem, al-'Alawi appears to have been selected as leader through the process of inspired dreams experienced by a number of *fuqarā'* (initiates) of the *tariqa* which were given divine attribution. Lings' monograph gives us a few accounts of such dreams as recounted by various adherents.[18] The biography also includes a chapter that is largely a translation of an autobiographical account of al-'Alawi's life in which the Shaykh makes reference to a number of marriages that had ended in divorce. The Shaykh's explanation of the divorces avoids any blame on the part of his ex-wives but, rather, attributes the failed marriages to his own neglect. He recalls, 'In a word, any shortcomings that there were were on my side, but they were not deliberate.'[19] Lings' publication is laced with the esoteric philosophy of Sufi teachings and doctrines. As an adherent of al-'Alawi, Lings describes with great ease and beauty the concepts and hierarchies of the Sufi *tariqa*, particularly the idea of unbroken chains of transmission (*silsilah*) as a mystic path to inner knowledge of the Divine. In doing so he labours at some length to establish the validity of al-'Alawi's *tariqa* as a new branch or pathway in the ancestral tree of the Shadhili and Daraqaawi spiritual orders. He comments that

'The shaikh al-'Alawi's descent from Abu 'l-Hassan ash-Shadhili through the chain of the 'Isawi *Tariqa* is not included [in al-'Alawi's 'spiritual chain' offered in his Appendix]. Moreover the ramifications of all the different branches, even if they were known, would be far too complex to be reproduced in one tree.'

He continues,

'The economy of this tree may be measured by the case of Hassan al-Basri (AD 640–727) who on his long life must have received various transmissions from many companions of the Prophet, whereas he is set down as the spiritual heir of one companion only.'[20]

In terms of the British-Yemeni connection to the 'Alawi *tariqa* via Shaykh Abdullah Ali al-Hakimi, Lings' work offers only a passing reference, reduced to a footnote, relating to the spread of the *tariqa* beyond North Africa. He says

'. . .The shaikh had many disciples, mostly seamen, who established *zawiyas* at various ports of calling including not only Cardiff but also subsequently, after his death, at Liverpool, Hull and South Shields, and inland at Birmingham.'[21]

Unfortunately, Lings' above concise account of the spread of the *tariqa* among the Muslims of Britain does not give an informed view of the spread of the *tariqa* as a result of al-Hakimi's missionary efforts.

British-Yemenis

Perhaps the earliest recorded study of the 'Alawi *tariqa* established in Britain among the burgeoning Yemeni Muslim community was that undertaken by the renowned Arabic philologist, the late, Professor R. B. Serjeant of the University of Cambridge, published in 1944.[22] His short paper was based on a fieldtrip to Cardiff conducted in 1943 in which he also notes that Yemeni communities had existed in both Cardiff and South Shields since before World War I. Accounting for the two hundred Yemeni families settled in South Shields at the time of his visit, he poignantly notes, 'nearly every one of which has lost a relative at sea during the present war.'[23] This bleak reality is a startling admission of the sense of duty and loyalty of British-Yemenis to their adopted country. Serjeant's paper also reminds us that smaller communities of Yemenis, or what he describes as 'colonies', were to be found in Hull, Liverpool, Birmingham and Sheffield, confirming Fred Halliday's later study of a British-Yemeni 'second wave' or inward migration from the port cities of original settlement to the industrial, urban metropolizes. By 1965, Badr ud-Din Dahya estimated that the migrant Yemeni population of the United Kingdom was around 12,000.[24] He confirms Serjeant's claim that the Arab migration to Britain began with the First World War, when Yemenis worked as stokers on British merchant vessels. Mashuq Ally says that during the war many Yemenis were also employed in the munitions and chemical factories in Manchester.[25] Muhammad Akram Khan further records that by the early 1940s the established Yemeni communities of Cardiff and South Shields were slowly, 'settling in Manchester and Liverpool',[26] trickling from their traditional docklands settlements to other urbanized industrial cities in Britain. Conversely, Fred Halliday contends that Liverpool was, 'from the 1900s onwards host to a small but distinctive Yemeni community'.[27] Humayun Ansari has described the early docklands communities as, 'close-knit and relatively self-contained' but usually divided internally becoming 'urban villages' and 'interacting with the broader society surrounding them in a selective fashion'.[28] Commenting on the 'Alawi *tariqa* in Cardiff Serjeant explains,

> The community is organised in the form of religious confraternity of the type known as *tariqa* or 'spiritual path'. The initiate entitled *faqir*, passes through various grades of spiritual attainment until he reaches that degree of understanding which entitles him to be called a *Sufi*, explained by the Arabs as 'one who has purified his heart'.[29]

He goes on to inform us that very few reach the higher station of *murshid* ('one who guides') or Shaykh.[30] The *tariqa* to which the British-Yemenis belong, Serjeant writes, is the *'Allawi* [sic] *tariqa'* – an off-shoot from the great Shadhili order that has spread across the Muslim world. The prescriptive *dhikr* employed by the *tariqa* has been described in some detail by Serjeant who attended a *dhikr* gathering at the Yemeni *zawiya* in Cardiff during his visit in 1943.[31] At this period, the *tariqa* was at its zenith with large numbers of adherents from the Yemeni communities throughout Britain. Experiencing the intense fervour of the *majlis* (ritual gathering) as their incantations and swaying increased, Serjeant observed,

> 'The action is so vigorous that I consider it nearly impossible for anyone to perform of his own accord. When the Sheikh perceives that the participants have had enough, he makes the dhikr stop; were he not to do so, they would continue until they dropped on the ground with exhaustion.'[32]

In the process of explaining the specific origins of the 'Alawi *tariqa*, Serjeant offers us a single tantalizing reference to the man solely responsible for introducing this particular form of Sufism to the British-Yemeni community, Shaykh Abdullah Ali al-Hakimi. Although in the brief reference Serjeant acknowledges al-Hakimi's pivotal role in bringing the *tariqa* to Britain, his claim that al-Hakimi is, 'from the town of Dhubhan in Southern Yemen',[33] is quite erroneous. Dhubhan is in the province of al-Hujariyyah, near to Ta'izz. However, Serjeant must be forgiven for his unintentional mistake as it is often wrongly assumed that the majority of Yemenis in Britain originate from the former British Protectorate of Aden established in 1839 in what eventually became part of South Yemen, then a separate state from North Yemen until reunification in 1990. Halliday notes that the Yemenis who came to Britain in the twentieth century were erroneously referred to as 'Adenis'.[34] In reality, of the Yemenis coming to Britain pre-1967 through the British Protectorate, only a few would have actually been Adenese, with most coming from the rural Northern highlands around Ta'izz or the Southern hinterlands of Tihamah. The migration of Shaykh Abdullah Ali al-Hakimi, as the community's spiritual and religious leader, coincided with a major change in the shipping industry and the first transformation of the British-Yemeni community from all-male, transient docklands communities to an urbanized industrial workforce. After the First World War, in which around 3,000 British-Yemeni sailors died in defence of Britain, the introduction of faster and more efficient oil-burning vessels saw many of the Yemenis without work. The labour intensive boilerman, or 'donkeyman' duties often allocated to Yemenis, Somalis and South Asians were no longer needed, and this forced many to seek work beyond their traditional maritime employment. A large number left the seaports for the industrial heartlands, and larger communities began to form in the cities of Manchester, Birmingham and Sheffield. The competition for jobs, not just at sea, had sparked-off a number of race riots, and the Yemenis, like the other South Asian and West Indian migrants, were easy visible scapegoats and targets for racism and discrimination. The influx of other migrant communities to the docklands area in Cardiff, where the Yemenis were concentrated, became known somewhat exotically as 'Tiger Bay', and the visible 'otherness' of the Yemenis has throughout their history in Britain been the 'reason' for racial violence against them. The origins of the Birmingham-Yemeni community date back to the late-1920s when Lascars were forced by both legal restrictions and a decline in jobs from the dock areas into the industrial heartlands. Further, when race riots, in 1919, spread throughout the port cities of Britain forcing the deportation of over 600 Yemeni Lascars, many sought other means of employment away from the racism experienced in the docklands.[35] The early Yemeni settlers in Birmingham influenced by the teachings of Shaykh al-Hakimi soon established a *zawiya* on Edward Road, Balsall Heath, led by a direct follower of al-Hakimi, Shaykh Muhammad Qassim al-'Alawi until his death in 1999. In the 1950s and 1960s, the community experienced a further migration of single males coming directly from the British Protectorate of Aden.

In South Shields where Shaykh al-Hakimi first settled the Muslim community was majority Yemeni numbering around 4,500 and catered for largely by Arab-owned boarding houses. Shaykh al-Hakimi noticed that many Yemenis had taken English wives and a significant number of them had converted to Islam, but educational provision and religious instruction for convert wives and their children were absent. In 1936, the Shaykh established Islamic studies classes and within two years the community purchased *The Hilda Arms*, a former public house, on Cuthbert Street, South Shields, converting it into the 'Zaoia Allaoia Islamia Mosque [sic]'. The establishment of this Islamic centre and other *zawaya* throughout the British-Yemeni communities transformed their religious identity, from one that had previously been somewhat peripheral, if not invisible, into a networked community with local religious centres and nationally coordinated activities such as the *tariqa's* religious processions and political activities of the Free Yemen Movement. As early as the 1950s a number of Yemenis in Eccles, Greater Manchester, had associated with the *tariqa* introduced by the Shaykh. They later established a *zawiya* at a house owned by Hassan al-Haidari, one of the earliest Yemeni migrants to Eccles, and he later became the first imam of the present Liverpool Road mosque. The *zawiya*, located at number 49 Peel Street, Eccles, was also al-Haidari's home, and the front room of his house was used for congregational prayers for about 20 years.[36] In 1982, a local newspaper feature referred to the *zawiya* stating, 'prayers were held in a room of a house but as the numbers attending public [congregational] prayers grew so people looked for a bigger place.'[37] It appears that as the community expanded the pressing need for a fully-fledged mosque and Islamic centre became a priority. Another account that also refers to the original *zawiya* states that although *it* initially served the burgeoning community, 'still there was a need for a proper mosque.'[38] However, in addition to the genuine need of a larger and more multifunctional religious centre, there may also have been theological objections within the community to the usage of the *zawiya* and growing reticence to the continued use of the *zawiya* appears to be three-fold. The primary objection was related to the 'ownership' of the mosque building because, according to the Qur'anic text, a mosque should not be ascribed to anybody or owned by a particular individual, rather, it belongs to the Muslim community *per se*. The verses that form the basis for this opinion according to the commentary of Abdullah Yusuf Ali are

> 'And who is more unjust than he who forbids that in places for the worship of Allah, His name should be celebrated? – whose zeal is (in fact) to ruin them? It was not fitting that such should themselves enter them except in fear. For them there is nothing but disgrace in this world, and in the world to come, an exceeding torment.' (2:114).[39]

And,

> 'And the places of worship are for Allah (alone): so invoke not any one along with Allah.' (72:18).[40]

Although the above-cited verses refer specifically to the prohibition of the early Muslims praying in the holy precinct at Makkah imposed on them by the pagan Arabs, the translator asserts that the inferred meaning establishes the principle of public or community 'ownership' of mosques. This is because Islamic law dictates that public places of worship must be dedicated exclusively to Allah for worship and this is a recognized canon among the *ijma'* (consensus) of Muslim jurists.[41] This religious ruling rendered the exclusivity of the *zawiya*, as a building owned by Hassan al-Haidari and dedicated to the *tariqa*, somewhat problematic for more orthodox Muslims. Secondly, the religious observances of the *tariqa,* its ascetic leanings, influences and practices, particularly the method of *dhikr* within the *zawiya* may have had a limited appeal among the growing community. More orthodox and conservative Muslims from the community began voicing their dislike of what they believed to be heretical practices. By this time large numbers of Yemenis were migrating directly from the Yemen, many influenced by modern reformist movements such as the Wahhabi[42] and the Salafi movements.[43] These ultra orthodox reformists would be averse to offering prayers in the *zawiya* as a place they might associate with *shirk* (polytheism). Thirdly, the *zawiya* was restricted to the ground floor of a terraced house and it could not accommodate all the necessary functions of a mosque which would include a large space for congregational prayer, a communal kitchen, adequate ablution facilities, a space for children's Qur'an, Islamic studies and 'mother-tongue' or Arabic language teaching, washing facilities for the deceased, living quarters for the imam or caretaker. The limited space of the *zawiya* also became impractical in a number of other ways as the community began to increase in population, diverse ethnicities and Islamic expressions. Further tensions arose as inter-tribal factions began to manifest in bouts of violence across the British-Yemeni communities. In the 1950s, transnational tribal tensions played out locally when Shaykh al-Hakimi promoted his Free Yemen Movement among the Yemeni community in Cardiff. Although respected as the imam of the mosque, he lost legitimacy for his political project simply because the majority of settlers in Cardiff belonged to the *Shamiri* tribe, led locally by Shaykh Hasan Ismail, his former deputy. The *Shamiris* were loyal to the Zaydi imam rule of the Yemen and both tribal and political tensions surfaced several times in the community when physical clashes and public brawls between the two factions broke out. Eventually, Shaykh Hasan's group established a rival *zawiya* in opposition to the Nur ul-Islam Mosque of Shaykh al-Hakimi. While the Nur ul-Islam Mosque still exists today in Cardiff, albeit in a new location, the 'Cardiff Islamic Centre' also exists almost on the old site of the Nur ul-Islam Mosque, as an originally government-aided building financed through the Colonial Office at a cost of £7,000 after it was destroyed by a bomb during the Second World War.[44] Today it exists as a purpose-built mosque that remains a tribute, not to Shaykh Abdullah Ali al-Hakimi but, his pro-Zaydi Imamate rival and one-time deputy of the 'Alawi *tariqa*, Shaykh Hassan Ismail. Today there exists only a remnant of the great missionary work established by Shaykh Abdullah al-Hakimi. And, while it is true that Sufism within British Islam is experiencing a renaissance possibly as a reaction to nihilistic, extremist and violent forms of Salafi and Wahhabi scriptural literalism, the particular legacy of al-Hakimi's Sufi *daw'ah* is, sadly, slowly evaporating.

Conclusion

The history of Sufi expression of Islam in Britain cannot be written without the inclusion of the unique emergence and spread of the 'Alawi *tariqa* among British-Yemenis. The establishment of this particular branch of Sufism is the result of the vision and undertaking of one man, Shaykh Abdullah Ali al-Hakimi (c. 1900–54). His extraordinary efforts not only transformed the British-Yemeni community from a disparate and invisible group of transient docklands settlers into a fully-fledged religious community that was both organized and dynamic locally and nationally but also resulted in the formation of a nascent and authentic manifestation of 'British Islam' that stretched from South Wales to North East England. The introduction of the 'Alawi *tariqa* to British-Yemenis also precipitated a significant identity shift from race and ethnicity in a distinctly discriminate and excluding minority context to a religious identity that was both geographically transcontinental linking Arabia, Africa and Europe, and spiritually universal developing a distinctly 'ummatic' sense of British-Yemeni Muslimness. The institutions and centres established by al-Hakimi and his followers created a tangible rootedness and cultural anchoring of a specific religious expression within the British context as the indigenous wives of Yemeni settlers were transformed as Muslim converts from peripheral entities into empowered individuals who were proud of their new found faith. Equally, the progeny of such 'mixed-race' marriages became the heirs to a unique and distinct form of Muslimness that inculcated a sense of cultural affirmation and religious authenticity. This inspired confidence within the British-Yemeni community as was openly manifest in very public processions organized across Britain marking significant Islamic festivals and events. Al-Hakimi was not simply a religious missionary and spiritual reformer, he also propagated very particular political views that sought radical reforms to the Yemen that had suffered from centuries of oppressive dictatorship under Zaydi Imamate-rule and more recent imperial and colonial division by both Ottoman and British expansionism. Al-Hakimi's political activism was less successful than his religious proselytizing and, where spiritual transformation and religious belonging instilled a unity of being and believing, the politics of revolution instead fissured and fractured the recently established sense of unity. Further, while al-Hakimi's politics was eventually vindicated with the overthrow of the Imam and the ousting of the British, eventually leading to reunification in 1990, he could not transcend the ancient, pre-Islamic reality of continued tribal bonds and allegiances that pervaded the diasporic, transnational facets of Yemeniness.[45]

Ultimately, it could be argued that al-Hakimi's forlorn political endeavours seriously impacted on his religious efforts, effectively ensuring the demise of the 'Alawi *tariqa's* Sufi mission across the British-Yemeni community. But al-Hakimi's mis-timed revolutionary politics were not the only factor in the waning of Sufism among British-Yemenis. Theological tensions began to emerge as a new wave of post-WWII, Yemeni migrants began to settle in the United Kingdom. They brought with them their version of puritanical and scriptural literalistic expressions of Islam, akin to the Wahhabi and Salafi reform movements, supported and promoted by Saudi Arabian 'petrol-dollars'.[46] This later migration of Yemeni settlers were extremely antithetical towards all forms of *Tassawuf*, which they interpreted as both religiously heterodox and culturally anachronistic, charging Sufism with not only compromising *tawhid* (the doctrine of the unicity of God) but also for the decline and malaise of the *umma* and the subsequent colonization of Muslim lands by European imperialism.[47] Ironically, the last decade has witnessed a resurgence of and growing interest in Sufism across Muslim communities in Britain and the West. This is partly due to a steadily declining influence of more puritanical and literal expressions of Islam as a post-9/11 and 7/7 reaction.[48] As a result, new generations of British and Western-born Muslims are rediscovering esoteric Islamic practices through the traditional *turuq* (plural of *tariqa*) of Sufism. In the process, there are a growing number of adherents to the 'Alawi *tariqa* in the United Kingdom. The renaissance of traditional Sufism within British Islam has witnessed an intellectual engagement that transcends the original charismatic and cultic aspects of the more popular manifestations of earlier Sufism as observed by Shaykh Abdullah Ali al-Hakimi and his community. These neo-classical forms of Sufism are more academically robust, and, as a result, an indubitable theological discourse is emerging as a potent antithesis to the seemingly discredited and defunct jihadi nihilism espoused by the Salafi and Wahhabi puritans who had gained a small, but significant, number of adherents among the previous generation of British Muslims.

Notes

1 A *hadith* of the Prophet cited in, Z. Bashier (1983) *The Makkan Crucible*, p. 18.
2 J. Salter (1872) *The Asiatics and England*. London: Selly Jackson and Salter, J. (1895) *The East in the West*. London: Partridge.

3 M. S. Seddon (2004) 'Muslim Communities in Britain: A Historiography' in *British Muslimsbetween Assimilation and Segregation*. M. S. Seddon, et al. (Eds). Markfield: The Islamic Foundation, pp. 7–14.

4 A *zawiya* (pl. *zawaya*) is, according to the Encyclopedia of Islam, 'lit. a "corner, nook (of a building)", originally the cell of a Christian monk and then in the Islamic context, a small mosque or oratory room . . . the term came to designate a building designed to house and feed travellers and members of local sufi brotherhood.' In Lewis, et al. (1986) *The Encyclopaedia of Islam*, Vol. XI, p. 44.

5 L. Martin (1971) *A Sufi Saint of the Twentieth Century*. London: George Allen & Unwin Ltd., p. 116, fn. 3.

6 Quoted in, F. Halliday (1992) *Arabs in Exile*. London: IB Tauris & Co. Ltd., p. 31.

7 R. Lawless (1995) *From Ta'izz to Tyneside*. Exeter: University of Exeter Press, p. 220.

8 Halliday (1992) Op. Cit., p. 30.

9 Ibid., p. 31.

10 Ibid., p. 31.

11 R. Lawless (1993) 'Sheikh Abdullah Ali al-Hakimi', http://al-bab.com/bys/articles/lawless93.htm, accessed 29/03/2010.

12 Ibid.

13 Ibid.

14 Ibid.

15 M. Lings (1961) *A Moslem Saint of the Twentieth Century*. London: George Allen & Unwin Ltd., p. 63, fn. 3.

16 Cited in Lings (1961) Op. Cit., p. 9.

17 The book was eventually posthumously published in 1941.

18 Ibid., pp. 64–6.

19 Ibid., p. 68.

20 Ibid., p. 74, fn. 1.

21 Ibid., p. 116, fn.3.

22 R. B. Serjeant (1944) 'Yemeni Arabs in Britain', *The Geographical Magazine*, 17, 4, pp. 143–7.

23 Ibid., p. 143.

24 B. Dahya (1965) 'Yemenis in Britain: An Arab Migrant Community', *Race*, 3, 4, p. 177.

25 M. M. Ally (1982) 'History of Muslims in Britain 1850–1980', unpublished MA thesis, University of Birmingham, p. 84.

26 M. A. Khan (1979) 'Islam and the Muslims of Liverpool', unpublished MA thesis, University of Liverpool, p. 42.

27 F. Halliday (1992) Op. Cit., p. 50.

28 H. Ansari (2004) *'The Infidel Within': Muslims in Britain since 1800*. London: Hurst & Company, p. 343.

29 Serjeant (1944) Op. Cit., p. 143.

30 'Shaykh' – lit., 'old man' but, understood to mean learned elder as in, tribal leader or religious scholar.

31 *Dhikr,* according to *The Encyclopaedia of Islam*, literally means 'reminding oneself'. In the Islamic context and particularly within the Sufi traditions, the act of *dhikr* is based on the Qur'anic verse, 'And remember your Lord when you forget, and say you: "Perchance my Lord will guide me to something nearer to right direction than this"' (18:24). See Daryabadi (2001) Op. Cit., p. 531. *Dhikr* then is, 'possibly the most frequent form of prayer, its mukabal ("opposite correlative") is fikr [q.v.] (discursive) reflection, meditation'; see Lewis, et al., Op. Cit., Vol. II, pp. 223–6.

32 Serjeant (1944) Op. Cit., p. 147.

33 Ibid., p. 143.

34 Halliday (1992) Op. Cit., p. 10.

35 See P. Fryer (1984) *Staying Power: A History of Black People in Britain*. London: Pluto Press, pp. 298–316. And, Seddon, Mohammad Siddique, '400 Years of Muslim Deportation from Britain', in *Q-News*, No.350.October 2003/Shaban 1424, pp. 18–21.

36 *Prayer Timetable 1993 To 2000*, Eccles, Eccles/Salford Mosque & Islamic Centre, 1993, p. 3.

37 C. Jim (1982) 'A visit to The Eccles Mosque', *The Eccles and Patricroft Journal*.

38 *Prayer Timetable* (1993) Op. Cit., p. 3.

39 A. Y. Ali (1989) *The Holy Qur'an: Text, Translation and Commentary*, p. 49.

40 Ibid., p. 1628.

41 See ibid., p. 49, fn. 117.

42 The *Wahhabis* or *Wahhabiyah*, are defined by *The Encyclopaedia of Religion*, as 'An Islamic renewal group established by Muhammad Ibn 'Abd al-Wahhab (d. ah 1206/1792 ce), the *Wahhabiyah* continues to the present in the Arabian Peninsula. The term *Wahhabi* was originally used by opponents of the movement, who charged that it was a new form of Islam, but the name eventually gained wide acceptance . . . The *Wahhabiyah* often refer to 'the mission of the oneness of God (da'wat al-tawhid)' and call themselves 'those who affirm the oneness of God', or 'Muwahhidun.' (italics are mine). For a detailed explanation, see J. O. Voll (1987) 'Wahhabiyah' in *The Encyclopaedia of Religion*, M. Eliade, et al. (Eds) Vol. 15, pp. 313–16.

43 The *Salafis* or *Salafiya*, are a reformist movement inspired by the modernist scholars like Muhammad 'Abdu and Rashid Rida from Egypt. *The Encyclopedia of Islam* describes the *Salafiya* as '[a] neo-orthodox brand of Islamic reformism originating in the late ninteenth century and centred on Egypt, aiming to regenerate Islam by a return to the tradition represented by the "pious forefathers"

(*al-salaf al-salih*, hence its name) of the primitive name.' See Lewis, et al. (1990) Op. Cit., Vol. VIII, pp. 900–9.

44 Halliday (1992) Op. Cit., p. 31.

45 For a detailed discussion on this subject, see M. S. Seddon (2009) 'Global Citizenry Ancient and Modern: British Yemenis and Tranlocal Tribalism' in *Citizenship, Security and Democracy: Muslim Engagement with the West*, W. Krause (Ed.), pp. 89–114.

46 See M. Raza (1993 2nd edition) *Islam in Britain*. Leicester:Volcano Press, p. 38.

47 See M. Ibn Abd Al Wahhab (trans. Al-Faruqi, Ismail, R.) (1991) *Kitab al-Tawhid*, pp. xv–xvii.

48 See Sadek Hamid (in this volume).

Bibliography

Ali, A. Y. (1989) *The Holy Qur'an: Text, Translation and Commentary*, Maryland: Amana Corporation.

Ally, M. M. (1982) 'History of Muslims in Britain 1850–1980', unpublished MA thesis, University of Birmingham.

Ansari, H. (2004) '*The Infidel Within': Muslims in Britain since 1800*, London: Hurst & Company.

Bashier, Z. (1983) *The Makkan Crucible*, Leicester: The Islamic Foundation.

Clark, J. (1982) 'A Visit to The Eccles Mosque', *The Eccles and Patricroft Journal*.

Dahya, B. (1965) 'Yemenis in Britain: An Arab Migrant Community', *Race*, 3(4).

Daryabadi, A. M. (2001) *The Glorious Qur'an*, Markfield: The Islamic Foundation.

Eliade, M. et al. (Eds) (1987) *The Encyclopaedia of Religion*, Vol. 15.

Fryer, P. (1984) *Staying Power: A History of Black People in Britain*, London: Pluto Press.

Halliday, F. (1992) *Arabs in Exile*, London: IB Tauris & Co. Ltd.

Ibn Abd Al Wahhab, (trans. Al-Faruqi, Ismail, R.) (1991) *Kitab al-Tawhid*, Ryadh: International Islamic Publishing House.

Khan, M. A. (1979) 'Islam and the Muslims of Liverpool', unpublished MA thesis, University of Liverpool.

Krause, W., (Ed.) (2009) *Citizenship, Security and Democracy: Muslim Engagement with the West*, London and Istanbul: The Association of Muslim Social Scientists, UK (AMSS) (UK) & The Foundation for Political, Economic and Social Research (SETA, Turkey).

Lawless, R., (1993) 'Sheikh Abdullah Ali al-Hakimi', http://al-bab.com/bys/articles/lawless93.htm (accessed 29/03/2010).

— (1995) *From Ta'izz to Tyneside*, Exeter: University of Exeter Press.

Lewis, B., et al., (1986) *The Encyclopaedia of Islam*, Vol. XI, Leiden: EJ Brill.

Lings, M., (1961) *A Moslem Saint of the Twentieth Century*, London: George Allen & Unwin Ltd.

— (1971) *A Sufi Saint of the Twentieth Century*, Berkley & Los Angeles: University of California Press.

Prayer Timetable 1993 To 2000, Eccles, Eccles/Salford Mosque & Islamic Centre, 1993.

Raza, M., (1993 2nd edition.) *Islam in Britain*, Leicester: Volcano Press.

Seddon, M. S., '400 Years of Muslim Deportation from Britain', *Q-News*, No.350. October 2003/Shaban 1424.

Seddon, M. S., et al., (2004) *British Muslims between Assimilation and Segregation: Historical, Legal and Social Realities*, Markfield: The Islamic Foundation.

Serjeant, R. B., (1944) 'Yemeni Arabs in Britain', *The Geographical Magazine*, 17(4).

5

Sufism in Britain: The *Da'wa* of Shaykh 'Abdalqadir as-Sufi[1]

Yasin Dutton

Other than a few limited references, there is very little in the literature about the *da'wa* ('call', 'invitation', that is, to Islam) of Shaykh 'Abdalqadir as-Sufi, which began in the late 1960s and continues to this day.[2] In this chapter, we aim to present a brief outline of the main events in the history of the Shaykh's da'wa, with special reference to the British situation, and also to highlight the main teachings of the Shaykh as they have developed over this historical period. We also append a select bibliography of the main works of the Shaykh and the translations of classical Muslim scholarship initiated and/or overseen by him.

Historical perspectives

Towards the end of 1967, a Scot from Ayr named Ian Dallas accepted Islam at the hand of the *imam khatib* (chief imam) of the Qarawiyyin Mosque in Fez, Morocco. He was henceforth known as 'Abdalqadir, and, later, Shaykh 'Abdalqadir as-Sufi. In the following year, the Shaykh met, and received instruction from, the learned scholar and Sufi, Shaykh Muhammad ibn al-Habib of Meknes, who told him to return to England and spread the *din* of Islam there, giving him authority as *muqaddam* (authorized representative) of the Shadhiliyya-Darqawiyya-Habibiyya *tariqa*. An account of such a meeting with a shaykh of instruction is given in the Shaykh's *The Book of Strangers* (1972), which in many respects is an autobiographical reflection of this early Moroccan period.[3]

Over the next few years, a number of other young British men and women became Muslim at the hand of the Shaykh and a small community of new

Muslims established itself in London, forming the nucleus of a *da'wa* movement that would, over the next few decades, spread to Malaysia and Indonesia in the East, and the United States and Mexico in the West, with a particularly strong presence in the United Kingdom, Spain and South Africa.

In 1970 and 1971, members of the new London-based group travelled to Morocco for the annual Moussem of Shaykh Muhammad ibn al-Habib, strengthening the links of the group with its Moroccan origins. At the end of 1971, members of the group went on Hajj, intending to meet up in Makka with Shaykh Muhammad ibn al-Habib, only to learn when they had arrived there that the Shaykh had died in Algeria on his way to the Hajj, aged well over 100 years.

In 1970 also, Shaykh 'Abdalqadir travelled to the United States, a journey which resulted in other individuals becoming Muslim and joining the group. In the early 1970s, further individuals became Muslim with the London group, which took up residence in a squat in Bristol Gardens, West London, where they founded the Society of Islam in England.

In addition to *The Book of Strangers*, this early period also saw the publication of the Shaykh's highly influential *The Way of Muhammad* (1975), described by the author as a 'meditation on the five pillars of Islam as viewed by someone who has taken them on and is savouring their meanings', and which was also intended 'to show that it was possible to grasp the meaning of Islam in terms of the European existential tradition'.[4]

1975 was the year when four Spanish men visited England and became Muslim at the hand of the Shaykh. In the following year, they returned to Spain, where they became the nucleus of a second community, which, by 1981, consisted of 30 men and was to grow much larger over the succeeding years.

1976 saw the move of the London-based community to Norfolk, where the Darqawi Institute was set up in Wood Dalling Hall in the Norfolk countryside, where the intention was to have, as far as possible, a self-sufficient community living according to the *shari'a*. Shortly afterwards the building now known as Ihsan Mosque – named after its benefactor – was acquired in Norwich, where the prayer, including the Jumu'a prayer, was first established in 1977 and has been ever since. 1977 was also the year when the Shaykh went into *khalwa* ('retreat') with his second shaykh, Shaykh al-Fayturi of Benghazi, Libya, who had received *idhn* ('permission') from the renowned Shaykh al-'Alawi of Mostaghanem, Algeria, and in turn passed on his *idhn* to Shaykh 'Abdalqadir after his *khalwa*, and who thus combined both the 'Alawi and Habibi *tariqas* in one person.

The late 1970s saw the publication of a number of key works of the Shaykh, including *Jihad: A Groundplan* in 1978, followed by *Resurgent Islam: 1400 Hijra* in 1979. During the same period the Shaykh oversaw the translation of the *Kitab ʿUsul al-Din* and *Kitab ʿUlum al-Muʿamala* by the Nigerian scholar ʿUthman dan Fodio (1754–1817), published in 1978 as *Handbook on Islam, Iman, Ihsan*; and also *The Darqawi Way*, a new translation of the letters of Shaykh al-Darqawi to his *murids* (1979).[5] The early 1980s saw the publication of further works of the Shaykh, including *Qurʾanic Tawhid* (1981), *Letter to an African Muslim* (1981), and *Kufr: An Islamic Critique* (1982). The Shaykh was also instrumental at this time in overseeing the translation of another key work, Qadi ʿIyadʾs famous summary of the Five Pillars of Islam according to Maliki fiqh, which was published in 1982 as *The Foundations of Islam*.

The late 1970s and early 1980s also saw the translation of Imam Malikʾs critically important work, the *Muwattaʾ*, which eventually saw the light of day, in an Azhar-approved edition, in 1982. This was also the year when Shaykh ʿAbdalqadir gave a series of discourses in Blanco, Texas, on Imam Malik and his method which were published soon after as *Root Islamic Education* (1982).

Meanwhile, following the political analysis of the Shaykh, and the emphasis on the need for amirate (see further below), the Norwich group had now organized itself around an *amir* ('leader') as political head of the community. One of the first activities of this new amirate was the organizing, in Norwich, of the First Maliki Fiqh Conference, in November 1982, attended by leading Maliki scholars from North Africa and the Gulf. The 1982 conference was followed by a second, hosted by the Spanish community in Granada, in November 1983, and a third, hosted by Shaykh Muhammad al-Shadhili al-Nayfar (who had attended both previous conferences), in Tunis in November 1984. (A fourth conference was hosted by Shaykh ʿAbd al-ʿAziz Al Mubarak, who had had a paper delivered in his name at the Norwich conference and had attended the Granada conference in person, in Abu Dhabi in April 1986.) 1984 also saw the first of what were to become regular visits to South Africa, initially to Durban and, two years later, to Soweto, just outside Johannesburg.

In 1987, the Norwich community hosted a pioneering conference on usury, a theme which had been highlighted by the Shaykh nearly ten years earlier in *Jihad: A Groundplan* and also *Resurgent Islam*.[6] The Norwich conference resulted in a publication entitled *Usury: The Root Cause of the Injustices of Our Time*, as well as an increased emphasis on the *haram* and destructive nature of the present-day banking system and the need to implement alternatives.

At the Fifth Conference on Maliki Fiqh, hosted by the Spanish community in Granada in 1991, the highly significant *Fatwa on the Unacceptability of Paper Money* was delivered by Umar Ibrahim Vadillo.[7] This was followed by renewed efforts to promulgate and reinstate a genuine *halal* currency based on real gold dinars and real silver dirhams, to be used in markets run according to the principles and precepts of Islamic law, where, as well as using *halal* currency, space could not be booked or rented but was available on a first-come, first-served, basis; thus the Birmingham Autumn Fair in October 1992, where the first English-minted dirhams were available; and the Berkshire Autumn Trade Fair in October 1993, characterized by *The Times* as 'the market that bans banknotes'.[8]

Thus it was that, during the 1970s and 1980s, a strong base in Sufism was wedded to a strong commitment to outward *fiqh*. Nor should it be forgotten that all of the outward events described above were accompanied by the inward practice of *dhikr* ('remembrance'). In this context, we might also note the Shaykh's reminder to his readers in the Preface to *Jihad: A Groundplan*, that 'half of the history of Islam is in the *ghayb* ("unseen"), for it concerns the destinies of millions saved from the fire throughout endless time by the good news of the mercy of Allah upon those who submit to Him'.[9]

From the 1990s on until the present day, there has been a consolidation of the above themes, both the outward aspects and the inward, with regular, usually annual, Moussems (religious festivals) emphasizing the inward aspects and regular meetings and conferences emphasizing the more outward aspects.

In 1991, after many years of refusal, the Spanish authorities finally gave permission for the community in Granada to build a mosque in the old Muslim area of the city, known as the Albaicin, overlooking the famous Alhambra Palace. (The land had been bought in 1981.) The new mosque was finally opened in July 2003 at a ceremony attended by dignitaries from within Spain and also from the Muslim world – including the Amir of Sharjah, who had contributed considerably in bringing the project to fruition in its final stages. Like the Ihsan Mosque in Norwich, the Granada mosque too has seen the daily establishment of the five prayers as well as the weekly Jumu'a prayer and considerable outreach activity.

A third, fully functioning mosque established by the Shaykh is the Jumu'a Mosque in Cape Town, South Africa, where the prayer has been fully established since 2006, and where a *zawiya* has been established alongside the mosque for weekly gatherings of *dhikr*. At the time of writing, a fourth mosque is in the early stages of being constructed in San Cristóbal, Chiapas, Mexico, where, at the instructions of the Shaykh, a small community was established in 1994 among the local Mayan Indians.

Key teachings of the Shaykh

The above is just an outline of some of the more memorable events and landmarks in the history of the Shaykh's *da'wa*, not just in England but elsewhere in the world, although much has, of course, been left out. In terms of ideas, a useful summary of the Shaykh's teachings – or rather his presentation of a complete and fully functioning Islam with both its inward and outward aspects intact – is contained in a pamphlet issued in 1991 at the time of the Gulf War. In this pamphlet, the following five points were highlighted:

1. To Establish Islam
2. To Establish Amirate
3. War Against Usury
4. The 'Amal of Madina
5. Dhikr of Allah

We shall look briefly at each in turn.

Establishing Islam

The Shaykh's position – and it is of course the position of all the traditional *'ulama'* of Islam – is that Islam is a whole and needs to be established in its entirety. It says in the Qur'an: 'Enter into Islam completely' (Q.2:208). This means, of course, inwardly and outwardly – in its political and economic aspects as well as its individual and spiritual aspects – although, of course, the two are not separate.[10]

This double-sided nature of Islam is evident at all levels, from the basics of the Five Pillars through to the finer details of Islamic law. It is particularly evident in the Pillar of Zakat – which the Shaykh has continued to put particular emphasis upon. Again and again throughout the Qur'an one finds the twin command to 'establish the prayer and pay the *zakat*' (e.g. Q.2:43, 83 and 110, and many other places), but, although the prayer is well established throughout the Muslim world – or should we say, throughout the world wherever there are Muslims – the pillar of *zakat* is almost entirely missing – in its traditionally correct form, that is. In our present time, *zakat* has effectively been reduced to private charity, hence the plethora of organizations aiming and claiming to collect and distribute people's *zakat* but which have absolutely no political authority – unless, of course, they are effectively claiming it for themselves. But this is not the traditional way. The Qur'anic command is *khudh min amwalihim sadaqa*, 'Take alms from their wealth' (Q.9:103), with the word *khudh*, 'take', in the singular, addressed originally to the Prophet and then, as the commentators affirm, addressed to those in leadership after him.[11] The Qur'an also refers to *al-'amilina 'alayha*, 'Those appointed to collect it (i.e. *zakat*)' (Q.9:60), as one of the eight categories of people entitled to receive *zakat*, with the word *'amil* ('official') indicating an official who has been appointed by the leader or his representative, in this case for the task of collecting *zakat*.

Zakat therefore necessitates politics. In fact, it is precisely this political nature of *zakat* that was the reason for the first fighting in Islam after the death of the Prophet. Certain tribes who had previously paid their *zakat* to the Prophet refused to do so to the first caliph, Abu Bakr, claiming that the verse in question ('Take alms from their wealth') was only addressed to the Prophet, and so no longer applied when he was dead. But Abu Bakr was adamant: 'Even if they were to refuse me a hobbling-cord which they used to pay to the Messenger of Allah, may Allah bless him and grant him peace, I would fight them for it. By Allah, I will fight anyone who makes a separation between the prayer and *zakat* (i.e. by accepting the one and rejecting the other)'.[12]

The same political background is necessary for the correct implementation of the pillar of fasting, since fasting in the month of Ramadan depends on the sighting of the new moon, and this sighting – that is, the testimony of it – should be verified by a *qadi* ('judge') – who is an official ultimately appointed by the *amir*, or leader; this sighting is then submitted to the leader who then announces the beginning of Ramadan to the community.[13] This political aspect of one leader/one announcement would thus obviate the problem faced every year with Muslims in different groups and/or countries beginning and/or ending the month on different days. In other words, the solution to the problem is not scientific, involving predictions of when the new month will begin, or, more correctly, when and where the first new crescent moon will be visible; rather, the solution to the problem is predominantly political, and involves the existence, or establishment, of amirate.

Establishing amirate

It says in the Qur'an: 'O you who believe, obey Allah, and obey the Messenger, and those in charge over you' (Q.4:59). The traditional commentaries make it clear that this obedience to 'those in charge over you' should be understood primarily as obedience to the political authorities, although there is a second meaning of 'those with knowledge'.[14] The Prophet also advised even a small group of three to appoint one of their number as *amir*: 'If three people set out on a journey, they should appoint one of themselves as *amir*'.[15] Leadership, then, is an expected feature of all groups, from the smallest to the largest.

Amirate is a feature of Islam that has been emphasized by the Shaykh since at least the early 1980s when, as we have seen, the Norwich community was organized around an amir. As has also been noted in the previous section, establishing amirate is effectively a prerequisite for the correct implementation of the two pillars of *zakat* and fasting, but it goes much further than that. Leadership is the basis of community, and Islam is first and foremost a religion of community. And leadership in this context means personal leadership – as implied in the singular command *khudh* referred to above – and not elections and committees and all the other structures that hide present day power realities. The Prophet said, in a well-known *hadith*, 'Whoever dies without having pledged allegiance (i.e. to an *amir*, or leader), dies a Jahili death', that is, a death characteristic of the Jahiliyya, or Time of Ignorance before Islam, when people lacked both guidance and any unified political leadership.[16]

This theme of leadership, in the sense of personal rule, has been a key theme in the Shaykh's writings, especially in more recent years. It is particularly evident in works such as *The Return of the Khalifate* (1996) and *The Muslim Prince* (2009). In *The Return of the Khalifate*, the Shaykh emphasizes what we have noted above, namely, that

> It is necessary for the establishment of the complete ethos of Islam that there is an Amir. From the authorisation of Jumu'a onwards, each obligation of Deen requires an empowered order. Thus leadership is an inescapable part of genuine Islam.[17]

In the Introduction to *The Muslim Prince*, the Shaykh notes how wealth and power necessarily go hand in hand but that the 'true policy of the Islamic Community' is based on a very different concept of wealth and power than that witnessed today. From an Islamic viewpoint

> Wealth is based on real-value instruments of exchange: Gold Islamic Dinar and Silver Dirham at the core, in a post-usury market. Power is based on personal rule, with the Amir at the head of affairs, ruling in consultation, openly and in trust.[18]

War against Usury

Usury – which we can and should define as the taking of *any* interest and not just that which is seen to be 'exorbitant' – is clearly prohibited in the Qur'an and strongly condemned in the *hadith* literature. In the Qur'an it says, about those who persist in taking usury even after they have been warned, 'then be informed of a war from Allah and His Messenger' (Q.2:279), while in the *hadith* it is described as being 36 times worse than illicit sexual intercourse, and also as consisting of 70, or 99, types of wrong action, the least of which is like that of a man having intercourse with his mother.[19]

This prohibition is well known to every Muslim and yet, despite this, it is still the case that the Muslims – indeed, the whole world – are using a monetary system that is usurious from beginning to end. It has been part of the teachings of the Shaykh from at least the early 1980s to highlight the usurious, and therefore *haram*, nature of the present monetary system. It was one of the points discussed in the 1982 First Maliki Fiqh conference in Norwich; a clear critique is also spelled out, for example, in the Shaykh's 1984 publication, *The Sign of the Sword*;[20] and it formed the major theme of the 1987 conference referred to earlier entitled 'Usury: The Root Cause of the Injustices of Our Time'.

This critique of the monetary system is, of course, not new. Writers in England in the first half of the past century, for example, were well aware of the issues. Jeffrey Mark, for instance, noted that 'all money now comes into existence as a debt to the banking systems of the world',[21] while Frederick Soddy summarized the situation succinctly by noting that money nowadays is 'imagined to exist for the purpose of charging interest on it'.[22] Nevertheless, it seems that there is very little critique in the Muslim world – indeed, anywhere – of fractional reserve banking, which is the technical term for the method whereby money is created out of nothing as a debt to the banking systems of the world, purely for the purpose of charging interest on it. Here is not the place to go into the details of this technique, but anyone who cares to go into it – in, for example, any first-year undergraduate economics textbook – will immediately see that it is usurious from beginning to end.[23] What is important to notice in the present context is that, among the worldwide Muslim community, it is the Shaykh, and, following him, his student Umar Ibrahim Vadillo, who have almost single-handedly brought this issue to the forefront of Muslim consciousness today.

An important corollary of this critique is the need to provide an alternative. Here again, the pioneering work of the Shaykh and Umar Vadillo on reviving the Islamic gold dinar and silver dirham as the currency of the Muslims has been paramount. The first modern silver dirhams, for example, were minted, and used, in Granada in 1992, closely followed by further coins minted in the next few years in the United Kingdom and South Africa. There are of course numerous problems in implementing this change, but already in Malaysia and Indonesia there have been significant advances, with dirhams and dinars available for people to acquire and use at an ever-increasing number of outlets, including, in the Malaysian case, a portion of the salaries of government employees in the state of Kelantan. And of course the model, once established, can be used elsewhere.

As the Malaysian-Indonesian case indicates, use of the gold dinar and silver dirham implies the provision of venues where these coins can be used. Already, as we have seen above, markets have been held where dinars and dirhams have been accepted – and expected – as the unit of currency, such as the Birmingham and Berkshire Fairs (1992 and 1993) mentioned earlier and, since that time, many others in Britain and elsewhere. Connected with this has been the work to resurrect the traditional marketplace where, in accordance with the Sunna, places cannot be reserved and anyone is free to come and sell his or her goods on a first-come, first-served basis.

The *'Amal* of Madina

As we noted earlier, the early 1980s saw the publication of a translation of Malik's *Muwatta'* and, shortly afterwards, the Shaykh's *Root Islamic Education* and, with these two, an overt concern with following the *'amal*, or 'practice', of the People of Madina. The *'amal* of the People of Madina is a principle that, in later formulations of Islamic *fiqh* and jurisprudence, is associated specifically with the Maliki *madhhab* to the exclusion of any others. This, however, is a misleading simplification since, in reality, the *'amal* of Madina is nothing other than a specific way of understanding the concept of *sunna* – indeed of Islam – and so the difference is not so much one of a different source of law as one of a different understanding of an agreed source of law.

The key feature of *'amal* – and, therefore *sunna* in its *'amal* understanding – is its non-textual quality. Just as *sunna* in Arabic refers originally to the normative practice of the Prophet and, by extension, of the Muslims, and only later becomes synonymous with the textual source of hadith (whether in written or spoken form), so too is *'amal* a non-textual concept which refers to what the people in Madina were *doing* – that is, their *'amal* – with regard to certain judgements of the law. This source is thus seen as being stronger than *hadith*, since it relates to the practice of a large body of people – the people of Madina – rather than reports related from or by individuals. This is why Rabi'a, one of the scholars of Madina, was noted as saying, 'One thousand from one thousand is preferred by me to one from one. One from one will tear the *sunna* right out of your hands.'[24] 'One thousand from one thousand' was the situation in Madina, where at least a thousand people learnt what they learnt and put into practice what they put into practice, based on what a thousand people had done before them; 'one from one', on the other hand, was the situation elsewhere, where single individuals, or at best a few individuals, transmitted simply what they personally knew about a particular issue. But 'one from one' was to become the standard throughout the Muslim world once the idea of *sunna* had become equated with *hadith* – usually, as we have said, transmitted by an individual or, at best, a few individuals. And it resulted in the compilations of Prophetic *hadith* which then became a second written source – identified as the Sunna – alongside the Qur'an.

What the concept of the *'amal* of Madina implies is a society, and not just individuals. It therefore also implies a transmission of knowledge-through-action that has been activated among, and witnessed by, the whole community and is not, therefore, the preserve of a scholastic elite. Thus for the Shaykh, Islam is not 'sustained by scholars – it is sustained by fuqaha, by people who pass legal judgement, who govern, and who control the social nexus of the Muslims in all aspects of life.'[25] And, since we are talking about a community with a leader, or *amir*, the concept of the *'amal* of Madina also implies a society where the men of knowledge are actively involved in the political and social affairs of their society alongside their *amir*.

These ideas about *'amal* form the backbone of *Root Islamic Education*, in which the Shaykh presents the work of the great Maliki scholar Qadi 'Iyad in his book *Tartib al-Madarik* about the characteristics and qualities of the *madhhab* of Malik. For the Shaykh, however, Qadi 'Iyad's argument is more than just an argument about *madhhab*, and why one should prefer one *madhhab* over another. Rather, 'Iyad's critique points to a purer and more original understanding of *sunna*, and thus of Islam. As the Shaykh says

> The madhhab of Malik is not Maliki in the sense of pertaining to Malik, it is that Malik recorded the 'amal of Madinah. I am saying there is one madhhab which is the madhhab of Islam and Malik was on it![26]

In particular, the importance of Madina, he says, is 'not some simple appreciation of the tremendous baraka of the place, but the political spiritual reality of the transformed people in it.'[27] He goes on to say

> This is the message of Madina – you are not a Muslim until your society is safe! You cannot preserve anything of ruhani lights or intellectual appreciation of intelligent worship as an individual in the deen of Islam if that blessing stops at the door of your house. There is no Muslim who is a private Muslim. There is no manhood without governance, and being governed in a way acceptable to you,

having accepted the deen of Islam. It is the definition of 'rijal', and without it you are as incomplete as if you were biologically incomplete.[28]

Dhikr of Allah

In the Qur'an, the Muslims are exhorted to 'remember Allah often' (Q.33:41), and this has been a key part of the Shaykh's teaching and practice from the earliest days. Of particular importance has been the daily recitation of Shaykh Muhammad ibn al-Habib's *wird* (set formulae of *dhikr*) which consists of the repetition of various well-known phrases in praise of Allah and His Prophet, along with certain verses of the Qur'an and prayers recorded from the Prophet, and including also some longer prayers written by Shaykh Muhammad ibn al-Habib himself. Beyond the general theme of praise of Allah and asking for blessings on His Prophet, a specific and recurrent theme is the reminder to put one's reliance in Allah. This *wird* takes about 20 minutes to recite, and is best done by people in a group, although it is also acceptable to do it by oneself.

Alongside the *wird*, the Shaykh has also emphasized recitation of the Qur'an. Again, this can be done in a group – following the standard North African practice of reciting a *hizb* (sixtieth portion) of the Qur'an in the mosque after both the dawn and sunset prayers – or by oneself. Such recitation usually also forms part of the weekly 'laylat al-fuqara' gatherings held by followers of the Shaykh in various parts of the world. These gatherings typically involve recitation of the Qur'an (often the last *hizb* of the Qur'an), followed by the *wird* and then various *qasida*s ('poems') from the *Diwan,* or collected poems, of Shaykh Muhammad ibn al-Habib. These poems deal with the teachings of *tasawwuf* and, in particular, the need to affirm both *shari'a* and *haqiqa* as part of a person's Islam.

These, of course, are all semi-formal types of *dhikr*. It should be remembered, though, that the aim is to remember Allah in all one's states and all one's times – the Qur'an refers to 'those who remember Allah, standing, sitting, and lying on their sides' (Q.3:191) – which equates to the meaning of *ihsan* ('excellence') in the famous Gabriel hadith where *ihsan* is defined as being 'that you worship Allah as though you can see Him and, even if you can't see Him, He can see you'.[29]

It should also be remembered that *dhikr* only has its meaning alongside an outward practice of the Shari'a. As the Shaykh says in *Jihad: A Groundplan*:

> Restored to the social and personal reality of a *deen*, it is possible for modern man to find in Islam the perfect way, combining as it does so elegantly and nobly, the science of inner knowledge and the science of social action . . . In the *sufi/fiqh*

conflict it is exclusivism, ritualism, and role-playing that must be eliminated. The truths of *Ihsan* remain and the Qur'anic injunctions of outwardness remain. The shari'at is nowhere denied, and gnosis is the promised gift to the *muhsin* when he 'watches the night'.[30]

One could thus say, summarizing the *da'wa* of the Shaykh, that it is epitomized in the *Diwan* of Shaykh Muhammad ibn al-Habib on the one hand and the Islamic gold dinar on the other. The first represents a particularly pure form of the teachings of *tawhid* and *tasawwuf* against a background of the actions of the Shari'a, and thus a purification of the inward; the second represents a purification of the outward through the re-creation of a business arena where one is *not* obliged to use usurious instruments to carry out one's daily business, nor to be under the effective, albeit indirect, rule of the banks. It should also be remembered that *zakat* – an eminently outward form of wealth re-distribution – is from an Arabic root which indicates purity. To pay one's *zakat*, therefore, is to purify one's wealth and, in the process, one's self. Thus it is that purification of the inward and the outward are inextricably bound together.

This, then, is a very brief introduction to the Shaykh's work and teachings. Alongside a development of ideas over time, following the Shaykh's identification and/or re-discovery of key texts, it is also possible to note a very strong continuity. Thus, for example, while the introduction of the gold dinar may be seen as a specific development in the teachings of the Shaykh, in reality it is, as we have seen, nothing other than the workings-out of the dual Qur'anic command to 'establish the prayer and pay the *zakat*' and the Qur'anic prohibition of usury, both of which themes have been in the Shaykh's teaching from at least the late 1970s. Similarly, there is no question that *dhikr* has remained an essential element in the Shaykh's teaching from the very earliest days. It is also the case that many of the earliest followers of the Shaykh are still with him, as are their sons and daughters and, increasingly, their grandchildren.

Finally, one should note that, although we began by referring to the development of Sufism in Britain, in which the Shaykh has undoubtedly played a major part, it is in fact more correct to talk, not about Sufism, but about Islam, and not about Britain, but about the world. Put differently, in the outward it is the three mosques of Norwich, Granada and Cape Town – and the people who pray in them – that best testify to the Shaykh's work and activity, while in the inward it is Allah who knows best about the quality of the people who pray in them.

Notes

1 This article is an expanded version of a paper originally presented at the 'Sufis and Scholars: The Development of Sufism in Britain' conference held at Liverpool Hope University on May 25 and 26, 2012. I am grateful to Professor Ron Geaves for his generous invitation to attend this conference. I wish also to express my thanks to Shaykh Abdalhaqq Bewley, Hajj Issa Bryce, Hajj Abdalhasib Castiñeira, Hafiz Ismail Perez and the late Hajj Abdallah Luongo for their clarifications of numerous points of fact in this work. Needless to say, any errors or misrepresentations are entirely my own responsibility. This work is based on research supported by the National Research Foundation. Any opinion, findings and conclusions or recommendations expressed in this material are those of the author and therefore the NRF do not accept any liability in regard thereto.

2 At the risk of overlooking much of the burgeoning scholarship on Sufism in the West, one might mention the following examples of references to the Shaykh's work: R. Geaves (2000) *The Sufis of Britain: An Exploration of Muslim Identity*, Cardiff Academic Press, pp. 70–1, 142–5; D. Westerlund 'Introduction: Inculturating and Transcending Islam', pp. 9–10, and idem (2004) 'The Contextualisation of Sufism in Europe' in *Sufism in Europe and North America*, D. Westerlund (Ed.), London and New York: Routledge Curzon, pp. 22–28; M. Hermansen (2009) 'Global Sufism: Theirs and Ours' in *Sufis in Western Society: Global Networking and Locality*, R. Geaves, M. Dressler and G. Klinkhammer (Eds), Abingdon: Routledge, pp. 34–6; H. A. Jawad (2012) *Towards Building a British Islam: New Muslims' Perspectives*, London and New York: Continuum, pp. 133, 156–8 (nn. 18 and 20), 166 (n. 9). It will be apparent that the present author's approach is somewhat different on this particular topic. Special mention should also be made of Aziz El Kobaiti Idrissi, *al-Tasawwuf al-Islami fi l-Maghrib: al-Athar al-Sufi al-Maghribi fi Baritaniya* (*'Islamic Sufism in the West: Moroccan Sufi Influence in Britain. Zawiya Habibiyya Darqawiyya as an Example'*), Matba'at Umayma/Manshurat al-Markaz al-Akadimi li-l-Thaqafa wa-l-Dirasat al-Maghribiyya, al-Sharqawsatiyya wa-l-Khalijiyya, Fez, 2008 (esp. pp. 105–24, 137–56), which contains an extended survey of the Shaykh's work and ideas in the particular context of its Moroccan origins. This is now available in English as: Aziz El Kabaiti Idrissi (2013), *Islamic Sufism in the West*, Norwich: Diwan Press.

3 Full bibliographical details of all the works of the Shaykh mentioned are given in Section A of the Selected Bibliography of the Shaykh's Writings appended to this article.

4 *The Way of Muhammad*, second edn, p. xi.

5   Full bibliographical details of the translations of classical Muslim works overseen
    by the Shaykh are given in Section B of the Selected Bibliography of the Shaykh's
    Writings appended to this article.

6   See, for example, *Jihad: A Groundplan*, p. 12: 'Thus we have seen banking swept
    into the realm of the *halal* without so much as a murmur from our brothers who sit
    uncomfortably, just back from the bank, letting the motion get passed in Makkah, a
    city now immersed in usury'; also *Resurgent Islam*, p. 22: 'The first and the greatest
    crisis in the United States of America was the crisis over the issue of banking. It was
    the attempt to avoid the curse of usury that led to the dramatic confrontation of the
    masons with the noble and idealistic men who had created America to be a place
    of honourable existence, and not dishonesty and exploitation . . . But the usurers
    won the day'. On the same page, there is also reference to Ezra Pound's *Cantos* as 'a
    massive epic poem denouncing the Masonic principle and the usury system, and
    calling on America to reject the banking network and reform its monetary system'.

7   This fatwa was published in: U. Vadillo (1991) *Fatwa on Paper-Money: Fatwa
    concerning the Islamic Prohibition on using Paper-Money as a medium of exchange,
    Granada, 18th of August of 1991*. Granada: Madinah Press.

8   *The Times*, October 30, 1993.

9   *Jihad: A Groundplan*. Norwich: Diwan Press, 1978, p. 8.

10 See, for example, al-Tabari, *Tafsir* (= *Jami' al-bayan fi tafsir al-Qur'an*), 30 vols
    (Dar al-Fikr, Beirut, n.d.; originally Cairo, 1330 (1912)), vol. 2, pp. 187–9; al-Sawi,
    Hashiyat al-Sawi 'ala l-Jalalayn, 4 vols (Dar al-Fikr, Beirut, n.d; originally Maktabat
    al-Tijariyya al-Kubra, Cairo, 1358 (1939)), vol. 1, p. 95; al-Baydawi, *Tafsir* (= *Anwar
    al-tanzil wa-asrar al-ta'wil*), 5 vols (Dar al-Kutub al-'Arabiyya al-Kubra, Cairo, 1330
    (1912)), vol. 1, p. 230.

11 See, for example, Ibn al-'Arabi, *Ahkam al-Qur'an*, 4 vols (Dar al-Ma'rifa, Beirut,
    n.d.; originally Cairo?, 1376 (1957)), vol. 2, p. 1011; al-Qurtubi, *Tafsir* (= *al-Jami' li-
    ahkam al-Qur'an*), 20 vols (Dar al-Kitab al-'Arabi, Cairo, 1387 (1967)), vol. 8, p. 251.

12 Ibn al-'Arabi, *al-'Awasim min al-qawasim* (al-Maktaba al-'Ilmiyya, Beirut,
    1405/1985; originally al-Matba'a al-Salafiyya, Cairo, 1371 (1951–2)), pp. 46–7.

13 See al-Wansharisi, *al-Mi'yar al-mu'rib wa-l-jami' al-mughrib 'an fatawi Ifriqiyya wa-
    l-Maghrib*, (Ed.) M. Hajji et al., 13 vols (Dar al-Gharb al-Islami, Rabat and Beirut,
    1403/1983), vol. 2, pp. 138–9.

14 See, for example, al-Tabari, *Tafsir*, vol. 5, pp. 93–4; al-Sawi, *Hashiya*, vol. 1, p. 226;
    al-Baydawi, *Tafsir*, vol. 2, pp. 94–5.

15 See, for example, al-Nawawi, *Riyad al-Salihin, Kitab adab al-safar: bab istihbab
    talab al-rifqa wa-ta'mirihim 'ala anfusihim wahidan yuti'unahu*, Manshurat Dar al-
    Nasr, n. pl., n.d., p. 297.

16 See, for example, Muslim, *Sahih*, ed., with marginal notes, by Muhammad Shukri
    ibn Hasan al-Anqarawi et al., 8 vols (Dar al-Fikr, Beirut, n.d; originally al-Matba'a
    al-'Amira, Istanbul, 1334 (1916)), vol. 6, p. 22 (= *Kitab al-Imara: bab al-amr*

bi-luzum al-jama'a 'inda zuhur al-fitan wa-tahdhir al-du'at ila l-kufr), and the commentary in the margin thereto.

17 *The Return of the Khalifate*, Cape Town and Erasmia: Madinah Press, 1996, p. 93.

18 Ibid., p. 12.

19 See al-Qurtubi, *Tafsir*, vol. 3, p. 364 (thirty-six times; ninety-nine types); Ibn Majah, *Sunan*, ed. Muhammad Fu'ad 'Abd al-Baqi, 2 vols (Dar Ihya' al-Turath al-'Arabi, n. pl., n.d.), vol. 2, p. 764 (= *Kitab al-Tijarat: bab al-taghliz fi l-riba*) (seventy types).

20 *The Sign of the Sword*, Norwich: Madinah Press, 1984, especially pp. 15–27.

21 J. Mark (1934) *The Modern Idolatry*. London: Chatto & Windus, p. 70.

22 F. Soddy (1926) *Wealth, Virtual Wealth and Debt*. London: George Allen & Unwin, p. 157.

23 See, for example, J. Sloman (2006) *Economics*, sixth edn, Harlow: Prentice Hall, where the author tells us that 'Profits are made by lending money out at a higher rate of interest than that paid to depositors' (p. 484), that 'Banks need to hold a certain amount of their assets as cash' (p. 483), but that 'Both cash and operational balances . . . earn no interest for banks. The *vast majority* of banks' assets are therefore in the form of various types of loan' (p. 484; emphasis added); C. R. McConnell and S. L. Brue (2005) *Economics: Principle, Problems and Policies*. New York: McGraw Hill, esp. pp. 252–65, where, having discussed the reserve ratios that banks must keep, for example, 1:10, or 10 per cent of their depositors' money – usually it is significantly less, although the authors' examples (e.g. pp. 253–5 and 263) mislead the reader into assuming it could be as much as 50 per cent – the authors go on to refer to such legally required reserves as 'leakages of money' that 'dampen the money-creating potential of the banking system' (pp. 263–44); D. Begg, S. Fischer and R. Dornbusch (2005) *Economics*, eighth edn, Maidenhead: McGraw Hill, esp. pp. 387–92, where the authors explain how the banks create many times the amount deposited with them in "overdrafts not fully backed by cash reserves" (p. 389), having previously noted that 'UK banks hold reserves that are only 2 per cent of the sight deposits that could be withdrawn at any time' (p. 387), and adding, somewhat disingenuously, 'Everybody knows what the banks are doing. Usually people do not mind' (p. 389). Compare this with J. K. Galbraith's comment that 'the means by which money is created out of nothing is so simple the mind is repelled' (J. K. Galbraith (1976) *Money: Whence It Came, Where It Went*. London: Pelican, p. 29).

24 See al-Qadi 'Iyad, *Tartib al-madarik wa-taqrib al-masalik li-ma'rifat a'lam madhhab Malik*, ed. Muhammad Tawit al-Tanji et al., 8 vols., second edn., al-Mamlaka al-Maghribiyya: Wizarat al-Awqaf wa-l-shu'un al-Islamiyya, Mohammedia, 1402–3/1982–3, vol. 4, p. 46; also *Root Islamic Education*, p. 60; ibid., second edn, p. 73.

25 *Root Islamic Education*, p. 23; ibid., second edn, p. 28.

26 *Root Islamic Education*, p. 95; ibid., second edn, p. 114.

27 *Root Islamic Education*, p. 44; ibid., second edn, p. 55.

28 *Root Islamic Education*, pp. 44–5; ibid., second edn, p. 55.

29 See, for example, al-Nawawi, *The Forty Hadith* (many editions), Hadith No. 2.
30 *Jihad: A Groundplan*, p. 48.

A select bibliography of the Shaykh's writings

It seems appropriate to append a list of the Shaykh's main writings and publications, some of which have been published under the Shaykh's Muslim name ('Abd al-Qadir as-Sufi/al-Murabit) and some under the name Ian Dallas. In the following list, arranged chronologically, those titles published under the Shaykh's Muslim name are coded with SAQ; those published under the name Ian Dallas with ID. We also include a separate list of translations, also arranged chronologically, of classical Muslim works overseen by him.

A. Works by the Shaykh

The Book of Strangers, Victor Gollancz, London, 1972. ISBN 0575014539. (ID).
The Way of Muhammad, first edn, Diwan Press, Berkeley and London, 1975. Library of Congress Catalog Card Number: 75–8119; second revised edn, Madinah Press, London, 2002. ISBN 1874216037. (SAQ).
Jihad: A Groundplan, Diwan Press, Norwich, 1978. ISBN 0950444693. (SAQ).
Indications from Signs, Iqra Inc., USA/Iqra Communications, Norwich, 1979. (ISBN not given.) (SAQ).
Resurgent Islam, Iqra Inc., USA/Diwan Press, Norwich, 1979. (ISBN not given.) (SAQ).
The Hundred Steps, Diwan Press, Norwich, 1979. ISBN 0906512077. (SAQ).
Letter to an African Muslim, Diwan Press, Norwich, 1981. ISBN 0906512131. (SAQ).
Qur'anic Tawhid. Two Discourses Delivered by Shaykh Abd al-Qadir to a Group of his Murids, Diwan Press, Norwich, 1981. ISBN 090651214X. (SAQ).
Kufr: An Islamic Critique, Diwan Press, Norwich, 1982. ISBN 0906512182. (SAQ).
Root Islamic Education, Diwan al-Amir Publications, Norwich, 1982. ISBN 0946430004; second revised edition, Madinah Press, London, 1993. ISBN 1874216053. (SAQ).
The Sign of the Sword, Madina Press, Norwich, 1984 (ISBN not known); second edn, Murabitun Publications, Norwich, 1991. ISBN 9781871207262. (SAQ).
For the Coming Man, Murabitun Press, Norwich, 1988. ISBN 1871207002. (SAQ).
The Ten Symphonies of Gorka König. A Novel, Kegan Paul International, London and New York, 1989. ISBN 0710303254. (ID).
The New Wagnerian, Freiburg Books, Granada, 1990. ISBN 844047475X; second edn, Editorial Kutubia Mayurqa, 2001. ISBN 8493051578. (ID).
Oedipus and Dionysus, Freiburg Books, Granada, 1992. ISBN 18714216029. (ID).

The Return of the Khalifate, Madinah Press, Cape Town and Erasmia, 1996. ISBN 1874216215. (SAQ).

Letter to an Arab Muslim, Kutubia Mayurqa, Palma de Mallorca, 2000. ISBN 8493051594. (SAQ).

Technique of the Coup de Banque, Kutubia Mayurqa, Palma de Mallorca, 2000. ISBN 849305156X. (SAQ).

A Commentary on Surat al-Waqi'a, Madinah Press, Cape Town, 2004. ISBN 0620319216. (SAQ).

The Book of Tawhid. Nine Discourses given between March 27th and May 29th 2004 at Al-Jami'a Mosque, Claremont, Cape Town, Madinah Press, Cape Town, 2006. ISBN 0620361263. (SAQ).

The Book of Hubb (Love of the Divine). Seven Discourses given between June 21st and September 1st 2007 at Masjid al-Mansur, Constantia, Cape Town, Madinah Press, Cape Town, 2007. ISBN 978–0620399111. (SAQ).

The Book of 'Amal. Eight Discourses given between October 27th 2007 and January 12th 2008 at the Nizamia Mosque, Tokai, Cape Town, Madinah Press, Cape Town, 2008. ISBN 978–0620404631. (SAQ).

The Book of Safar. Six Discourses given between July 5th 2008 and October 17th 2008 at the Jumu'a Mosque of Cape Town, Madinah Press, Cape Town, 2009. ISBN 978–0620441100. (SAQ).

The End of the Political Class, in *Political Renewal: The End of the Political Class* by Ian Dallas, and *The House of Commons and Monarchy* by Hilaire Belloc (first published 1920), Budgate Press, Cape Town, 2009. ISBN 978–0620445733. (ID).

The Muslim Prince, Madinah Press, Cape Town, 2009. ISBN 978–0620434553. (SAQ).

The Interim is Mine, Budgate Press, Cape Town, 2010. ISBN 978–0620486187; paperback edition, 2011. ISBN 978–0620515498. (ID).

The Engines of the Broken World: Discourses on Tacitus and Lucan, Budgate Press, Cape Town, 2012. ISBN 978–0620532501. (ID).

Commentaries, Madinah Press, Cape Town, 2012. ISBN 978–0620523820. (SAQ).

B. Translations initiated and/or overseen by the Shaykh

The Tawasin of Mansur al-Hallaj, trans. Aisha Abd ar-Rahman at-Tarjumana, Diwan Press, Berkeley and London, 1974. Library of Congress Catalog Card Number: 7421376.

Sidi 'Ali al-Jamal of Fez, *The Meaning of Man*, trans. Aisha 'Abd ar-Rahman al-Tarjumana, Diwan Press, Norwich, 1977. ISBN 0950444669 (cloth); 0950444650 (paper).

Shaykh 'Uthman dan Fodio, *Handbook on Islam, Iman, Ihsan (Kitab Usul ad-Deen and Kitab al-Mu'amala)*, trans. Aisha 'Abd ar-Rahman al-Tarjumana, Diwan Press, Norwich, 1978. ISBN 0950444685.

The Darqawi Way: The Letters of Shaykh Mawlay al-'Arabi ad-Darqawi. Letters from the Shaykh to the Fuqara, trans. 'Aisha 'Abd ar-Rahman at-Tarjumana, Diwan Press, Norwich, 1979. ISBN 0906512069.

The Diwans of the Darqawa: Shaykh Ibn al-Habib, Shaykh al-'Alawi, Shaykh al-Fayturi, Shaykh al-Harraq, trans. 'Aisha 'Abd ar-Rahman at-Tarjumana, Diwan Press, Norwich, 1980. ISBN 0906512107.

Muhyiddin Ibn al-'Arabi, *The Seals of Wisdom (Fusus al-Hikam)*, trans. 'Aisha 'Abd al-Rahman al-Tarjumana, Diwan Press, Norwich, 1980. ISBN 096512093; paperback edition, Madinah Press, ISBN 096512093.

Shaykh al-'Alawi, *The Two Invocations: The Unique Name* and *The Prayer on the Prophet*, Diwan Press, Norwich, 1980. ISBN 096512050; second edn, *Shaykh Mustafa al-'Alawi on The Unique Name and on The Treasury of Truths of Shaykh Muhammad ibn al-Habib*, Madinah Press, Bandung, 2001. ISBN 9799668808.

Imam Malik, *Al-Muwatta*, trans. 'A'isha 'Abdarahman at-Tarjumana and Ya 'qub Johnson, Diwan Press, Norwich, 1982. ISBN 0906512174; second revised edn, Imam Malik ibn Anas, *Al-Muwatta of Imam Malik ibn Anas: The First Formulation of Islamic Law*, trans. Aisha Abdurrahman Bewley, Kegan Paul International, London and New York, 1989. ISBN 0710303610.

Shaykh al-'Alawi, *Knowledge of God. A Sufic Commentary on al-Murshid al-Mu'in of Ibn 'Ashir* (a translation of the author's *al-Minah al-Quddusiyya*), trans. 'Abd al-Kabir al-Munawarra and 'Abd as-Sabur al-Ustadh, Diwan Press, Norwich, 1982. ISBN 0906512166.

Qadi 'Iyad, *The Foundations of Islam*, Diwan Press, Norwich, 1982. ISBN 0946430012; second edn, *Foundations of Islam According to the Ahl al-Madinah*, Madinah Press, Inverness, 2001. ISBN 9799548632.

Qadi 'Iyad ibn Musa al-Yahsubi, *Muhammad Messenger of Allah: Ash-Shifa of Qadi 'Iyad*, trans. Aisha Abdarrahman Bewley, Madinah Press, Granada, 1991. (ISBN not given); second revised edn, Madinah Press, Cape Town, 2011. ISBN 1874216262.

Qadi Abu Bakr ibn al-'Arabi, *Defence Against Disaster, by Accurately Determining the Position of the Companions After the Death of the Prophet, May Allah Bless Him and Grant Him Peace (al-'Awasim min al-Qawasim)*, Madinah Press, Cape Town and Erasmia, 1995. ISBN 0620196882.

Shaykh Ahmad ibn Ajiba, *The Basic Research. Al-Futuhat al-Ilahiyya fi Sharh al-Mabaahith al-Asliyya* (a commentary on the poem of Ibn al-Banna of Saragossa), trans. Abdalkhabir al-Munawara and Hajj Abdas-Sabur al-Ustadh, text revised and edited by Shaykh Abdalqadir as-Sufi, Madinah Press, Cape Town, 1998. ISBN 0620232455.

The Noble Qur'an: A New Rendering of Its Meaning in English, trans. Abdalhaqq and Aisha Bewley, Bookwork, Norwich, 1999. ISBN 1874216363; second revised edn, Bookwork, Norwich, 2012. ISBN 978–0953863945.

Shaykh 'Abdul-Hayy al-'Amrawi and Shaykh 'Abdul-Karim Murad, *Sufis and Sufism: A Defence*, trans. 'Aisha 'Abd ar-Rahman at-Tarjumana, Madinah Press, Cape Town, 2004. ISBN 0620319208.

The One or the Many? Transnational Sufism and Locality in the British Būdshīshiyya

Marta Dominguez-Diaz

It is generally taken for granted that when religions turn global, they develop not only international networks but 'universal' identities. According to this view, religious movements that have settled into a multiplicity of geographic contexts engender increasingly homogenized forms of religious identity. This gives rise to global communities in which locals are imbued with a sense of belonging that stretches far beyond their localities. By doing so, they embrace religious features not necessarily customary to their 'culturally bounded' *milieus*. Members of transnational religious groups, are, thus, assumed to abandon local manifestations of religious praxis by appropriating and embodying 'global forms' of religious expression (Levitt, 2001a) and adopting 'universalist' religious discourses. Furthermore, they often bring these newly formed expressions to the cultural *loci* from which it initially originated.[1]

In the case of the scholarly study of Sufism, the supposedly 'universal' character of transnational Sufi Orders (ar. pl. *ṭuruq,* sing. *ṭarīqa*) is something that academia has mostly overlooked; the study of transnational *ṭuruq* being still in its infancy, with most research having dealt either with Orders in their original contexts or with their European or American groups (e.g. Raudvere, 2002; Lassen, 2009). Very few have incorporated a more embracing transnational dimension (e.g. Nielsen, Draper and Yemelianova, 2006; Villalón, 2007; Werbner, 2005). This chapter wants to contribute to the scholarly debate on the religious identity of transnational religion by presenting a case within an international Sufi organization. The Moroccan *ṭarīqa* Qādiriyya al-Būdshīshiyya originated in the Berber-dominated North Western province of Oujda but has, in recent times, become a transnational religious phenomenon. As a result of this process,

it has incorporated members from urban *milieus* in Morocco and abroad and
has surpassed its traditional ethnic boundaries, coming to accept members from
a variety of backgrounds. Today this *ṭarīqa* is present across the globe, from
West Africa to Latin America but has predominantly settled in North America
and Western Europe.

This chapter proposes a comparative perspective in which the British enclaves
of the Order will be analysed *vis-a-vis* the rest of European groups.[2] The chapter
suggests that in order to understand the British groups of the Būdshīshiyya,
we need to scrutinize them in a comparative manner, by incorporating an
understanding of how they relate to other European groups. It argues that
some of the religious features of the British Būdshīshiyya make more sense if
looked at in relation to the religious features of other Būdshīshiyya groups. It
proposes a comparative perspective among the British and other European
enclaves of the Order, discussing whether or not transnational Sufi Orders hold
a transnational religious character, or develop distinct religious identities in the
new lands in which they set down roots. The chapter discusses the similarities
and differences of British and non-British European groups of the Order and
tries to evaluate the relevance these features have to the overall religious identity
of *ṭarīqa*. It aims to clarify the extent to which it is fair to consider the various
groups of the Order in a similar or differentiated way. By doing so, the chapter
ultimately reflects on how religious identity is being transformed when a Sufi
Order becomes international. Does the character of a *ṭarīqa* remain intact
when transplanted into a multiplicity of cultural regions? Do Sufi Orders re-
territorialize homogenously or diversely? To what extent can different enclaves
of a given *ṭarīqa* be analyzed as participating in a unified religious phenomenon
occurring worldwide – as members of transnational *ṭuruq* often claim – and
to what extent do individual enclaves need to be approached with a greater
consideration of their distinctiveness?

I contend that there are some noticeable differences between the British and
non-British groups of the Order in Europe and that a comparison between them
shed light on such contrasting features. Būdshīshiyya's British groups consist
mainly of young people who were generally not connected to Moroccan culture
or forms of religiosity prior to joining this *ṭarīqa*. In contrast, most enclaves
of the Order in the rest of Western Europe and in North America are related
to the migrational flows of the Moroccan diaspora. As a result, most groups
outside Morocco – with the exception of the British groups – either contain a
sizeable proportion of members born in Morocco or a large number of second-
generation and third-generation Moroccans born and raised in the West. These

second-generation and third-generation Moroccans are still largely connected to Moroccan culture through family relations and regular visits to the land of their parents and grandparents.

Conversely, in the United Kingdom, devotees (ar. pl. *fuqarā'/ faqīrāt*; sing. *faqīr/a*)[3] are mainly white British converts and Muslims of South-Asian background. This chapter explores the extent to which the particular circumstances in which the Būdshīshiyya evolved in Britain has determined a religious identity distinct from that of other Western groups.

The Būdshīshiyya in Europe is made up of small groups of followers scattered all over Western Europe.[4] Some of them are congregated by Moroccan migrants who tend to maintain a tight relationship with their homeland and who have little interaction with the groups attended by non-Moroccans.[5] These are 'Moroccan hubs': *Darija* (the Moroccan dialect of spoken Arabic) is the spoken language, the food eaten is Moroccan, and traditional *jilābāt* are worn for ritual performances. 'Cultural strangers' rarely enter this kind of group and integrate.[6] As far as I am aware, such Būdshīshiyya groups, exclusively made of migrants, do not exist in the United Kingdom. On the other hand, aside from incorporating the groups made of migrants, the Būdshīshiyya in Europe also contains 'hybrid'[7] enclaves: groups that tend to combine a variety of members with diverse backgrounds. Religiously speaking, 'hybrid' groups of the Būdshīshiyya are made up of different peoples who have all taken the conscious decision to join this *tarīqa*. The decision is ritually symbolized by performing the rite of *bay'a*.[8]

The variety of religious paths followed by the devotees of 'hybrid' groups can be broadly divided into the following. First, converts to Islam, by which we mean non-Muslims (religious and non-religious) who formally join the Būdshīshiyya by undertaking the Islamic rite of conversion (ar. *shahada*). Many will prefer to be called reverts[9] (in French often referred to as *reconverties*). Similar to that which happens with other converts, they emphasize a belief that all humans are naturally born with *fitra,* an innate 'feeling' of God's existence. As a result, they view their acts of conversion as a 'return' to this original state of instinctive belief.[10] For some of these 'convert' *fuqarā',* however, the Order turns out to be their 'springboard' to Islam: having converted to Islam to join this *tarīqa*, some leave it after a time but remain practising Muslims.

Second, 'revert' Muslims: those who were born Muslim and, after a period of religious disengagement, returned to the practice of Islam.[11] In the case of the Būdshīshiyya, these often are European born people: the daughters and sons (and grandchildren) of Moroccans who migrated to Europe over the past 30 years or so. No such reverts are to be found in the British groups, perhaps because the rates of Moroccan migration to the United Kingdom seem to be much lower than to the rest of Western Europe.[12]

Finally, the Order contains a large proportion of 're-affiliated' Muslims. Re-affiliation within the Būdshīshiyya is characteristic of the British groups, which, for this reason, are distinctive in comparison to the rest of the European enclaves. Re-affiliated Muslims are those who leave one particular denomination or sect, in order to join another within the same religion. In the case of the Būdshīshiyya, re-affiliated members are typically British-born youngsters whose South Asian parents and grandparents (largely of Pakistani origin) migrated to the United Kingdom around the last three decades. 'Re-affiliated Muslims' were born and brought up as Muslims, and can be differentiated from 'reverts' in that they deem themselves to have believed continuously in the tenets of the Islamic faith.

How did British devotees come to be attracted to the Būdshīshiyya? First, there seemed to be a group of British converts open to exploring North African Sufism by adopting an eclectic, post-modern approach referred to by Ian Draper (2002) as the 'Glastonbury Experience'[13] and/or by joining orders such as the Darqawiyya (a Moroccan branch of the Shadhili order whose European sub-branch is better known by its former name, the Murabitun) and other European branches of the Shadhiliyya (Geaves, 2000). These groups have gained relative popularity in Britain over the last 30 years, attracting not only converts but also members from local Muslim communities –including South Asian communities These first converts' more eclectic interest was later turned into an attraction for more 'traditional' forms of Moroccan Sufism and getting into contact with Sīdī Hamza's teachings followed.

Despite their differences, there are various features shared by the Order right across Western Europe – for example, in what is referred to as the social profile of its adherents. Both the British and non-British groups of this *ṭarīqa* have tended to consolidate in poor urban areas. Although a significant proportion of these 'hybrid' groups were founded by middle and upper class people with an initial intellectual drive for Sufism[14] (in the United Kingdom and France, for example), over the years it is the less well-off members who have kept the Order running.[15] The Order has acquired a house in the borough of Argenteuil (Paris). This house is considered by members to be the center, the *zāwiya*,[16] of the Order in Europe. The higher ranks of religious authority within the Order in Europe are either based in Morocco and regularly visit Argenteuil, or are permanently based in Argenteuil. More recently, followers from Birmingham have also established their own *zāwiya* catering for the religious and community life of its British devotees.[17] If we look at the French and the British *zāwiyāt*, one soon becomes aware of the similarities between the two. They are both located in underprivileged areas. The lodge in Argenteuil is a three storied house, situated in the second most populous area among the so-called *villes de banlieue* of Paris. The neighbourhood is also one of the poorest *banlieues* of the French capital. Similarly, the Birmingham group and the central British *zāwiya* is in the Borough of Small Heath, which is also a socially deprived area. These ghettoized urban areas, commonly referred to as 'ethnic enclaves' – one is predominantly North African, the other South Asian[18] – are often associated with the realities of economic migration: high concentrations of council housing and high unemployment rates.[19] A significant proportion of members are from the neighboring areas. Similarly, the groups in smaller cities also congregate in poor urban areas – usually in private homes where the followers live.[20] There are also resemblances between the British and non-British followers in terms of age. the typical European Būdshīshiyya devotee tends to be quite young (usually below 30), while a small few are below the age of 18. Perhaps as a result of this youthful disciplehood, commitment to the Order tends to be strong, constituting the centre of most devotees' social lives – a *fuqarā*'s friends usually being made up of peer members of the group.[21]

Similarities between the British and non-British groups cannot only be observed at a social level but also at a religious one. Transnational *ṭuruq* often consist of culturally diverse and geographically dispersed groups that ultimately share respect and religious devotion for a shared Sufi master (*walī 'Allāh*)[22] and Sufi ritual performance (*dhikr*).[23] Būdshīshiyya *faqīrāt* are certainly proud of the diverse amalgam of people that the Order brings together. The diversity of the discipleship is often viewed as a proof of the authenticity of the Būdshīshiyya's leader saintly attributes, a manifestation of his *walaya* (Godly granted authority). All the *fuqarā*' pay their utmost respect and devote 'spiritual love' (*maḥabba*) to Sīdī Hamza – a sentiment central in the talk of his devotees and even the main theme of a published biography of the hip hop singer Abd al Malik, perhaps the Order's most famous disciple.[24]

There is consensual respect for religious authority, which follows the pyramidal pattern characteristic of North African Orders.[25] At the top Sīdī Hamza, *shaykh al-tabarruk* of the Order – literally the one attaining *baraka*.[26] Accordingly, he is generally believed to be divinely guided and incapable of sin. After him, members of his closest family, including his son Sīdī Hamida, governor (up until the spring of 2012), of the Berkane province where the central *zāwiya* sits; his grandson Sīdī Mounir; the son of Sīdī Hamza's eldest son, Sīdī Jamal and the person in-charge of the European branches (also believed moreover to be the future inheritor of Sīdī Hamza's *baraka*.

Sīdī Mounir represents the highest authority of the Order in Europe. He is a young, Western-educated man,[27] perceived by many as a 'cultural broker' between the more traditional generation of his father and the newer more 'modern' disciplehood of both the European groups and the younger followers of the Moroccan cities. British followers alongside the rest of the European devotees, consider him a source of spiritual inspiration. Contrary to the figure of his father, however, from whom very little is heard (Sīdī Hamza very rarely leaves the central *zāwiya* and seldom speaks to his followers),[28] Sīdī Mounir represents a new form of authority that involves not only bodily saintly power but also dialectical persuasion as well. Thus, he is the author of various articles translated into European languages that circulate widely among European members of the Order.

There is yet another type of newly emerging religious authority within the Order, represented by people like Faouzi Skali. Skali, not a member of the Būdshīshiyya family but certainly someone with influence within the Order, graduated in Anthropology at the Sorbonne with a thesis on Moroccan Sufism. His Wikipedia site is indicative of what he represents for many Būdshīshiyya devotees: '. . . *ecrivain francophone, il se situe entre l'Orient et l'Occident et œuvre pour le dialogue des hommes et des cultures. . .*'. Although he has no bearing on the authority structure in a traditional sense, (since he is unrelated by blood to Sīdī Hamza) he is respected and followed by members and mentioned by them as an inspirational source. Sometimes his name is praised and mentioned with more recurrence than that of the leading *shaykh*. Skali embodies a modern approach to Sufism, advocating a cosmopolitan form of religious life. He is a public figure: the director general of the Spirit of Fes Foundation and the famous festival of 'Sacred' music hosted at the city, frequently appearing, also, in the media and having authored several books on Sufism.

Both Skali and Mounir epitomize the most visible side of the Order's leadership and, one might argue, a new type of 'more informal' charisma. Their message seems to be proving its effectiveness in helping the *tarīqa* to garner new adherents, younger and literate, particularly in urban areas of Morocco and Europe. Overall, the success of the Order beyond its original enclave seems to be partly related to these new ways of conceptualizing religious authority. Both British and other European followers manifest a similar devotion not only for the leading *shaykh* but also for others like Mounir or Skali.

Although the hierarchy of the Order is entirely based on a masculine line of descent, female members of the Būdshīshiyya family do hold a remarkable status. Sīdī Hamza's daughters are often evoked for their benevolence and hospitality, for embodying the attributes of an adequate female Sufi, particularly among European followers (British and non-British). Immediately below them the hierarchy of the Order has a series of *muqaddimāt*, or secondary authorities, who are the emissaries of the central authority of this *ṭarīqa* in the diverse locations. Each enclave therefore, consists of a local *muqaddim/a* and a group of devotees. The *muqaddim/a*'s role mainly consists of leading the weekly ritual gatherings. This is the reason why there has to be two *muqaddimun* for each enclave – as ritual performance of the weekly *waẓīfa* is gender segregated.[29] Although the respect for this hierarchy certainly holds true among all the members of this *ṭarīqa*, the ways in which this respect is embodied and actually understood varies substantially among devotees with different cultural backgrounds.

For example, an impression one gets by conducting fieldwork is that young Moroccan devotees seem, sometimes, to look for consent from the Order in relation to decisions they make in life (e.g. regarding choosing careers or partners), an attitude that does not seem common among European followers. Whereas in Morocco a dimension of religious authority is related to the act of commanding *sharīʿa* observance, the responsibility of following religious law in Europe seems to be left up to the devotee. This can be linked to a shift in approach to religious authority and religious norms towards the more individualized form of religiosity which is increasingly common in European Islam (Cesari, 2004; Peter, 2006). The Būdshīshiyya is a *ṭarīqa* in which adherence to *sharīʿa*, as developed by the *Mālikī maḏhab,* is formally encouraged. While Moroccan followers adhere to a behavioral code that is compliant with the cultural etiquette of where they live, individual ways of interpreting religious law translates into a kaleidoscope of attitudes towards law among European followers.[30] In this regard, a significant difference between British and non-British groups is the often laxer approach to *sharīʿa* observance among continental European followers; Cases of non-compliance with *sharīʿa* are seemingly more common in France, Belgium and Spain. Such non-compliance ranges from cohabitation with a partner with whom members do not have a formalized or religiously valid Islamic marriage, to women married to non-Muslim men, or to cases of devotees who happen to be regular smokers or dog owners. Although these instances do not make up the rule but are the exception (and do occur, in unusual cases, within the more 'traditional' membership of Morocco as well!), they are much less frequent in British than in non-British European groups.

A tentative explanation for this phenomenon may come from the fact that a significant number of *faqīrāt* in Belgium, France and Spain come from families in which there was no *sharīʿa* endorsement, either because they were not formerly Muslims or were 'culturally but not observant' Muslims – daughters of Moroccan, secularized parents uninterested in complying with *sharīʿa* norms. There is also the case among the continental European followers of girls who grew up in more 'traditional' Moroccan households (i.e. coming from the Moroccan countryside) in which *sharīʿa* rulings were observed, as stated by them, '*more fervently than back in Morocco*'. These devotees sometimes see their parents' attitude towards religious law as a somewhat backward approach that there is little point in implementing in Western European societies. In some cases, it is not converts but the above-mentioned category of reverts who refuse to adhere to certain aspects of an Islamic behavioural code. Although a substantial proportion of British devotees were brought up in South Asian households (culturally Muslim and religiously observant environments), such criticisms are perhaps less common among British *faqīrāt*. The more observant attitude that seems to prevail among the British groups can be seen in relation to the wider context in which European Islam has developed, British Islam has been shown to be generally more *sharīʿa*-observant and conservative than the Islam consolidated in continental Europe.[31] Furthermore, the non-existence of revert Muslims among the British groups may also help to explain this phenomenon.

A quite different picture may have emerged, however, from the Order in the United Kingdom a few years ago. The study of the British Būdshīshiyya in the United Kingdom conducted by Draper back in 2002, presents a *ṭarīqa* much more influenced by laxer approaches to *sharīʿa*, a somewhat more eclectic approach to Sufism, influenced by New Age religiosities, and less inclined to the religious conservatism characteristic of British groups today. This highlights the importance of introducing a temporal dimension into the study of transnational *ṭuruq*. The remarkable degree of adaptability to social change distinctive of transnational Orders[32] means that they can undergo enormous transformations in relatively short periods of time. In more recent times, the New Age approach seems to have decreased significantly, together with the 'traditionalist' (i.e. Guenonian) approach held by some of the older members.[33] The more conservative approach of younger members to Islam has also gained wider representation. Overall, we might argue that the British Būdshīshiyya has moved towards religious conservatism, in accordance with the changes in Muslim discourses at a wider societal level. Recent studies have suggested that *sharī'a*-centered tendencies have gained increasing popularity in recent years among Muslims all across Europe, and particularly in the United Kingdom.[34]

However, an overall, more conservative approach among British devotees does not necessarily mean better acceptance from the rest of devotees. *Faqīrāt* in continental Europe who have met British followers have described their British peers as somehow 'culturally different': *'some of them are Pakistani Sufis who sometimes do things according to their own culture'.* This perception can be based not merely on more obvious physical appearances but also on the use by some British members of the terminology more common in South Asian Sufism (e.g. more recurrent use of words such as *murīd* instead of *faqīr* to refer to other devotees, or *pīr* instead of *walī* to refer to a Sufi master).[35]

Whatever the basis for this perception, there seem to be attempts to erase the South Asian character of British groups, as is manifest in the fact that the official website of the Būdshīshiyya in the United Kingdom puts far more emphasis on Moroccan identity than its equivalents in Arabic, French and Spanish.[36] For example, the websites of the Birmingham and London groups display activities such as talks accompanied by 'Moroccan mint tea'[37] and publicize events such as *Qur'ānic* recitation[38] and Sufi chanting (*samā*), always clarifying that such practices are to be be performed in the Maghribi style. By contrast, reference to the Moroccan character of the Order is largely absent in the rest of Būdshīshiyya websites. Moreover, a similar trend occurs in a group of *faqīrāt* in the South of France, who founded, in 2003, the Sufi music group Rabi'a, named after the notable medieval mystic. This group has achieved fame since its founding. Although they chant in the Moroccan style known as *Qasida*, no reference is made to the Moroccan character of the group in any of their interviews, nor in their website. Instead, the cosmopolitan character of the formation is underlined *"[Rabi'a] est composé de femmes issues d'horizons culturels divers (France, Mali, Maghreb, Andalousie, Portugal), que la voie soufie a réunies et qui suivent l'enseignement du même guide spirituel, sidi Hamza al-Qâdiri Boudchich."*[39] On the whole, it seems rather logical that those are groups with no Moroccan component that find a need to re-affirm a Moroccan identity that may surface more naturally in groups with an existing Moroccan cultural dimension. On the other hand, the British references to Moroccan culture may indicate that the *tarīqa* emphasizes its Maghrebi identity as a strategy to overcome the overwhelming dominance of the South Asian cultural *milieu*.

The performative aspect is central to our understanding of the evolution of the Būdshīshiyya from a local *zāwiya* to a transnational organization.[40] Until approximately three decades ago, the Order was defined as endorsing a *tabarrukiyya* character, which meant that initiation was highly selective, a process in which the commitment of the aspirant to the Order was continually tested (Ben Driss, 2002: 139–40). If the *faqīr* succeeded, he (only males were then permitted) entered an elite group, entirely dedicated to religious instruction. According to some elderly locals, this class of religious student was highly respected by people, and the local *zāwiya* was sometimes opened to the public, becoming a place of social gathering for the communities of the area, where most of the religious celebrations and festivities would occur.[41]

During the late 1970s and 1980s, the *tarīqa* tried to change the membership's ethnic basis.[42] This new orientation towards a more diverse disciplehood has been understood by its members as an 'educational' (*tarbawiyya*) endeavour – aiming to make Sufism accessible to everyone – and it is portrayed as such in scholarly accounts (Ben Driss, 2002; Draper, 2002; Haenni and Voix, 2007; Sedgwick, 2004a; Tozy, 1990; Voix, 2004).[43] To reach its target, the discourses and institutional ethos of this *tarīqa* changed considerably, adopting a proselytizing style, with which it actively began, first, to publicize the organization among university students and secondary school pupils in the main Moroccan cities, and, at a later stage, to do the same abroad. In contrast to the previously strict criteria which applied to the recruitment of *fuqarā'*, the new Būdshīshiyya made it possible for anyone – regardless of their gender, background and/or previous knowledge or commitment to Islam – to become a *faqīr/a*. From that moment onwards, there was no need to abandon your family duties or occupation to become a member.

In doctrinal terms, the main results of this change are twofold. First, the importance hitherto attached to a personalized mode of transmitting knowledge has been replaced by a new concept in which spiritual love (*maḥabba*) is perceived as the tool for knowledge acquisition. In this, the Būdshīshiyya seems to follow a pattern typical of certain Sufi movements born in the twentieth century (e.g. the Gülen movement), in which the idea of direct initiation has disappeared along with the teaching role of the *shaykh* (Hermansen, 2009: 29). Secondly, ritual has taken on an unprecedented relevance. In the absence of a setting in which doctrine could be fully explained and apprehended, it is ritual action which has become preponderant. Religious knowledge has been substituted by religious practice.

As a result of the internationalization of the Order, members can no longer perform ritual practices all together on a regular basis. This is the reason why the Order organizes regular meetings to gather members from various geograpies to enact together a bigger, louder *waẓīfa* session. These encounters enhance a sense of *camaraderie* among the followers otherwise difficult to attain (particularly among the followers of smaller groups). In contrast to the previous context, in which all members knew each other, these international meetings are intended to bring people with no regular relationship with one another, together. After all, such encounters aim to create some sense of the previous *locality* that has been lost also evidencing the role of ritual in engendering social solidarity, as Durkheim has famously demonstrated (1912). These encounters show the power of ritual in reinforcing the sense of belonging to a religious group, as scholars have long suggested (e.g. Marshall, 2002).

According to what many devotees have said, attendance to local weekly *waẓīfa* sessions tends to seal the belonging of the person to the local group, whereas being part of international gatherings activates a feeling that one is part of something bigger, and more meaningful. A proof to devotees that this is the case is that Būdshīshiyya international gatherings unite people beyond cultural and social boundaries. Several of the people who have been attending a local group for a short while, but are still reluctant to consider themselves members of the Order, are often persuaded by peer members to attend one of these international encounters.[44]

However, British devotees are not regularly seen at international encounters, neither in Morocco nor in Continental Europe. Perhaps, language may play a more crucial role into the inner dynamic of the Order than is generally acknowledged. The fact that most British *fuqarā'* are unable to communicate in French, the most commonly spoken vehicular language in this *ṭarīqa*, may partly explain their absence. There is probably an added dimension which relates to the internal dynamics of the leadership of the Order. In France, for example, some of those in the higher ranks are members of Sīdī Hamza's family. Visiting the central lodge in Madāgh and getting to meet Sīdī Hamza and the members of his family is, equally, recommended. The hospitality[45] shown by them to any visitor (independent of their interest in becoming a member), together with the sacred essence that *fuqarā'* believe the *shaykh* emanates, are aspects considered 'convincing' of a more committed affiliation. As is the case of international gatherings, locals report having seen far fewer English-speaking visitors than French, or even Spanish-speaking ones.

Whatever the causes, one might assume that the largely British absence in those crucial events and places affects, in some way, the relationship between the British groups and the rest of European. However, further research would be needed to formulate a conclusive statement on the precise ways in which intra-*ṭarīqa* relations are affected by the lack of enduring contact between British and non-British European groups, as well as to elucidate their relation to the Order as a whole.

In conclusion, studying the case of the British Būdshīshiyya through a comparative lens opens up a set of questions for further research which are, more holistically, relevant to an increasingly nuanced understanding of the Būdshīshiyya. This study points towards the relative importance of the emigrational element in defining religious identities across borders in the Būdshīshiyya *ṭarīqa*.

Shall we think of the Būdshīshiyya worldwide as a primarily diasporic religion? That is to say, to what extent are the transnational Moroccan households and communities, around which much of the Būdshīshiyya religious life in Europe revolves, responsible for shaping the overall identity of this *ṭarīqa*? Despite the very sporadic contact between Moroccan and 'Hybrid' groups in Europe, it seems clear that the Order endows a substantial part of its identity to the Moroccan character and thus has to be analysed within the context of the Moroccan Diaspora. As a socio-religious reality, the Būdshīshiyya participates in the migration experience of some young Moroccans in Europe, yet the extent to which it shapes the identity features of the Order beyond Morocco and its diaspora component remains to be determined. By analysing those groups which do not contain Moroccans (British groups, namely), in contrast to those groups containing Moroccans (the rest of Western European groups), we also gain a first impression into how relevant the Moroccan element is transnationally. Overall, this provides an empirical window into one way in which religious globalization actually evolves and transforms, within a myriad of diverse cultural influences.

Analysing the British groups from a comparative perspective has elucidated trends of continuity and transformation of UK enclaves in relation to the more similar development that the Order has experienced in the rest of Western Europe. In particular, the emergence of the Order in the United Kingdom seems largely unconnected to the roots of the Order in Continental Europe. The very reduced size of the Moroccan diaspora in the isles is likely to have played a role. Its original connection to the 'Glastonbury experience', an eminently British New Age phenomena, and the South Asian background of many British devotees, seems to have contributed to its distinctiveness, with an appropriated Moroccan identity being more recurrently emphasized among British circles, instead of the more 'universalist' trends *in vogue* in France, Belgium or Spain, where the Moroccan element may surface more naturally. A certain degree of differentiation may also be noticed in the weaker interaction British devotees have with their continental peers *vis-a-vis* the central lodge. This chapter has also explored ways in which a Sufi Order participates in, and is being shaped by, the social *milieus* in which it exists. Thus, the Būdshīshiyya in the United Kingdom seems to be, religiously speaking, more conservative and more 'sharī`a-endorsing' than groups in the rest of Western Europe. This is in accordance with wider societal trends and the features of Islam in the respective European countries.

However, despite the marked differences, between European and British groups, this article has also discussed how the British Būdshīshiyya participates in the wider transnational phenomena of the Būdshīshiyya that constitutes this *ṭarīqa*, evidencing some features that appear to be very similar in all the European groups. Among those, we see the social profile of the Order with a vast proportion of young, underprivileged, migrant descendants' devotees and a much smaller proportion of white, more liberal, older converts to Islam. Middle-class devotees took the initial drive but are, nowadays, a minority within the *ṭarīqa*. In addition, similar way of performing ritual practices, along with a respect for a twofold leadership (a 'traditional' leader whose charisma is *physically* manifested and a more 'modern' leadership, whose charisma is *intellectually* defined) is typical of the whole European disciplehood, including British groups.

Overall, this chapter contends that transnational Orders like the Būdshīshiyya, far from developing homogenized forms of religious identity, re-root into new cultural contexts diversely. In doing so they are influenced by the processes that take them to these new lands and are to be seen, therefore, as more complex religious phenomena than they are generally given credit to be.

Notes

1 *The transnational villagers of* Levitt (2001b) is an interesting fieldwork-based research about how identity (including religious features) develops when people relate to a multiplicity of cultural settings.

2 There are very few scholarly works on the Būdshīshiyya. Although studies of the political dimensions of the Order in Morocco are not scarce (e.g. Tozy, 1999; Zeghal, 2008, 2005), there is a lack of research into the Būdshīshiyya from a religious studies perspective. Primary published sources include Ben Driss (2002), Ben Rochd (2002) and Qustas' (2007). The unpublished PhD thesis of Draper's (2002) is one of the few works available, together with some articles (Sedgwick, 2004a; Haenni and Voix 2007; Voix, 2004). The data gathered for this article is mainly the result of fieldwork research carried out as part of my doctoral thesis for the School of Oriental and African Studies between 2006 and 2009. During this time, I was in contact with

current and former members of the Order –mostly women – from various European and Moroccan locations. I did visit some of the European groups when they met for their weekly ritual gatherings and talked to people from Berkane, the town who sits closest to the central lodge (ar. *zāwiya*) of the Order in Madāgh, in the North-Eastern province of Oujda. I did also attend an international gathering of followers in Paris in February 2008 and go on pilgrimage (ar. *ziyāra*) with European devotees in March 2008 for the Būdshīshiyya's major celebration, the *Mawlid*, time in which approximately 70,000 followers congregate in the lodge to visit the current leader of this *ṭarīqa*, Sīdī Hamza and celebrate the birth of the Prophet Muḥammad. Also a valuable source of information has been the written and media materials produced by members of the Order up to the present videos of Sīdī Hamza on Youtube, forums of followers, groups on Facebook, official webpages, booklets, pamphlets and books. Some aspects of this ethnographic experience were discussed in an article; see Dominguez Diaz (2011).

3 *Faqīr/a* in Arabic means 'poor', and in popular parlance it is used for a homeless person, a pauper or a beggar. Among North African Sufis, the term is used as a synonym for disciple. The traditional connotations of the term describe someone who entirely accepts the will of God and has no private property, considered to be indispensable attributes of the *faqīr*. Today reformed Sufi Orders such as the Būdshīshiyya use the term simply to refer to a member of the Order, irrespective of his/her degree of spiritual commitment.

4 In Western Europe, we have identified the following groups: five in Paris, the biggest of which, situated in Argenteuil, is also the home of the central *zāwiya* of the Order on the continent; also there are groups in Aix-en-Provence, Avignon, Bayonne, Bordeaux, Lyons, Marseilles, Montpellier, Nantes, Nice, Strasbourg, Toulouse, Vauvert, Brussels, Barcelona, Girona, Manchester, Nottingham, London, Bradford and Birmingham. The Birmingham group is in the Borough of Small Heath, and is home to the central British *zāwiya*. Recent groups are being formed in Italy and the Netherlands, although further research would be needed on these particular enclaves.

5 The Moroccan Diaspora is a very significant emigrational phenomenon in European demographics – it is expected to become the biggest non-European Diaspora group in Europe in the next decade, for further information see, Bilgili and Weyel (2009).

6 The phenomena of keeping a cultural character seems to be common among migrant groups in the diaspora whether South Asian (e.g. Werbner, 2005) Turkish (e.g. Jonker, 2006), Persian (e.g. Lewisohn, 2006) or North African (e.g. Dominguez Diaz, 2010b).

7 I am borrowing here Hermansen's (1996) widely used threefold classification of Sufism in Western contexts: (a) Hybrid, groups that link themselves with a larger Islamic tradition and are generally composed of members of Muslim origin and

converts; (b) Perennials, which are groups that do not relate Sufism to Islam and tend to be classified among 'New Age Movements'; and (c) Transplants, which are *turuq* whose followers are migrants living in Western contexts, and which tend to reproduce the structure, organization and rituals of the original *tarīqa*.

8 *Bayʿa* is the term generally used in Arabic to refer to an 'oath of allegiance' pledged to a religious or political institution or leader. In the Būdshīshiyya, it signifies a vow of allegiance to Sīdī Hamza. Most of the Būdshīshiyya's European members refer to it as *the pact*. This rite existed before but in its present form is distinctive of Modern Sufi Orders and to some other Islamic transnational groups today. On the opposite, the majority of Muslims around the world are born within a particular denomination and do not make decisions involving the internalization of a particular belief system or subsystem. Accordingly, scholars have identified the issue of voluntarism as being characteristic of European and North-American Islam, a key distinctive feature developed by Islam as a result of its encounter with the secular systems of the Western world. For further information on European Islam's voluntarism see Cesari (2004: 128).

9 This phenomenon of reversion is in French generally referred as *reconversion religieuse* and not as *reversion* as an English reader might expect; it however, refers to the same discourse described above and it follows the same sort of rationale.

10 An account of this kind of rationale within the Būdshīshiyya can be for example found in the narrative of this French follower, http://saveurs-soufies.com/forum/6-T%C3%A9moignage-et-coins-des-convertis%28e%29s/2018-cheminement-et-reconversion#2021, (accessed July 20, 2012).

11 Observation of reversion throughout the *Būdshīshiyya* indicates that if conversion is to be defined as an act that involves '*not just adopting a set of ideas but also converting to and from an embodied worldview and identity*' (Sachs Norris, 2003: 171), then we should infer that religious reversion as it occurs in the *Būdshīshiyya* is indeed a form of religious conversion, as some authors have already argued in relation to religious conversion and reversion in general (Gilliat-Ray, 1999).

12 For more data on the features of the Moroccan migration to the United Kingdom, see Bakewell, de Haas and Kubal's (2011) report, http://imi.ox.ac.uk/pdfs/research-projects-pdfs/themis-pdfs/themis-scoping-study-morroco, (accessed August 20, 2012).

13 The reference to Glastonbury refers to a British type of post-modern approach to spirituality, and it has been specifically explored in his 2004 article 'From Celts to Kaaba: Sufism in Glastonbury.' This phenomenon responds to the needs of a 'pick and mix' religious culture typical of Western societies. Jeremy Carette and Richard King (2005) have scrutinized processes of appropriation and commodification experienced by the re-territorialization of Asian religions in the West. They suggest that key features of non-Western religions have been 'translated into a

modern Western context, but there is generally a failure to appreciate that this is not the total picture' (2005: 87), what has come to be known as a 'pick and mix attitude' typical of Modern Western Spirituality. In their view, this evidences an attempt at commodifying others' cultures, making them available for selective re-appropriation, re-packing and re-selling. As a result, religious traditions are presented in an individualist gaze, eliminating the cultural and philosophical intricacies when translated into circles of Western followers. I content that these features are also often to be found among members of the Būdshīshiyya. Interestingly, whereas Carette and King seem to imply this is a feature of New Age religiosities, the case of the Būdshīshiyya seems to indicate that these are processes that occur at a much larger scale within Western societies. For example, *fuqarā'* who were keen to become Muslims and adopt a way of life respectful with religious law do often evidence a very individualistic approach to Islam uncommon among members of the Order in rural Morocco. This is a feature shared by both British and non-British members of this *ṭarīqa*.

14 This is in consonance with other studies of religious conversion, people first feeling attracted by an intellectual side of religion only turning into a more bodily oriented approach after an initial phase (Zebiri, 2007).

15 The Order in Belgium and Spain is not big enough as to be able to pay for a building of their own; meeting there are more informal and are held at a follower's home. The choosing of the home often rotates, as there are sometimes problems to find a person willing to offer her house for the gathering. It is no clear whether the number of British devotees is substantial enough as to explain the availability of a separate lodge, or whether this is evidence of a certain degree of autonomy and differentiation from the rest of European enclaves.

16 Term used in the Būdshīshiyya and other Moroccan Sufi orders to refer to the central lodge where the highest authorities of the Order reside. It might also be used in a more generic way to designate any of the places where a group of followers gather together to perform collective ritual sessions and is considered as the center of various congregations, for example, the one in Argeteuil, the one on Birmingham. The *zāwiya* of the Būdshīshiyya is located in the town of Madāgh (North Eastern Morocco).

17 The British lodge is ran by a charity called *Amina Trust* set up by some of the first members of the Order in the UK. Their website is indicative of the thriving social life of the center, http://thezawiya.co.uk/, (accessed August 1, 2012).

18 In the Birmingham borough of Small Heath 63.33% of the population are 'South Asian' or of 'South Asian' descent. This ethnic group comprises 18.49% of the population of the city of Birmingham and 4.09% of the population of England. According to the 2001 National Census, see: http://neighbourhood.statistics.gov.uk/dissemination/LeadTableView.do;jsessionid=ac1f930d30d6e1e0fec2349f4998

bf26bf2dd7124a78?a=7&b=560960&c=Small+Heath&d=14&e=13&g=372561&
i=1001x1003x1004&m=0&r=1&s=1272463089123&enc=1&dsFamilyId=47&nsj
s=true&nsck=true&nssvg=false&nswid=1003, (accessed May 2, 2012). Similarly,
Argenteuil has a notable population of North Africans or people of North African
descent. It would be difficult to provide accurate statistical figures because of the
lack of relevant data of this kind in France.Data available from 2010 suggests
that unemployment rates in Argenteuil peaked at 16 per cent compared to the
national average of 10 per cent. Similarly, the unemployment rate in Small Heath
in 2010 was 17.9 per cent – making it the constituency with the highest rate after
Ladywood – whereas the national rate is almost half that at 8 per cent. For further
information, visit *L'encyclopédie des Villes de France*, available at: www.linternaute.
com/ville/ville/accueil/1459/argenteuil.shtml and Residence-based unemployment
rates by parliamentary constituency, United Kingdom, January 2010 www.
parliament.uk/commons/lib/research/rp2010/rp10–013.pdf (both accessed May
3, 2010). A dramatic increase in these figures is to be expected due to the ongoing
economic crisis.

19 In 2010, unemployment rates in Argenteuil peaked at 16% compared to the
national average of 10 per cent. Similarly, the unemployment rate in Small Heath
today is 17.9 per cent – making it the constituency with the highest rate after
Ladywood – whereas the national rate is almost half that at 8 per cent. For further
information, visit *L'encyclopédie des Villes de France*, available at: www.linternaute.
com/ville/ville/accueil/1459/argenteuil.shtml and Residence-based unemployment
rates by parliamentary constituency, United Kingdom, January 2010 www.
parliament.uk/commons/lib/research/rp2010/rp10–013.pdf (both accessed May
3, 2010). A dramatic increase in these figures is to be expected due to the ongoing
economic crisis, yet accurate figures are not currently available.

20 Although geographically speaking the area that the Būdshīshiyya covers is certainly
vast, one needs to remember that, with the exception of the two lodges, groups in
Western Europe can often be very small, many of them consisting of less than ten
people.

21 Accordingly, many see the Būdshīshiyya at the center of their lives and the most
important thing that has ever happened to them; they often attach a sense of
predestination to their joining. In this sense, the Būdshīshiyya exhibits some –
yet not all – of the features attributed by Wallis to New Religious Movements of
the 'world-rejecting' type: they imbue in people a sense of 'deindividuation' and
a feeling of being 'reborn' which encourages them to break with their past life
(1984: 19). Remarkably, however, other characteristics of Wallis' 'world-rejecting
movements' (e.g. communal life, millennialism and authoritarian leadership) are
not to be found in this Sufi order. In fact, it would seem that the European groups
of the Būdshīshiyya represent the 'world-accommodating' pattern rather than

the 'world-rejecting' one. Second, the 'world-accommodating movements' make a distinction between the spiritual and the mundane. Religion is not linked with social matters, but instead constitutes a source of personal solace and nourishes the interior life (1984: 35). However, as Fichter (1975) has argued, this does not necessarily indicate a lack of social concern, since 'the conviction is that a better society can emerge only when people have become better' (see Fichter in Wallis 1984: 36). It is particularly striking that when a movement of this type has been inspired by, or has its genesis in, Islam, religion disappears from the public realm (where it typically manifests itself in the Muslim world) and situates itself in the private sphere. This is very often the case with the European Būdshīshiyya. Adherence to world-accommodating movements does not necessarily have profound consequences for the devotee's routines and lifestyle, as such movements do not set forth an strict code containing precise details on how to live – only that their followers should behave in a more or less religiously inspired way. Devotees, by and large, carry on with their conventional lives as accountants, shop-keepers, housewives, students and so on. Hence these movements adapt to the world rather than affirm or reject it. Whilst belief and ritual performance are presented as being of potential benefit to the individual, religious practice and worship are performed collectively (Wallis, 1984: 36). According to the majority of their members, movements of this type restore an experiential element to the spiritual life and replace certainties which are perceived as having been lost; these movements are common in societies with a perceived sense of religious institutions having become increasingly relativised (Wallis, 1984: 37).

22   *Walī 'Allāh* (pl. *awliyā' 'Allāh*) is a term that can be translated as manager, guardian, protector, and also intimate or, most commonly, friend. *Walī 'Allāh* is generally used as 'friend of God', and it is the term used to designate a Muslim saint, one who intercedes for others as Allah's deputy or vice-regent on earth. In some cases but not in all, these saints are leaders of Sufi Orders, like the leader of the Būdshīsshiyya

23   It is generally translated into English as 'remembrance'. Ritual commonly performed by Sufis that consists of mentioning a previously memorized formula. *Dhikr djāli* refers to the performed ritual when the formula is uttered aloud, whereas *dhikr khāfi* refers to the one practiced either in silence or in a low voice. Both can be performed either individually or collectively. When performed collectively is referred among members of this Order as a *wazīfa* (pl. *wazīfāt)*. The ritual consists of reciting and/or chanting litanies consisting of various formulas in repetitive ways. These rituals are distinctive to every order, with slight differences that define the distinctiveness of each *tarīqa*. For example, the use of musical instruments is allowed in some orders and forbidden in others, the reaching of ecstasy of some of the members is frequent in some orders and rarer in some others.

24 In his book *Qu'Allah Bénisse La France* (2004) he describe his religious journey from being interested in other Islamic religious choices available at the poor suburbs of the main European cities becoming a Būdshīshiyya follower.

25 The same pattern of religious authority is characteristic of North-African Sufism as Clifford Geertz (1971) once observed. See also an example of an Order with the same authority structure in Karrar's (1992) study of a Sudanese branch of the Qādiriyya. The Qādiriyya in general and thus the Būdshīshiyya – as a branch of the wider Qādiriyya – follows the classical al-Mīrghanī category of Sufi religious authority (Karrar, 1992: 126).

26 Term generally translated as 'blessing'. It refers to the spiritual potency or power that holy individuals, places and/or objects are believed to have. Since its existence is believed to be tangible, it is believed that it can be transmitted to those who come into contact with the person or thing that possesses it.

27 About his education a website of the Order reads: '*Sidi Mounir Qadiri Boutchich was born in Morocco. He grew up in the family of the Qadiri Boutchich and his earliest education was obtained from this Pure source. He graduated from Oujda University in Literary Science in 1994, and completed his Degree in Law at the Dar al Hassania Institute, Rabat, in 1996. His search for knowledge brought him to France where he has studied for a wide range of Degrees, followed by a Masters in Social Anthropology at the Europe-Maghrib Institute in Paris 2001. He recently completed his Doctorate in Islamic Law at the Sorbonne-Paris, where he researches Communication and Sufism. He is also known for his many publications on Sufism, the latest being 'The Sufi presence in an age of Globalisation(2004).*' http://sufiway.net/ar_Sufism_SidiMounir_ISEG.html (accessed August 18, 2012).

28 There is only a series of Sīdī Hamza 'sayings', quotes written following a classical style of Sufi literature with recurrent reference to Sufi symbolism and metaphors which contrasts with the more direct style of his descendants' writings, made in prose with a clear, less symbolic way of expressing ideas. Both Sīdī Hamza's sayings and Sīdī Mounir's articles are available online in various European languages including English, http://tariqa.org/qadiriya/texts/sayings.html, http://sufiway.net/ar_Sufism_SidiMounir_ISEG.html, (both accessed August 18, 2012).

29 As these gatherings are gender divided, people in the Būdshīshiyya mostly meet members of the same sex only. In smaller groups, where interaction often goes beyond ritual performances, male and female members meet outside and come to know each other. However, these encounters occur almost always in the presence of the whole or most of the group and, consequently, very few members have ever met with a member of the other sex in a private setting. This gender divide is found everywhere, in Europe and in Morocco, and was also determining the type of fieldwork I could conduct. As a result most of the followers of the Order I met were female devotees.

30   The most contentious aspect of this individualized approach appears when there
     is display of attitudes considered as unlawful when they visit the central lodge
     in Madāgh – for example, young European followers have been seen smoking
     outside the main lodge creating some outrage among the locals. Albeit permitting
     Europeans to decide by themselves the extent to which they behave 'islamically',
     subtle attempts have been made to try to instill a sense of *sharī'a* respect among
     European members, by means of 'education' and 'information', and approach that
     is also manifested in some of the articles posted in the websites of the Order in
     French and Spanish.

31   An illustrative example of this has been presented in a comparative study that
     examines the views of young European Muslims on sexuality, being the British
     far more reluctant to tolerate homosexuality than their French or German co-
     religionists. See Butt (2009) at: www.guardian.co.uk/uk/2009/may/07/muslims-
     britain-france-germany-homosexuality (accessed May 7, 2010). Interesting also is
     a recent move towards a more liberal approach to religion among Young British
     Muslims in general in relation to the previous generation. In particular, British
     Muslim youth differ from older Muslims and non-Muslim British peers on that
     they attribute a greater salience to Islam for their personal identity, even though
     they pray and read scripture less, but support plural interpretations of Islam more
     than their elders. Besides, it has been shown that, Muslim youth increasingly show
     liberalizing social attitudes across generations on gay marriage and legal abortion
     (Kashyap and Lewis, 2012).

32   On the malleable nature of *ţuruq* to the rapid changes of modernity, see, for
     example, Voll (1995: 116).

33   'Universalist' discourses within Sufism tend to either be characterized by 1)
     New Age approach characteristic of the 'pick and mix' post-modern approach
     to spirituality in which the connections to a more 'mainstream' Islamic tradition
     may be compromised (e.g. in some of this groups, not the Būdshīshiyya though,
     converting to Islam may not be required) or 2) Guenonian approach, in which
     being part of one of the by them considered 'Major Traditions' which includes
     Islam, is viewed as a source or return to a Primordial source of Spiritual Awareness.
     For a more detailed explanation of the religious ideology of Guenonianism
     see Sedgwick (2004b) and Dominguez Diaz (2010a). A very useful source for
     information on Guenonian religious groups including Sufi ones is Mark Sedgwick's
     blog *traditionalists,* http://traditionalistblog.blogspot.ch/, (accessed July 27, 2012).
     Both tendencies are to be found among members of the Būdshīshiyya, although
     these trends are seem to be somehow in decline.

34   See for example the outcomings of the reporthttp://home.medewerker.uva.
     nl/m.j.m.maussen/bestanden/ASSR-WP0503%20maussen.pdf, (accessed July 4,
     2012).

35 Further research would be needed to elucidate whether it may also refer in some instances to observing *sharīʿa* in accordance to Hanafism characteristic of countries such as Pakistan and Bangladesh and not to the Malikism, adhered to in Morocco. The differences between Hanafism and the Malikism may range from things like prayer (Hanafis consider some prayers compulsory that are only recommended by the Maliki) to food practices (seafood being allowed by Malikis and forbidden by Hanafis, for example) or certain issues of marriage and family law. Additionally, some cultural traditions that may be common in South Asian households in Europe are strongly discouraged by the religious authorities in the Būdshīshiyya.

36 See for example, the French website http://saveurs-soufies.com/ and the Spanish one http://tariqa.org/espanol/index.php.

37 See for example, the website of the central zawiyya in the UK, http://sufiway.net/zawiya_birmingham.html.

38 This is commonly referred as *warch* (Arabic transliteration in French) the specific method for Quranic reading characteristic of North-African Sufism.

39 http://ensemblerabia.net/, (accessed July 17, 2012).

40 Part of my work has focused on the analysis of ritual practices in relation to the internal dynamics of the Order, see for example Dominguez Diaz (2010c).

41 This twofold nature of disciplehood is the kind of membership that many Orders follow today (e.g. the Egyptian Khalwātiyya studied by Chih, 2004). On the one hand, for the bulk of followers affiliation remains restricted to prayers, congregational *dhikr* sessions and occasional visits to the leader. On the other hand, there is a group of more committed members that live in the *zāwiya* and are considered to be at a higher level of spiritual realization.

42 Adherence to Sufi Orders in Morocco tends to follow ethnic and geographical patterns.

43 Tozy, Sedwick and Haenni and Voix's articles only briefly comment on this fact. The most detailed studies of the Order have been done by Draper and Ben Driss, both members of this *ṭarīqa* at the time of writing their texts.

44 By getting to know each other, it seems, people create stronger bonds and are keener to stay in the group after the common initial stage of fascination is overcome. This may even so be the case in religious organizations in which membership is formalized in very casual ways. In the Būdshīshiyya, membership is determined by geography in the original enclave – being from the Madāgh region is often understood as to be a disciple of Sīdī Hamza – but beyond the North-eastern area of Morocco, membership is sealed by undertaking the rite of *bayʿa*. This is however a rather symbolic endeavor, no one is forced to undertake this commitment, with several attendees being regular at the weekly meetings without being formal members. It may be suggested that not having a requirement for a very strong personal commitment generates a flexible organization, one that can

guarantee that a higher number of followers are to be part of the order at a given time, despite durability may become an issue in the long-term. This again may be a typical aspect of the malleability of Sufi Orders. In any case, in a religious organization with a very simple and voluntary affiliation process, attendance can be translated as belonging. The fluidity typical of this kind of religious membership adds up relevance to the role that international meetings have in instilling a more homogenous sense of religious identity to the organization.

45 Hospitality is has been a very meaningful, religiously inspired and morally driven act in Moroccan society for a long time as Geertz rightly noticed (1971: 34).

Bibliography

Argenteuil, L'encyclopédie des Villes de France (2010) http://linternaute.com/ville/ville/accueil/1459/argenteuil.shtml (accessed May 3, 2010).

Bakewell, O., de Haas, H., and Kubal, A. (2011). 'The Evolution of Moroccan Migration to the UK'. Scoping Study Report, International Migration Institute, University of Oxford. http://imi.ox.ac.uk/pdfs/research-projects-pdfs/themis-pdfs/themis-scoping-study-morroco (accessed August 20, 2012).

Ben Driss, K. (2002) *Sidi Hamza al-Qadiri Boudchich. Le Renouveau du Soufisme au Maroc*, Beirut: Albouraq.

Ben Rochd, E. R. (2004) *Douze Siècles de Soufisme au Maroc*, Casablanca: Dechra.

Bilgili, Ö. and Weyel, S. (2009) 'Migration in Morocco: History, Current Trends and Future Prospects. Migration and Development Country Profiles'. Migration and Development Country Profiles Report, University of Maastricht. http://mgsog.merit.unu.edu/ISacademie/docs/CR_morocco.pdf (accessed July 12, 2012).

Carrette, J. and King, R. (2005) *Selling Spirituality: The Silent Takeover of Religion*, London and New York: Routledge.

Cesari, J. (2004) *When Islam and Democracy Meet: Muslims in Europe and in the United States*, New York: Palgrave Macmillan.

Chih, R. (2004) 'The Khalwatiyya Brotherhood in Rural Egypt and in Cairo'. In: R. Hopkins and N. Saad (Eds). *Upper Egypt: Identity and Change*. Cairo: American University in Cairo Press.

Dominguez Diaz, M. (2010a) 'Traditionalism'. In: D. A. Leeming, K. Madden and S. Marlan (Eds). *Encyclopedia of Psychology and Religion,* London: Springer.

— (2010b). 'Revisiting Moroccan Sufism and Re-Islamisizing Secular Audiences: Female Religious Narratives in the *ṭarīqa Qādiriyya Būdshīshiyya* in Morocco and Western Europe Today'. Unpublished PhD thesis, University of London, School of Oriental and African Studies.

— (2010c). Performance, Belonging and Identity: Ritual Variations in the British Qādiriyya. *Religion, State & Society*, 38, London: Taylor and Francis.

— (2011) Shifting Fieldsites: an Alternative Approach to Fieldwork in Transnational Sufism, *Fieldwork in Religion*, 6/1. London: Equinox.

Draper, M. (2002) 'Towards a Postmodern Sufism: Eclecticism, Appropriation and Adaptation in a Naqshbandiyya and a Qadiriyya Tariqa in the UK'. Unpublished PhD thesis, University of Birmingham.

Draper, M. (2004) 'From Celts to Kaaba: Sufism in Glastonbury'. In: D. Westerlund (Ed.). *Sufism in Europe and North America*, London: Routledge Curzon.

Durkheim, É. (1912) *The Elementary Forms of the Religious Life: A Study in Religious Sociology*, London: Allen & Unwin.

Geaves, R. (2000) *The Sufis of Britain: an Exploration of Muslim Identity*, Cardiff: Cardiff Academic Press.

Geertz, C. (1971) *Islam observed: religious development in Morocco and Indonesia*, Chicago: University of Chicago Press.

Gilliat-Ray, S. (1999) 'Rediscovering Islam: A Muslim Journey of Faith'. In: C. Lamb and M. D. Bryant (Eds). *Religious Conversion: Contemporary Practices and Controversies*. London: Cassell.

Haenni, P. and Voix, R. (2007) 'God by All Means . . . Eclectic Faith and Sufi Resurgence Among the Moroccan Bourgeoisie'. In: M. Bruinessen and J. Day Howell (Eds). *Sufism and the 'Modern' in Islam*. London: Tauris, pp. 241–56.

Hermansen, M. (1996) 'In the Garden of American Sufi Movements: Hybrids and Perennials'. In: P. B. Clarke (Ed.). *New Trends and Developments in the World of Islam*. London: Luzac.

— (2009) 'Global Sufism. 'Theirs and Ours'. In: M. Dressler, R. Geaves and G. Klinkhammer (Eds). *Sufis in Western Societies. Global Networking and Locality*. London and New York: Routledge.

Jonker, G. (2006) 'The Evolution of the Naqshbandi-Mujaddidi: Sulaymancis in Germany'. In: J. Hinnells and M. Jamal (Eds). *Sufism in the West*. London: Routledge Curzon.

Karrar, A. S. (1992) *The Sufi Brotherhoods in the Sudan,* London: Hurst.

Kashyap, R. and Valerie A. L. (2012) British Muslim Youth and Religious Fundamentalism: A Quantitative Investigation. *Ethnic and Racial Studies*, 1–24.

Lassen, S. C. (2009) 'Growing Up as a Sufi. Generational Change in the Burhaniya Sufi Order'. In: M. Dressler, R. Geaves and G. Klinkhammer (Eds). *Sufis in Western Society. Global Networking and Locality*. London and New York: Routledge.

Levitt, P. (2001a) Between God, Ethnicity, and Country: An Approach to the Study of Transnational Religion, Oxford: University of Oxford, Transnational Communities Programme.

— (2001b) *The Transnational Villagers*, Berkeley: University of California Press.

Lewisohn, L. (2006) 'Persian Sufism in the Contemporary West: Reflections on the Ni'matu'llahi Diaspora'. In: J. Malik and J. Hinnells (Eds). *Sufism in the West*. London: Routledge Curzon.

Malik, A. (2004) *Qu'Allah Bénisse La France,* Paris: Albin Michel.

Marshall, D. A. (2002) Behavior, Belonging, and Belief: A Theory of Ritual Practice. *Sociological Theory*, 20(3), 360–80.

Maussen, M. (2005) 'Making Muslim Presence Meaningful. Studies on Islam and Mosques in Western Europe', Amsterdam School for Social Science Research Report. http://home.medewerker.uva.nl/m.j.m.maussen/bestanden/ASSR-WP0503%20 maussen.pdf, (accessed July 4, 2012).

Nielsen, J. S., Draper, M. and Yemelianova, G. (2006) 'Transnational Sufism: the Haqqaniyya'. In: J. Malik and J. Hinnells (Eds). *Sufism in the West*. London: Routledge Curzon.

Peter, F. (2006) Individualization and Religious Authority in Western European Islam. *Islam and Christian-Muslim Relations*, 17(1), 105–18.

Qustas, A. (2007) *Nibrās al-Mudīr*, Marrakesh: al-Ahmadi.

Raudvere, C. (2002) *The Book and the Roses: Sufi Women, Visibility, and Zikir in Contemporary Istanbul*, Istanbul: Swedish Research Institute.

Sach Norris, R. (2003) '"Converting to What?" Embodied Culture and the Adoption of New Beliefs'. In: A. Buckser and S. D. Glazier (Eds). *The Anthropology of Religious Conversion*. Lanham: Lexington Books.

Sedgwick, M. (2004a) 'In Search of the Counter-Reformation: Anti-Sufi Stereotypes and the Budshishiyya's response'. In: M. Browers and C. Kurzman (Eds). *An Islamic Reformation?*. Lanham: Lexington Books.

— (2004b) *Against the Modern World: Traditionalism and the Secret Intellectual History of the Twentieth Century*, Oxford and New York: Oxford University Press.

Tozy, M. (1990) 'Le Prince, le Clerc et l'Etat: la Restructuration du Champ Religieux au Maroc'. In: G. Kepel and Y. Richard (Eds). *Intellectuels et Militants de l'Islam Contemporain*. Paris: Seuil.

— (1999) *Monarchie et Islam Politique au Maroc*, Paris: Presses de la Fondation nationale des sciences politiques.

UK National Census. (2011) http://neighbourhood.statistics.gov.uk/dissemination/ LeadTableView.do;jsessionid=ac1f930d30d6e1e0fec2349f4998bf26bf2dd7124a78?a= 7&b=560960&c=Small+Heath&d=14&e=13&g=372561&i=1001x1003x1004&m=0 &r=1&s=1272463089123&enc=1&dsFamilyId=47&nsjs=true&nsck=true&nssvg=fal se&nswid=1003 (accessed May 2, 2012).

Unemployment by Constituency, House of Commons Library (2010) http://parliament. uk/documents/commons/lib/research/rp2010/rp10–013.pdf (accessed May 3, 2010).

Villalón, L. A. (2007) 'Sufi Modernities in Contemporary Senegal. Religious Dynamics between the Local and the Global'. In: M. Bruinessen and D. J. Howell (Eds). *Sufism and the 'Modern' in Islam*. London: Tauris.

Voix, R. (2004) Implantation d'une Confrérie Marocaine en France: Mécanismes, Méthodes, et Acteurs. *Ateliers*, 28, 221–8.

Wallis, R. (1984) *The Elementary Forms of the New Religious Life*, London: Routledge & Kegan Paul.

Werbner, P. (2005) *Pilgrims of Love. The Anthropology of a Global Sufi Cult*, Karachi: Oxford University Press.

Zebiri, K. P. (2007) *British Muslim Converts: Choosing Alternative Lives*, Oxford: Oneworld Publications.

Zeghal, M. (2005) *Les Islamistes Marocains: le Défi à la Monarchie*, Paris: Découverte.

— (2008) *Islamism in Morocco: Religion, Authoritarianism, and Electoral Politics*, Princeton: Markus Wiener.

7

Conversion Narratives among the Alami and Rifa'i Tariqa in Britain

Julianne Hazen

Despite predictions of decline, in the twenty-first-century Sufism has demonstrated resilience and a remarkable ability to adapt to different societies and attract new members.[1] This chapter explores the contemporary presence of Islamic Sufism in Britain by looking at reasons why individuals are drawn to its circles. Although immigration of Sufi Muslims to the West plays an important role in sustaining and increasing the membership of Sufi orders in Britain, involvement of native Britons and immigrants without prior affinity to Sufism also contributes significantly. Arguably, contemporary Sufism is filling a need for spiritual reconnection with God in an increasingly materialistic and secular society and serves to unite individuals across diverse religious and ethnic backgrounds.

A Glance through the Literature

Although literature on Sufism in the West has increased since the early 1990s, it remains uncommon to address why individuals join Islamic Sufi movements.[2] However, the literature does provide a useful backdrop for approaching this topic. A number of studies discuss reasons why Westerners join universal, non-Islamic Sufis movements, such as the writings of Hermansen (1998), Wilson (1998) and Genn (2007).[3] Several studies also explore conversion to Islam through Sufism, including Köse (1996), Smith (1999) and Jawad (2006).[4] In addition, research on particular Sufi *tariqas* (orders) frequently indicates briefly how the movements attracted local followings.[5] For example, Stjernholm (2009) describes how the

Naqshbandi-Haqqani became established in London. In my doctoral study, I included an in-depth chapter exploring why the *murids* (students of the *shaykh*) joined the Alami *tariqa* in the United States.[6] They were mostly Americans who had embraced Islam and their adult children who were raised Muslim, in addition to a few Muslim immigrants from South Asia.

This chapter attempts to show that Sufism serves as an outlet for those who are disenchanted with materialistic existence and seeking spiritual fulfilment. Most who join Sufism express a feeling that something was incomplete or unsettled in their lives. This may have manifested itself very subtly or overtly as a sense of meaningless, perceived spiritual void, lack of intimacy with the divine, or desire for a like-minded community. This appears to be applicable for both non-Muslims and Muslims, as this study substantiates. The continued affiliation to Sufism of Muslim immigrants who arrive in the West already holding membership in a Sufi order, in contrast, is frequently associated with a desire to uphold ethnic and religious identity and retain a connection to their homelands.[7]

Westerners are often attracted to Sufism by creative expressions such as Sufi poetry, anecdotal stories, dancing and music.[8] The internet is also playing a role in spreading awareness of Sufism and Sufi movements, thus attracting new members to both Islamic and universal Sufism.[9] Ali Köse, in his 1996 study of British converts to Islam, found that many who associated with Sufism were rejecting Western culture and values, including materialism, over-secularization and the established religious traditions.[10] They frequently expressed discontent with their former religious traditions, and many had a history of depression and other psychological struggles.[11] It is common for Westerners to experiment with various New Age and alternative religious movements before joining Sufism.[12] Western women, in particular, are sometimes attracted to the Sufi Path as an alternative to restrictive religious traditions in which they were raised.[13] Sufism is unique because it offers experiential avenues through which to pursue a personal relationship with the divine while being grounded by an established monotheistic religion.[14]

Regarding reasons why Muslims in the West join Sufism, the literature implies that the main influences are leadership qualities, personal magnetism and ethnicity of the *shaykh*. Itzchak Weismann (2007), for example, states that Shaykh Nazim's Naqshbandi-Haqqani tariqa tends to draw Muslim members of two types: South Asians who are attracted by the *shaykh's* charisma and ethnic Turks who turn to him as a scholar who can interpret Islam for the contemporary world.[15] In addition, Shaykh Nazim attracts Westerners who are in search of 'spiritual enlightenment'. The writings of Pnina Werbner demonstrate that Sufi movements are periodically reinvigorated by charismatic *shaykhs*, particularly those who undergo challenges by travelling outside the Muslim world and morally 'conquering' previously non-Muslim space, thereby both developing and demonstrating charisma.[16] According to sociologist Max Weber, charisma refers to:

> ...a certain quality of an individual personality by virtue of which he is considered extraordinary and treated as endowed with supernatural, superhuman, or at least specifically exceptional powers or qualities. These are such as are not accessible to the ordinary person, but are regarded as of divine origin or as exemplary.[17]

Over time, Sufi movements experience a natural 'waxing' and 'waning' as leadership and socio-cultural elements shift.[18] For Muslims who are disenchanted with British society, Sufism provides an alternative to movements espousing radical and Islamist ideals.[19]

My earlier study involving 35 *murids* of the Alami *tariqa* in NY, confirmed that the desire for a more meaningful, personal certainty of God is a primary motivating factor for joining Sufism.[20] It also found that personal, transformational experiences play a critical role in the decision, which is not usually discussed in the literature. In addition, the charisma of the *shaykh*, a desire for intellectual spiritual development and yearning for spiritual healing were important elements. Contrary to Köse's (1996) study, my research did not find rejection of cultural norms to be a predominant reason, as only two of the respondents reported dissatisfaction with Western society.[21]

Sufism in Britain: The Alami and Rifa'i Tariqa

This study involved survey and interview research with 21 British Muslims affiliated with Sufism. Most of the research participants were either members of Shaykh Asaf's Alami *tariqa* or Shaykh Fadhlalla Haeri's loosely connected Rifa'i Sufi community. In addition, the study included two *murids* of Shaykh Kabir Helminski's Mevlevi Threshold Society and an individual who did not specify allegiance to any particular *shaykh*, all three of whom took part in the Sufi activities in Luton along with a number of *murids* of Shaykh Fadhlalla.

The Alami *tariqa* and Shaykh Fadhlalla's community are transnational, Islamically oriented Sufi movements that have been present in Britain since the mid-1980s. These Sufi movements are related by the Rifa'i connection in their spiritual lineage (*silsila*), but differ in subtle ways regarding their structure and leadership. The Alami Order, with its reverence to long-standing *tariqa* traditions, represents a form of contemporary, but traditional Sufism that has acculturated to modern Western culture. Shaykh Fadhlalla, on the other hand, prefers not to be identified with any formal *tariqa*.[22] In the spirit of unity and universalism, he refers to himself as a 'post-*tariqa shaykh*'. Regardless of these distinctions, they are 'two sides of the same coin', as several *murids* in Luton explained, meaning that the essence of their teachings is the same. They have developed distinct transnational frameworks meant to be socially relevant to the lifestyles of contemporary individuals seeking spiritual awareness across ethnic and physical dimensions.

The Alami *tariqa* is led by Shaykh Asaf of the Balkans, who received his *hilafetnameh* (title of leader/*shaykh*) from the late Shaykh Yahya of the Khalwati-Hayati *tariqa* in Ohrid, Macedonia, and the late Shaykh Jemali of the Rifa'i *tariqa* in Prizren, Kosovo.[23] His *silsila* is traced back to the time of the Prophet Muhammad through both Shaykh Ahmad al-Rifa'i al-Husseini, founder of the Rifa'i *tariqa*, and Shaykh Muhammad Hayati Sultan, founder of the Hayati branch of the Khalwati *tariqa*. Shaykh Asaf is highly educated in both Islamic and Western institutions, having memorized the Qur'an by the age of 13 and later earned four doctorate degrees (MD, DVM, PhD., DSc).[24] He presently lives in the United States and serves as the director of the Uranium Medical Research Centre, Inc., and, in this capacity, uses his knowledge to increase understanding of global nuclear effects. He is also an internationally recognized poet, and his literary works are included in the Vatican's *Anthology of Spiritual Poetry on Christ*.[25]

Previously identified with the Rifa'i *tariqa*, Shaykh Asaf was given permission to establish the Alami branch in the mid-1980s. In Arabic, *alami* means 'of the world, universe, creation'.[26] Although it is common for the name of the *tariqa* to indicate the founder and leader of a Sufi order, in this case it describes its larger purpose. Identifying this Sufi order as the Alami *tariqa* signifies that Sufism is not limited to a particular place or ethnic population. Also, this *tariqa* is dedicated to relieving the suffering of humankind through the programs of the non-profit, humanitarian organization World Life Institute, which was established in 1987.[27] While the main headquarters of the Alami *tariqa* are in New York State, *murids* and small communities are spread across the globe in Britain, the Balkans, Western Europe, Scandinavia, Turkey, the Middle East, South Asia and South Africa. Shaykh Asaf visits Britain periodically and holds annual Sufi gatherings in Europe.

Shaykh Fadhlalla Haeri is from Karbala, Iraq, and descends from a lineage of distinguished spiritual leaders. Similarly to Shaykh Asaf, he also bridges the East and West, having memorized the Qur'an at a young age and pursued higher education in Europe and the United States. He founded a number of companies in the Middle East and worked as a consultant in the oil industry. Shaykh Fadhlalla received his *hilafetnameh* from Shaykh Abdalqadir as-Sufi of the Shadhili *tariqa*, Shaykh Asaf of the Rifa'i *tariqa*, as well as from the Chishti *tariqa*.[28] Currently, though he does not identify with any of the formal *tariqas*, preferring to be without titles and more universal in his approach to Sufism. Shaykh Fadhlalla established Sufi communities in the United States, Britain and the Middle East. In the 1980s and 1990s, he resided in Berkshire, England, before moving to South Africa. He continues to visit Britain a few times a year. Shaykh Fadhlalla is known for establishing the Zahra Trust, a charitable organization, and the Academy of Self Knowledge (ASK), which offers online courses for spiritual advancement. He published an autobiography, *Son of Karbala*, in 2006.

Religious conversion

Historically, Sufism is recognized for its role in spreading Islam, and it continues to play an important part in Europeans becoming Muslim.[29] Islam is the second largest religion in Britain, with an estimate of nearly 2.5 million adherents.[30] Conversion to Islam in Britain has nearly doubled in the last decade, with figures as high as 100,000, according to the comprehensive study conducted by Faith Matters,[31] although the 2011 Census is more conservative, estimating 60,000. Unfortunately, it is not possible to estimate the number of those involved in Sufism because there is no central registration, and joining a Sufi movement is typically a private event. In addition, those pursuing the Sufi Path may not be willing to identify themselves or discuss their membership. Historically, 'Sufi' has rarely been used in reference to individuals, likely because of the contradiction in the ideal selflessness of a Sufi and the implied egotism of someone who would claim the title for him or herself.[32] Although members of the same Sufi movement frequently live in proximity of one another, forming a Sufi community, it is also common for members to be scattered around the world individually or in satellite communities, contributing to transnational networks.[33]

Traditional Sufi *tariqas* have a strict concept of membership, with an inner circle of individuals who are official *murids*. The formal ceremony of joining Sufism and becoming a *murid* is called 'taking *intisab*'. In *The Sufi Code of*

Conduct, Shaykh Asaf discusses the step-by-step transformational process through which someone interested in Sufism traverses.[34] After finding a Sufi *shaykh* who is willing to accept *murids*, an initial step that may take many years of searching, it is up to the individual to evaluate the *shaykh* for spiritual advancement and sincerity towards God. Simultaneously, the *shaykh* assesses the potential student for genuineness, spiritual advancement and compatibility. Following this period of assessment, which can be very lengthy (several years) or short (a few minutes), the *shaykh* may invite the seeker to take *intisab*. This ceremony involves a reaffirmation of the declaration of faith (*shahada*) and an oath of allegiance to the *shaykh* (*bayah*). In the Alami *tariqa*, *intisab* takes place in a private, formal ceremony in which only other *murids* are present.[35] Thereafter, the student and shaykh are considered to be spiritually linked. This *bayah* is believed to have origins in the Qur'an (48:10), 'Verily, those who give you their allegiance, they give it but to God Himself'. The *wali allah* (friends of God, saints; that is, Sufi *shaykhs*) are considered to be the spiritual successors of the prophets.

Since joining a Sufi movement involves a religious change, it may be identified as a type of religious conversion. According to Lewis Rambo and Charles Farhadian (1999), religious conversion refers to 'changing from one religious tradition to another, changing from one group to another within a tradition ... [and] the intensifying of religious beliefs and practices'.[36] Religious conversion is understood as a complex, on-going process that takes place in the socio-cultural context of life. Although it may involve an extraordinary transformational event, it is not primarily defined by it.[37] Elaborating on the conversion process, Rambo (1993) provides a flexible seven stage model: context, crisis, quest, encounter, interaction, commitment and consequences.[38] This study is concerned with the time leading up to and including the commitment to join Sufism.

Sufism is historically and traditionally connected to Islam. However, particularly in the West, a significant number of spiritual movements have developed that refer to themselves as Sufis, but have little or no connection to Islam. Thierry Zarcone suggests that Europeans who have joined Sufism, particularly those influenced by René Guénon and other Western writers, often idealize Sufism, which then becomes separated from its history and distinct from its counterpart in Islamic societies.[39] Regardless of the reality that a number of Westerners involved in Sufi movements have not formally embraced Islam, this study focuses on those who joined Sufi movements that uphold Islam as essential to Sufism. Formal involvement in the Alami and Rifa'i *tariqa* requires the *shahada*. It should be noted that in Arabic, there is no direct translation of religious 'conversion'.[40] Instead, the concept of becoming Muslim is described by the verb *aslama*, meaning literally 'to submit'. The Qur'an (4:125) identifies a Muslim as someone who 'submits his whole self to God, does good, and follows the way of Abraham, the true in faith'. Particularly among certain groups of Muslims, embracing Islam is identified as a 'reversion' instead of a 'conversion'. This is because the Qur'an (7:172) states that all souls bowed to God prior to being born, indicating that everyone was born in a state of obedience to God (i.e. a Muslim). Therefore, embracing Islam later in life is considered by many Muslims to be a return, or reversion, to the original belief in God.[41]

While it is useful for academic purposes to view joining Sufism as a religious conversion, this approach is unsuited for those who are informally involved in Sufism. This includes Muslims who have an inclination towards the Ahl-as Sunna wa-jamaat (literally meaning 'the people of the Prophet's way and the community') but have not taken *bayah* with a *shaykh*.[42] This relationship is particularly common among ethnic communities whose culture respects elements of Sufism, such as those in South Asia. Also, 'conversion' is inappropriate for spiritual seekers who frequently participate in various spiritual paths without strict or lasting dedication. Since they uphold essential truths common to many religions, spiritual seekers may not view changing from one religious path to another in the same light as those who focus on doctrinal differences. Paul Heelas (2000) suggests that 'a turning within' more accurately describes those on an 'ever-changing quest'.[43] Admittedly, conversion can be 'awkward', as Donald Taylor (1999) discusses in his three categories of conversions called 'inward, outward and awkward'.[44] He suggests that Sufism falls into the awkward category, particularly when it does not involve ceremonial rituals or indicate full acceptance of the beliefs and practices of Islam on behalf of the individual.

Since human experiences have commonalities and shared elements, several theme-based categories have been identified among conversion narratives. John Loftland and Norman Skonovd (1981) suggest six common motif experiences: intellectual, experimental, mystical, affectional, revivalism and coercive.[45] A later study by Ali Köse and Kate Miriam Loewenthal in 2000 found the intellectual, experimental and affectional motifs to be the most prevalent, having each been reported by about 67 per cent of their British research participants who converted to Islam.[46] The affectional and mystical motifs were more common among those involved in Sufism, indicating that personal feelings and unusual experiences played a more common role in their conversion to Islam.

Marcia Hermansen (1999) discusses 'Sufi-oriented narratives' as a distinct genre within conversion narratives.[47] Her research indicates four common themes among these narratives including emphasis on the importance of adhering to *shari'ah* law, the search for a spiritual teacher, the inner transformation into a Muslim, and critiques of Western culture. Another theme that may be added is focus on the journey. The physical and spiritual journey can be observed in autobiographies such as *The Book of Strangers* by Scottish-born Ian Dallas, who is also known as Shaykh Abdalqadir as-Sufi of the Murabitun Movement.[48]

Although conversion narratives in the form of first-person autobiographies provide valuable insight into the experience, they have limitations for academic research. The narratives may be inadequate regarding important details, lack accuracy and influenced by external factors, such as cultural biases, gender and common literary styles of the time.[49] Although these concerns are present in this study, it is expected that they are lessened since each research participant responded to similar questions on the survey and/or during the interview. However, there is no way of assuring that the narratives accurately relay the facts of what happened. The possibility remains that they could have been influenced by numerous factors, including my own involvement in the Alami *tariqa* in the United States. Being an insider, I had the advantage of familiarity with the philosophy and lived practices of Sufism and was able to relate to the conversion narratives through my own experiences.

Research in Britain

Research was conducted in May 2012 with 21 Sufi adherents in London, High Wycombe, Wembley, Oxford and Luton. The study involved a written survey to gather basic data, which was returned by 20 individuals, and 12 semi-structured interviews to elicit original conversion narratives. Individuals were invited for interviews based on snowball sampling and availability. All surveys and interviews were confidential, and original names have been replaced by pseudonyms. There were more women (15) than men (6) involved in the study, and all except four were raised Muslim. Half of the participants were introduced to Sufism through a family member. Nine indicated Shaykh Asaf as their teacher, eight Shaykh Fadhlalla, one both Shaykh Fadhlalla and Shaykh Asaf, two Shaykh Kabir Helminski and one did not name a *shaykh*, having been influenced by the Shi'a tradition of *irfan* (gnosis). The earliest *bayah* among the research participants happened in 1985 with Shaykh Fadhlalla, and the three most recent occurred in 2011, one with each of the three *shaykhs* mentioned above. The eldest *murid* at the time of the study was 74, and the youngest was 18. Nearly everyone had pursued higher education, including 10 who had pursued post-graduate study. The courses of study included a law degree, postgraduate study in social work, healthcare, geography and classes in holistic healing and accounting.

Although all respondents lived in the United Kingdom at the time of this research, except for one who had recently moved, only seven (33%) were born in Britain. The others originated from Pakistan, India, Germany, Uganda, Algeria, Morocco, South Africa, and the United States. The most common ancestral background, indicated by 65 per cent of the respondents, was South Asian (Pakistani, Bangladeshi or Indian). Following this, four indicated having African ancestry (North African, West African and African American), and four had Western European ancestry. As anticipated, most of the research participants were first or second generation immigrants to Britain. Only the three participants with British ancestry indicated that they were more than the third generation to have lived in the United Kingdom.

On the survey, the research participants were first asked to describe how they came to the Sufi Path in an open-ended question. This was followed by a request to indicate their five primary reasons for joining Sufism from nine pre-determined options, which were based on the literature. The survey question was as follows:

Please rank your top five reasons for deciding to become a *murid*:
(Ranking scale: 1 = primary reason, 5 = least important)
___ Personal, mystical experiences
___ Charisma/leadership style of the *shaykh*
___ Desire for spiritual healing
___ Dissatisfaction with previous religious/spiritual path
___ Desire for intellectual spiritual development
___ Desire for a more meaningful, personal certainty of God
___ Supportive community of faith
___ Fulfilling an expectation of family or community
___ Dissatisfaction with dominant social and moral norms
      Please specify:_____
___ Other:_____

Reasons for joining Sufism

Based on the survey results, the most common reason for joining Sufism was a desire for a more meaningful, personal certainty of God (Table 7.1). This was also indicated most often as the primary reason for joining Sufism, by just over half of the respondents (55%). This confirms that individuals who join Sufism are looking for spiritual fulfilment and a deeper relationship with the Divine, regardless of whether their religious background was Islam or another tradition. Following this primary motivation, three answers received the same number of responses, tying for second, third and fourth places. These include personal, mystical experiences, charisma/leadership style of the *shaykh* and desire for intellectual spiritual development. The high ranking of mystical experiences indicates that 70 per cent had out of the ordinary, transformational events that helped to confirm that this path was right for them. Likewise, the charisma and personality of the *shaykh* played a critical role for individuals connecting to this spiritual path. The significant number who indicated desiring for intellectual spiritual development shows that these Sufi movements respect and encourage the pursuit of spiritual as well as academic knowledge. The fifth most common reason for joining Sufism was the desire for spiritual healing, indicated by half of the respondents.

The research participants were asked on the survey to indicate their top five reasons for becoming a *murid*. These are the un-weighted results from 20 responses.

Strikingly, these are the same top five reasons that were indicated by the Alami *murids* in the United States, with only slight differences in percentages. The largest distinction was in the number who indicated having a desire for a more meaningful, personal certainty of God. This was documented by 75 per cent in

Table 7.1 Most Common Reasons for Joining Sufism

Rank	Reason	Total Responses (out of 20)
1	Desire for a more meaningful, personal certainty of God	15
2/3/4	Personal, mystical experience	14
2/3/4	Charisma/leadership style of the shaykh	14
2/3/4	Desire for intellectual spiritual development	14
5	Desire for spiritual healing	10

the United Kingdom compared to 89 per cent in the United States. Also, a few more in the United States than in Britain noted having had personal, mystical experiences (70% compared to 83%). However, this variance may be due to the difference in wording, since the broader word 'transformational' was used in the American survey instead of 'mystical'. Charisma of the *shaykh* and desire for intellectual spiritual development received more responses among British participants (70% compared to 60%), and desire for healing received nearly equal percentage of votes in both studies (50% compared to 49%).

Although their survey responses were remarkably similar, the conversion narratives of the *murids* in the United States and Britain differed dramatically. In contrast to my previous research with Alami *murids* in the United States, most of the research respondents in Britain were raised Muslim. Only four had been raised non-Muslim (19%). Since both Shaykh Fadhlalla and Shaykh Asaf transcend sectarian divides, it is unsurprising that there were a mix of participants from Sunni and Shi'a backgrounds. In total, 11 indicated Sunni upbringings and 6 Shi'a. Although the identity labels are useful for analyzing their conversion narratives, a vast majority of the research participants did not identify with these labels at the time of the research and preferred to be simply called Muslim. In the discussion below, the conversion narratives are explored further for trends and themes.

Those raised Muslim

Among those born and raised Muslim, many joined Sufism as a way to connect with the essence of Islam. They expressed that before joining Sufism they had difficulty fitting in with other Muslims and did not feel fulfilled by attending the mosques. They had observed hypocrisy and superficiality in the rituals, which initiated an inquiry into what was 'true' Islam as opposed to cultural religious practices. In contrast to many non-Muslims who join Sufi movements, most of the Muslims in this study were not actively seeking a spiritual guide and did not experiment with other religions or spiritual paths. Many were introduced by a professional acquaintance or family member, typically a spouse, who invited them to a *dhikr* circle (gathering to remember God). Among the reasons that attracted them to join Sufism were the way the *shaykh* practised Islam without hypocrisy and explained concepts, as well as his charismatic, striking personality. The affectional, mystical, and intellectual motifs of Köse and Loewenthal's (2000) study were prominent in their conversion narratives, as was Hermansen's (1999) theme of 'inner transformation into a Muslim'.

Although this study did not confirm dissatisfaction with mainstream Western cultural values as a major reason for joining Sufism, the findings indicate that an important factor was discontent with Islam as it was practiced in mainstream mosques. Only 4 of the 20 survey respondents indicated dissatisfaction with social norms in their top 5 reasons for joining Sufism. For example, Abdul Kareem struggled to connect with other Muslims and questioned the Shi'a practices, particularly concerning the apparent increase in 'bipolar' behaviour during Muharram – how many Shi'a were distraught and upset in the mosque, but content and happy after leaving it. Farida also explained that she found Islam oppressive as a child because of the overbearing threats of hellfire. She knew she was blessed to have been raised Muslim, but the Islam she witnessed did not resonate with her. Attending Shaykh Fadhlalla and Shaykh Asaf's talks allowed her to grasp the transformational message of Islam. Another research participant, Nabiha, described how she had prayed for approximately nine years for personal guidance and a community that properly followed Islam and with which God was pleased. She was bored with life and knew there was more to it but could not find fulfilment from attending the mosques. When she was invited to *dhikr* and eventually met Shaykh Asaf, she knew exactly that this was an answer to her prayers.

Khalid's conversion narrative provides another interesting example of this. He was introduced to Shaykh Fadhlalla in 1985, making him the first to become a *murid* among the research participants. Also, he was one of the few who experienced a crisis moment in his life, after which he went in search of a guide. Khalid explained that he became aware of the meaninglessness of a life that is focused on material pursuits. Soon after, he began praying regularly and went on Hajj. While circumambulating the Kaaba, he grasped the *kiswah* (cloth covering the Kaaba) and demanded that God give him guidance. About a month after returning to Britain, he attended Muharram commemorations, during which he was fully aware of the insincerity and shallowness among those present. Outside the mosque, he interacted with an American Muslim selling books and was invited to lunch. The lunch, unknown to him beforehand, was attended by Shaykh Fadhlalla. Describing the events, Khalid said, 'I walked in, and I was shocked. I was overwhelmed by love . . . I just stood there looking at him. I thought of the *mizan* (balance, metaphorical pursuit of justice and harmony in all endeavours). This guy has this balance.' In his talks, Shaykh Fadhlalla unabashedly reproached the elitist attitude found among Shi'a, the focus on victimhood, and sense that the world owed them something. Khalid was astounded. He had intended to visit Iran in search of a guide, but instead had found one in London. Proudly, Khalid stated during the interview, 'I can claim back my heritage from those who hijacked Islam'. He attributes the Sufi path to helping him connect with the inner meaning of Islam.

Another critical factor that Khalid's narrative highlights is the role of charisma. In the survey results, the charisma and leadership of the *shaykh* was tied for the second most common reason for joining Sufism. The sense that Shaykh Fadhlalla and Shaykh Asaf were imbued with exceptional qualities was widespread throughout the conversion narratives. Charisma of the *shaykh* is closely linked to the prevalence of personal, mystical experiences. Several indicated that the initial interactions with their *shaykhs* were very powerful. For example, Farida commented that she was 'mesmerized' by Shaykh Asaf's words and knew instantly that he was her teacher. A few described having had dreams in which the *shaykhs* appeared. Leena mentioned a transformational moment at a Sufi gathering in which she sensed being called and looked up to see Shaykh Fadhlalla watching her. In addition, Kareema spoke of how her father, who was on his deathbed, astounded the doctors by living eight weeks longer than predicted. Her family, which was initially suspicious of her involvement in Sufism, attributed his improvement to the healing *dhikr* prescriptions advised by Shaykh Fadhlalla. Others mentioned the powerful group *dhikrs* of both *shaykhs*.

Köse and Loewenthal's (2000) affectional motif was particularly prominent in the conversion narratives of two whose parents were involved in Sufism in Britain. Anna was six years old when her British mother embraced both Islam and Sufism. After this, she was raised in a spiritual Muslim environment but still attended Christian worship services sometimes with her friends. When she was 14, Anna decided to take the *shahada* while attending a Sufi gathering hosted by Shaykh Asaf. Since Shaykh Asaf had been an important part of her life and almost like family, she felt a special bond with him. Although eager to become a *murid* at the age of 15, Shaykh Asaf rarely accepts students under the age of 18, at which point Anna took *bayah* and officially joined the *tariqa*. Likewise, Taqwa felt a strong connection to Shaykh Fadhlalla because both of her parents were *murids* and she had spent time with him and his grandchildren in South Africa. She was highly influenced by her parents' deep respect for Shaykh Fadhlalla. Around the age of 13 or 14, her understanding developed as to why her parents regarded him so highly, and she decided to dedicate herself to following his teachings, too. In total, only three indicated that they were fulfilling an expectation of their family among their top five reasons for joining Sufism.

One research participant, who was raised in the United States by parents who embraced Islam and joined Sufism, had a very different experience. Through his family's interactions with various *shaykhs* in the United States and his travels in Pakistan and Iran, Dawud became aware of the potential danger of misguided spiritual leaders. Although he had not taken *bayah* with anyone, Dawud considers himself to be involved in Sufism and identifies particularly with the Shi'a tradition of *irfan*, or gnosis. The practice of not making allegiance with living *shaykhs* is common among some Sufi orders, for example, the Iranian Oveyessi Sufi mystic tradition.[50]

Those raised Non-Muslim

Among the four research participants who had been raised non-Muslim, their religious backgrounds were Christianity, Agnosticism and Hinduism. Three of them were looking for spiritual guidance and joined Islam through Sufism. Layla was the most active in her search for spiritual direction, and her story corresponds with Köse and Loewenthal's (2000) 'experimental' motif and Hermansen's (1999) Sufi theme of 'searching for a spiritual teacher.' Prior to learning about Sufism, Layla was involved in Christian mysticism, Buddhism and Hinduism but did not stay long with any of them. She had three spiritual guides in succession, starting with a Christian mystic who told her pre-emptively, 'You are a Sufi'. A few years later, Layla discovered a book by Irina Tweedie and was amazed and encouraged by her personal journey with a Sufi master. Unsure of how to proceed and locate a Sufi *shaykh*, it was two years until a breakthrough – someone she knew professionally told her about Shaykh Asaf. After writing to him, Layla experienced an overwhelming feeling that this was the guide for whom she had been waiting. In 1996, she flew to the United States to meet him and, while there, took the *shahada* and *bayah*.

Hassan was the only research participant with a non-Abrahamic religious background. Born in Uganda, he was raised Hindu by his Indian parents, and they moved to Britain when he was 10. Years later, he was introduced to Sufism through his wife, who was actively searching for a spiritual path and guide. When she started attending *dhikrs* in London and listening to Shaykh Fadhlalla's talks, Hassan would sometimes join her. Slowly, his interest and commitment increased, and about three years after his wife joined Sufism, he also embraced Islam and was accepted as a student by Shaykh Fadhlalla.

In contrast to those looking for spiritual guidance, Safiya encountered Sufism without intending to find it. Her conversion narrative has elements of Köse and Loewenthal's (2000) affectional, experimental and intellectual motifs but is not strictly defined by any of them. Instead, it is best described as an example of a 'journey' Sufi conversion. Safiya was born in India near the end of British imperialism, after which her family moved to Britain. Following her university study, she took a teaching position in Northern Nigeria and settled into life there, marrying a Muslim who had three other wives, and bearing two children. She lived and worked there for 16 years, 4 years beyond the sudden death of her husband, before returning to Britain with her young boys. At that point, she had not become Muslim mostly due to how she perceived Muslim women to be treated. As a Christian/Agnostic, she felt she had better standing in Nigerian culture.

Back in Britain, Safiya attempted to reconnect with Christianity, but disagreed with some of the theology, and her children found Sunday School to be uninteresting. In her teaching position, she interacted with Muslims of different backgrounds and was strongly influenced towards embracing Islam by a Shi'a Muslim. Eventually, in 1992, Safiya took the *shahada*. Although she had accepted the Islamic faith, she faced difficulty being Muslim. She struggled to keep it up on her own and embody the new socio-cultural identity, such as not participating in the Christmas holidays, which were a beloved part of her family's activities. She also did not appreciate the sectarian tensions that became apparent to her after embracing Islam. Experiencing a crisis of faith, Safiya called an Islamic help-line and was given the phone number of a 'Sufi' woman, who was one of Shaykh Fadhlalla's wives. Up until that point, she had not encountered Sufism. After speaking with Shaykh Fadhlalla's wife and another woman, she found she had a better sense of inner stability. She was then invited to a *dhikr* circle.

Even though Safiya found the worship event a little disconcerting, for example, the soulful and breathy repetitions of God's Names, she continued attending mostly because she enjoyed the company of the people. They were from diverse ethnic backgrounds and had a 'sweetness to them' that she had not experienced at other Muslim gatherings. She appreciated how respectfully the men treated the women. Also, it was appealing because English was the main spoken language. After briefly meeting Shaykh Fadhlalla, Safiya continued to attend the gatherings for two years without further interaction with him. During this time, she read books and listened to his talks, taking time to determine whether to accept him as a guide. She appreciated that he was a bridge between

East and West and liked his personality and how he accepted questions. At the age of 56, she took *bayah* with him.

Reactions from family members

Although Sufism is a common cultural aspect of Islam in many Muslim countries, particularly South Asia, many research participants who were the first in their families to join a *tariqa* encountered tensions with their Muslim family members and friends. This appeared to be worse for those from a Shi'a background. For their families, Sufism was frequently considered to be a deviation from Islam. The survey responses were very telling: 'Our close friends regard us as being out of Islam'. Kareema's family thought she was getting involved with a cult. Another described her interactions with her family like a 'friendly war'. During an interview, Abdul Kareem conveyed his experience with an elder member of his family who approached him and expressed worry about their brother's involvement in Sufism. Since their father had recently died, the elder brother spoke about the need to uphold the Shi'a traditions of their family, and he expressed his desire to 'retrieve' their other brother from his folly. Much to the elder brother's shock and dismay, Abdul Kareem replied that he had met their brother's *shaykh* and thought quite highly of him. To this, the elder brother replied, mostly to himself, that they had 'lost another one'. Similarly, another found her family to be antagonistic until they had the opportunity to meet Shaykh Asaf during his *ziyarah* (pilgrimage) to the holy sites in Iraq. This unplanned meeting, which demonstrated to them his love and respect for Ahlel Bayt (the family of the Prophet Muhammad) appeared to relieve their worry.

A few research participants grew up in families that participated in Sufi orders, and they had very different experiences from those who were the first in their families to join. For example, Nabiha's family in North Africa had been involved in Sufism for many generations, but at the time they did not know of a living *shaykh* in either their hometown or in Britain. To discover a Sufi circle in London was astounding for her. Her immediate family has been supportive, and they have had direct interactions with the *shaykh*. Another research participant was initially unaware of her family's involvement in Sufism. Tasneem was worried about her parents' reaction until she was reminded that they have a heritage of belonging to a Sufi order in South Asia, which they have become disconnected from since moving to Britain. They have been generally supportive of her decision to take *bayah*, although they did not know much about Shaykh Asaf at the time of this study.

Final thoughts

This chapter both suggests some initial answers to the question of why individuals in Britain join Sufism and encourages further research into this topic. The research participants had very different backgrounds, demonstrating the appeal of Islamic Sufi movements throughout contemporary British society. A common experience, particularly among those raised Muslim, was to feel unfulfilled by ritualistic religious practices and desire spiritual fulfilment. Some were actively seeking a spiritual guide, but many were not. Most commonly, they were invited to *dhikr* circles through a family member or professional acquaintances. Alternatively, there were those raised as non-Muslims who were seeking spiritual guidance and embraced Islam and Sufism. It was more common for this to be a combined conversion experience, although one research participant embraced Islam before learning about Sufism. This study confirmed Köse and Loewenthal's (2000) findings that intellectual, affectional, experimental and mystical were common types of conversion experiences. Although discontent with materialism and secularism was present, this study did not substantiate joining Sufism as a way of rejecting Western cultural values, which contradicts the findings of Köse's (1996) study. In addition, there were many more women than men involved in the study, possibly supporting the idea that women in the West are more likely to turn to Sufism as a spiritual outlet.[51]

The charisma of the *shaykh* and, likewise, experiencing mystical, transformational events, played critical roles in the decision to join Sufism. They served to indicate that this path would be exceptional and confirm that it was 'right' for the individual. Although charisma is discussed in the literature,[52] mystical experiences are not frequently cited, except in Köse and Loewenthal's (2000) study. Also, the ethnicity of the *shaykh* appears to have somewhat influenced the participants, as those with Shi'a backgrounds were more likely to self-identify as Shaykh Fadhlalla's *murids*. However, it is notable that none of Shaykh Asaf's *murids* were from the Balkans, nor were any of Shaykh Fadhlalla's from Iraq, their birthplaces, indicating that ethnicity was not a major factor among the participants. Although artistic elements, such as sacred music and whirling, are often presented in the literature as attractive for non-Muslims,[53] they are not integral parts of the traditions of the Alami or Rifa'i *tariqa* and, therefore, were not discussed in this research. Future research, including in-depth studies of particular *tariqas* and comparative studies, would be valuable to developing this topic.

Notes

1   A. J. Arberry (1969) *Sufism*. London: Allen and Unwin, p. 122; J. Baldick (1989) *Mystical Islam*. London: IB Tauris, p. 153; M. van Bruinessen and J. D. Howell (Eds) (2007) *Sufism and the 'Modern' in Islam*. London: IB Tauris & Co Ltd, pp. 8–10.

2   See Y. Haddad and J. Smith (Eds) (1994) *Muslim Communities in North America*. Albany: State University of New York Press; D. Westerlund (Ed.) (2004) *Sufism in Europe and North America*, London: Routledge Curzon; J. Malik and J. Hinnells (Eds) (2006) *Sufism in the West*. London: Routledge; M. van Bruinessen and J. D. Howell (Eds) (2007) *Sufism and the 'Modern' in Islam*. London: IB Tauris & Co Ltd.; R. Geaves, M. Dressler and G. Klinkhammer (2009) *Sufis in Western Society: Global Networking and Locality*. New York: Routledge; C. Raudvere and L. Stenberg (Eds) (2009) *Sufism Today*. London: IB Tauris.

3   M. Hermansen (1998) 'In the Garden of American Sufi Movements: Hybrids and Perennials' in *New Trends and Developments in the World of Islam*, P. Clarke (Ed.), London: Luzac Oriental, pp. 155–78; P. Wilson (1998) 'The Strange Fate of Sufism in the New Age' in *New Trends and Developments in the World of Islam*, P. B. Clarke (Ed.), London: Luzac Oriental, pp. 179–210; T. Zarcone (1999), 'Rereadings and Transformations of Sufism in the West', *Diogenes*, 47, 3, 110–22; C. A. Genn (2007) 'The Development of a Modern Western Sufism' in *Sufism and the 'Modern' in Islam*, M. van Bruinessen and J. D. Howell (Ed.), London: IB Tauris & Co. Ltd, pp. 257–77.

4   A. Köse (1996) *Conversion to Islam: A Study of Native British Converts*. London: Kegan Paul International; J. Smith (1999) *Islam in America*. New York: Columbia University Press; H. Jawad (2006) 'Female Conversion to Islam: The Sufi Paradigm' in *Woman Embracing Islam: Gender and Conversion in the West*, K. van Nieuwkerk (Ed.), Austin: University of Texas Press, pp. 153–71.

5   G. Webb (1994) 'Tradition and Innovation in Contemporary American Spirituality: The Bawa Muhaiyaddeen Fellowship' in *Muslim Communities in North America*, Y. Y. Haddad and J. I. Smith (Eds), Albany: State University of New York, pp. 81, 75–108; I. Weismann (2007) *The Naqshbandiyya: Orthodoxy and Activism in a Worldwide Sufi Tradition*. New York: Routledge, p. 167; S. Stjernholm (2009) 'A Translocal Sufi Movement: Developments among Naqshbandi-Haqqani in London' in *Sufism Today*, C. Raudvere and L. Stenberg (Eds), London: IB Tauris, pp. 85, 83–102.

6   J. Hazen (2011) *Contemporary Islamic Sufism in America: The Philosophy and Practices of the Alami Tariqa in Waterport, New York.* PhD diss. SOAS, University of London. http://eprints.soas.ac.uk/13816/1/Hazen_3369.pdf (accessed October 13, 2012).

7   R. Geaves (2000) *The Sufis of Britain: An Exploration of Muslim Identity.* Great Britain: Cardiff Academic Press.

8   M. Hermansen (1998); J. Smith (1999), p. 69.

9   G. Schmidt (2004) 'Sufi Charisma on the Internet' in *Sufism in Europe and North America*, D. Westerlund (Ed.), London: Routledge Curzon, pp. 109–26; M. J. Rausch (2009) 'Encountering Sufism on the Web' in *Sufism Today*, R. Catharina and L. Stenberg (Eds), London: IB Tauris, pp. 159–76.

10 A. Köse (1996), p. 156.

11 pp. 150, 153.

12 A. Köse (1996), p. 194; I. Weismann (2007), p. 167.

13 J. Smith (1999), p. 72; H. Jawad (2006); C. Helminski (2003), *Women of Sufism: A Hidden Treasure.* Boston: Shambhala.

14 R. Geaves (2000), p. 142; J. Hazen (2011), p. 248.

15 I. Weismann (2007), p. 167.

16 Werbner, P. (2003) *Pilgrims of Love: The Anthropology of a Global Sufi Cult*, Bloomington: Indiana University Press, pp. 329–31.

17 M. Weber (1978) *Economy and Society: An Outline of Interpretive Sociology.* (2 vols.); G. Roth and C. Wittich (Eds). Berkeley, CA: University of California Press, p. 241.

18 R. Geaves (2000), p. 117.

19 P. Werbner (1996), p. 329; Geaves, R. (2006), p. 147.

20 J. Hazen (2011), p. 165.

21 A. Köse (1996), p. 194; J. Hazen (2011), p. 191.

22 D. Westerlund (Ed.) (2004) *Sufism in Europe and North America.* London: Routledge Curzon, p. 22.

23 J. Hazen (2011), p. 89.

24 For a more complete biography of Shaykh Asaf, see J. Hazen (2011), pp. 89–90.

25 See 'Veronikin Rubac' and 'Rio De Janeiro' in V. Lončarević (2007) (Ed.), *Krist u hrvatskom pjesnistvu. Antologija Duhovne Poezije*, Split: Verbum, pp. 600–1.

26 H. A. Salmoné (1978) 'Alami' in *An Advanced Learner's Arabic-English Dictionary.* Beirut: Librairie Du Liban.

27 J. Hazen (2011), p. 99.

28 Shaykh Fadhlalla Haeri (2006) *Son of Karbala.* Winchester, UK: O Books, p. 163.

29 Y. Dutton (1999) 'Conversion to Islam: The Qur'anic Paradigm' in *Religious Conversion: Contemporary Practices and Controversies*, C. Lamb and M. Bryant (Eds), London: Cassell, p. 163, pp. 151–65.

30 HMG Estimation based on 2008 figures and 2011 Census data.

31 M. A. Kevin Brice (2010) *A Minority within a Minority: A Report on Conversion to Islam in the United Kingdom. On behalf of Faith Matters.* http://faith-matters.org/images/stories/fm-reports/a-minority-within-a-minority-a-report-on-converts-to-islam-in-the-uk.pdf (accessed November 2, 2012).

32 C. Ernst (1997) *The Shambhala Guide to Sufism*. Boston: Shambhala Publications Inc., p. 26.

33 P. Werbner (2003); Van Bruinessen and Howell (2007); Geaves, Dressler and Klinkhammer (2009).

34 Shaykh Asaf (2004) *Sufi Code of Conduct*. Björboholm, Sweden: Stiftelsen Författares Bokmaskin.

35 Other *tariqas* are less strict on this and have allowed the *intisab* ceremony to be observed by non-*murids* or recorded and posted on the internet. See the YouTube video of Muhammad Ali taking *bayah* with Shaykh Hisham Kabbani in 2001: http://youtube.com/watch?v=UtmuEqmNUfQ (accessed April 27, 2011).

36 L. Rambo and C. Farhadian (1999) 'Converting: Stages of Religious Change' in *Religious Conversion: Contemporary Practices and Controversies*, C. Lamb and M. Bryant (Eds), London: Cassell, pp. 23, 23–34.

37 L. Rambo (1993) *Understanding Religious Conversion*. New Haven: Yale University Press, p. 5.

38 L. Rambo (1993).

39 T. Zarcone (1999), 'Rereadings and Transformations of Sufism in the West', *Diogenes*, 47, 3, pp. 110–22, p. 117. There is disagreement as to whether or not Guénon converted to Islam and, if he did, how this should be interpreted.

40 Y. Dutton (1999), p. 151.

41 H. Jawad (2006), p. 155.

42 R. Geaves (2000), p. 72.

43 P. Heelas (2000) 'Turning Within' in *Previous Convictions: Conversion in the Present Day*, M. Percy (Ed.). London: SPCK, pp. 58–70, 58–76.

44 D. Taylor (1999) 'Conversion: Inward, Outward and Awkward' in *Religious Conversion: Contemporary Practices and Controversies*, C. Lamb and M. Bryant (Eds). London: Cassell, pp. 41, 35–50.

45 J. Lofland and N. Skonovd (1981) 'Conversion Motifs', *Journal for the Scientific Study of Religion*, 20, pp. 373–85.

46 A. Köse and K. M. Loewenthal (2000) 'Conversion Motifs among British Converts to Islam', *The International Journal for the Psychology of Religion*, 10, 2, pp. 101–10, p. 101.

47 M. Hermansen (1999) 'Roads to Mecca: Conversion Narratives of European and Euro-American Muslims'. *The Muslim World*, 89, 1 (January): pp. 56–89. http://macdonald.hartsem.edu/articles/hermansenart1.pdf (accessed May 4, 2011).

48 I. Dallas (1972) *The Book of Strangers*. New York: Pantheon Books.

49 M. Hermansen, (1999), p. 56.

50 See K. Spellman (2004) 'A National Sufi Order with Transnational Dimensions: The Maktab Tarighat Oveyssi Shahmaghsoudi Sufi Order in London', *Journal of Ethnic and Migration Studies*, 30, 5, pp. 945–60, pp. 950–1. This practice is based on the tradition of Oveys Gharani, who is said to have received spiritual teachings directly from the Prophet Muhammad, although he resided in Yemen and had never physically met the prophet of Islam.

51 See the writings by H. Jawad (2006).

52 P. Werbner (1996); I. Weismann (2007).

53 J. Smith (1999), p. 69.

Part Three

Case Studies

8

Online Sufism – Young British Muslims, their Internet 'Selves' and Virtual Reality

Sariya Cheruvallil-Contractor

Introduction: Virtual religion

Religion is a buzzing, hyperactive and fascinating confluence of divine revelation, prophetic guidance, scripture, ritual and spirituality. From a theological standpoint, in the monotheistic religions, this heaving, moving and constantly changing mass has a constant centre – God – the certainty of whom is a source of solace for believers of all predilections. From a sociological perspective, the focus is more fluid – people who are much more changeable and whose faith, beliefs and practice determine the societal ramifications and impact of religion.

While the divine and scriptural authority of God remains unchanging, authority within religious practice engages with and responds to the social contexts, needs and eccentricities of religious people. Religion must therefore adapt to diverse cultures, traditions and now also to changing technologies – the twentieth century has seen believers tuning into religious radio and TV channels and they now often log on to online religious forums. Although most academics agree that the internet affects various aspects of people's lives, it is not often integrated into various discourses within the social sciences. This chapter hopes to partly bridge this gap, by contextualising the internet into discussions about Sufism as articulated by young people. This chapter avoids detailed analysis of esoteric or spiritual aspects of Sufism but rather examines how young Muslims express and enunciate their particular Sufi beliefs on various internet forums.

Real location religious forums often tend to be dominated by community elders, and young people may not always have the opportunity to interrogate their faith. The online world, on the other hand, gives young people the anonymity to explore their faith and to ask the questions that they want answered. While this can be dismissed as online-social-network prattle, a closer reading unearths the strong verbal and non-verbal statements that young people make about their faith, beliefs and religious dogmas. In this online world, the spoken word is replaced by the written word, emoticons replace expressions and actions, but nevertheless young people still articulate religious understandings and positions which are uniquely their own and inherently real. It is within this context of 'virtuality', reality and 'virtual realities' that this chapter explores young people's articulations of their Sufi beliefs.

Strands of exploration

This chapter was conceptualized as a relatively simple article exploring the 'Online Sufism' of young British Muslims, however as I researched various sources and also undertook more in-depth explorations, previously unanticipated strands of sociological enquiry began to emerge. There is so much more scope here for further exploration, that I have begun to realise that this contribution will take a more headline approach that seeks to introduce the subject to the reader rather than delve into it in great detail, with the latter task being the subject of ongoing and future work by this author.

With regard to the 'various strands' which I found of academic interest, first as a sociologist, I recognize the divergences and convergences within contemporary Sufi practice. There are diverse Sufis and their diverse Sufisms,[1] within which are embedded further diversities in practical Islamic theology, transformative ritual and spiritual self-reflection. Open communication lines and democratic access on the internet allow these diversities, which were traditionally quite separate, to converge creating spaces for agreements and disagreements. It is fascinating to explore the outcomes of such convergences where none hitherto existed. Within Muslim practice, it is argued that Sufism has always been more inclusive towards women. In digital contexts, social barriers between the sexes and the ages become even more permeable.

There is the further complication that although it is a widely accepted term, as an 'ism', Sufism cannot be definitively defined or even be understood except perhaps in the hearts and minds of those who practise and hence *experience* this esoteric route to Islamic spirituality and spiritual accomplishment. The origins of the term are debated, with Shah arguing that it is a new term[2] and that it is nothing but authentic Islamic practice.[3] It is also presented as the emotional side of Islam, and according to Werner and Basu it is the realm of emotional discourse as opposed to theologian's discussions.[4] My work with young people brings their perspectives and experiences to this debate – how do young people understand their Sufisms?

During the writing of this paper, it was enlightening to reflect upon my own intentions for writing an article on Sufism and also that of prospective readers. In the preface to his seminal book *What is Sufism?*, Martin Lings writes that although his readers may not have any specialized knowledge, he pre-supposes that they would have a deep and searching interest in spiritual things that originally leads them to explore a subject such as Sufism.[5] Ling's Sufism was influenced by the Traditionalist's version of perennialism and shows through in the above assertion but can still push me to ask 'Has my own Sufi practice encouraged the writing of this article?' Haeri seems to agree when he says that writing about inner awakening is only really possible if one has experienced it, just as understanding such books is only really possible if one genuinely desires, or has already attained such awakening.[6] This chapter is further complicated by the fact that it is written from a sociological rather than a theological standpoint.

Finally, there is Durkheim's dichotomy between the sacred and the profane. My research on young people's online Sufisms adds to the many fronts where this dichotomy is challenged. On online forums, deep spiritual understandings and ontological discussions seamlessly co-exist with profane everyday chit-chat. Does this weakening of the sacred-profane dichotomy suggest a philosophical strand within this essentially sociological exploration?

Methodological reflections: Researching the Esoteric online

As an ethnographer, I have always worked within what I call a Feminist-Pragmatist epistemological stance.[7] This is a collaborative approach to research that works well in the Sociology of Religion, wherein sociologists explore deeply held religious and spiritual values that are experienced and felt by believers but which outside religious/spiritual contexts are difficult, if not impossible, to measure or weigh. This is where my 'Feminist-Pragmatist' becomes relevant. It situates knowledge in the experiences of individuals and in the consequences of their actions[8] thereby giving weight to those who feel, experience, say and do. To go back to Lings and Haeri, this research process was driven and informed not only by my own Sufi practice but also by those Sufis who participated in this research. Thus 'experience' rather than 'observation' becomes the thrust of this research – individuals become 'meaning makers' and we together clarify people's interpretations of their shared world. There are problems with a research stance, such as this one, in which the boundaries between researcher and researched are blurred and criticality perhaps becomes less possible, but then was it ever possible? There are strengths to this collaborative approach to research including better engagement with research participants, greater control for them and more democracy in the research process.

Social interactions in our twenty-first-century world are in a state of transition – moving from offline to online contexts. While these will hopefully never be fully digitized, sociologists are observing an increasing reliance on digital technologies to express values, allegiances and multi-faceted identities. Therefore an interest in digital research methodologies among Sociologists of Religion comes as no surprise and it is now not infrequent to find research projects and papers that explore online faith communities or particular aspects of a faith communities' online practice.[9] However, there has been significantly less focus on the methodological challenges associated with such online research and so I spend a few paragraphs here reflecting on the 'digital' nature of this research.

From a practical point of view, the research involved the identification of an online discussion forum that was used by Sufi Muslims. Most of this chapter is based on observations of discussions on this forum – what were these online Sufis saying and how did this impact on their Sufi practice. I sometimes participated in discussions and occasionally initiated discussion threads. This was a qualitative research project and as in offline research it was vital to capture coherent and multiple narratives. Observations were therefore spaced in two 3-month phases. This chapter is based on a number of discussions that were observed during these two phases. Later on in this chapter, three specific discussions have been highlighted as case studies to give readers a flavour of these online discussions. The narrations of these online Sufis are important because according to El-Nawawy and Khamis, current research about online Muslim communities is sometime limited in scope because it rarely analyses content.[10]

Although this research was situated in digital contexts, it mostly followed a classical ethnography framework, the difference being that for this Virtual Ethnography or 'Netnography' project, the methods had to be altered to suit the online world. So 'participant observation' and 'discussion groups' (both traditional methods) were combined into a mutated form of online content analysis of discussion threads. It was still possible to observe what people were doing and discussing, but this was typed text rather that the spoken word. The signifiers

I looked for and the observations I made were now digitized – 'forum posts', 'emoticons', 'font size' and 'font colour' were the signs I looked for rather than the spoken word, emotions and body language. Was a participant 'SHOUTING' because s/he was using capital letters or was s/he simply emphasizing a point?

There are significant ethical considerations that a researcher must be aware of in online research about religion and religious experience. Religion is an emotive and sensitive subject. With regard to the Muslim community, this is further complicated by socio-political suspicions around islamophobia and extremism. In online discussions about religion, distinctions between the public and private become blurred – while comments are usually posted in 'public' forums, the intentionality behind posts may not always be for them to be public, although this is difficult to measure. Researchers must also be aware of anonymity – which is something that many online posters may take for granted. Posters may perceive their comments as not being traceable back to them, however, technology allows this to be done quite easily and netnographers must constantly remain aware of possible inconsistencies within understandings and expectations of anonymity that exist in the online world. With regard to my own ethical practice, the website and posters will remain anonymous and quotes used are all paraphrased to limit the possibility that an individual participant is identified.

The Online Muslim community

This research involved observations of discussions on an online Sufi discussion forum. At the beginning, it is important to note that not everyone in the *Umma* (global Muslim community) has access to internet[11] and that a limitation of the 'virtual Umma' is that views captured on it are more representative of young techno-savvy Muslims who are mostly based in the West or in urban contexts. While there will be exceptions to this generalization, this was generally ratified by the limited statistics that I was able to access about this website. These statistics indicated that a large number of registered users were based in India and Pakistan. However, qualitative examinations of forum discussions clearly indicated that the most frequent users were young British and European Sufis, with more men than women participating in discussions.

The website that forms the basis of this research has a Sufi *Barelvi* stance, but I observed a recent shift towards a more ecumenical stance that welcomed discussions from other Sufi *tariqas* and also other Muslim groups. The stated aim of the website was to preserve traditional Islamic standpoints including the teachings of the *sahaba* (companions of Prophet Muhammad), *ahle bayt* (family of Prophet Muhammad), *tabiun* (second generation of Muslims who came after the *sahabah*) and blessed *Awliyah* (Friends. usually refers to Sufi shaykhs and leaders of *tariqat*) from the various *tariqat*. It respects all four Muslim schools of thought. With regard to resources in addition to discussion forums, it provided resources that are typically found on Islamic websites including Qur'an and *hadith* databases, Islamic calendar, prayer time calculator, etc.

The discussions – How and what were the 'online Sufis' discussing?

The discussions on the online forum are extremely varied and include discussions on favourite *nasheeds* (Islamic songs usually but not always sung in praise of God or the Prophet Muhammad), *nasheed* singers, current affairs, poetry and art. In a mirroring of music culture in general, it was interesting to see self-proclaimed 'fans' of various *nasheed* artists loyally proclaiming the merits of their favourite singer. There is a significant amount of banter (e.g. – I am really bored what do I do?). Given the European and mostly British nationality of most users, the election victory of the Conservative party in 2010, the formation of the coalition government, the politician George Galloway's by-election victory in Bradford were all discussed on the forum over the last two years while the research for this paper was being undertaken.

From a religious perspective discussions include prayer requests, information requests (a commonly asked question – is xyz food *halal* (or permissible?) or seeking advice about relationships. A number of discussion threads criticized 'more literal forms' of Islam which were often described as inaccurate or as being innovations or *bida* (innovation). Finally given the Islamic Sufi nature of the forum, there are quite intense theological and spiritual discussions about finer details of faith and Sufi practice. Disagreement is also evident between posters even in theological debates where divergent standpoints are presented (in some cases opinions were quite revolutionary and it is likely that these would not have been made in offline conversations). This variation is indicative of the diversity that is possible within a social group that is distinctively 'religious' and Sufi. It is also indicative of a social group that is 'young'.

There is clear indication of the role of the internet in creating 'safe' social spaces for young Muslims to discuss and debate their faith to an extent that would not be possible offline. The internet seems to allow an element of populism in this process of *Ijtihad*[12] where young people can use the internet to access diverse scholarly opinion and to thus inform their own understandings of religious doctrine and then share these understandings with their peers. These young people negotiate dichotomies that are complicated by divergence in the ways in which they are perceived online and offline, for example, between anonymity and identity or between reality as perceived in the real world, the virtual world and in Sufi practice. Nevertheless they present narratives about their beliefs, in this case Sufism, that are both coherent and enlightening. According to Bunt, online Muslims

> have applied technical innovation to galvanise an audience unsatisfied with convention, for which the Net is a natural place to acquire knowledge and converse with peers.[13]

Although the internet democratizes religious debates, there is also a recognized concern as reported by El-Nawawy and Khamis that 'it can also lead to further confusion'.[14] Such 'confusion' is sometimes evident in discussions and ranged from confusions due to different schools of thought having different rulings about certain subjects. Furthermore occasionally even within schools of thought, different opinions are possible and so for the more naïve among posters, information received in response to queries could be quite bewildering. Such complications and the difficulty to resolve all queries online was something that forum users recognize and posters with complicated queries often in addition to some information received the added advice to 'approach your local *imam* or a scholar'.

There is also the issue of inaccuracies in advice/information received on forums. For such issues, the website being observed had formal and informal hierarchies in place. The formal hierarchy involved moderators whose duties included ensuring that language used on forums was decent and appropriate; forums were neat and tidy; discussions were not replicated; that trouble-makers and spammers were suitably dealt with; and other such administrative tasks. The informal hierarchies were formed when certain users were recognized by others as more 'knowledgeable' and that their posts/advice were therefore more accurate.

Achieving such recognition from peers was a long process that involved developing a reputation for writing posts and responses that are well researched and which appropriately drew upon Islamic fundamentals. It is within such informal hierarchies and as a result of the communication and interactions facilitated by them, that the dynamics of identity and identification begin to emerge. Personalities begin to develop for various forum users. Some of these 'personality traits' are purely aesthetic such as user names, signature tag lines, profile pictures, standard use of a unique font style across all posts and use of emoticons. For example, a user may use bold electric blue comic sans font to display a more fun loving character, another user may use a deep green font to express love for the Prophet as symbolized by the Green dome of his mosque in Medina. Others may end all posts with an emoticon shaped like a rose. Signature lines also contribute to posters online identities and these included verses of the Qur'an, poetry excerpts and slogans.

These visual and narrative signifiers are meaningful to those who use them and also those who perceive them and were usually vested with Sufi meaning. A few examples of signature taglines include: 'From Darkness to Light' and 'Light upon light that perhaps signify the journey that all Sufis must make as their *nafs* (self) travels towards higher levels of spiritual clarity. Another user called herself 'A Bird in Medina' portraying her deep love for Prophet Muhammad and the city she loved. A user's style became a label through which he or she was recognized even before the material s/he posted was read by other users. One user for his signature quoted a sentence supposedly from the jurist Imam Shafi which again illustrates this young person's deep desire for knowledge and sincerity in the pursuit of knowledge:

> All humans are dead except those who have knowledge; And all those who have knowledge are asleep, except those who do good deeds; And those who do good deeds are deceived, except those who are sincere; And those who are sincere are always in a state of worry.

Forum users also gradually adopted, developed and sustained 'character traits' that extend beyond visual and narrative signifiers. Some are known to be kind and compassionate and in case of debates and online arguments, it was not unusual for regular forum users to await advice and inputs from these more compassionate users. Others are 'angry young men and women' who had snappy and revolutionary answers that challenged the authority online and offline. On the forums, there were users who were recognized as 'jokers', 'poets', 'scholars' and 'philosophers'. There were also troublemakers and critical friends. A few users assume the role of 'patriarch' offering advice and solace to the 'younger ones'. It is significant that in order to sustain their assumed roles, the visual, lingual and other signifiers had to be larger than life. These exaggerations seemed to compensate for the lack of multi-dimensional *real* conversations that are not possible in these virtual discussions. Strong bonds are evident across forum users and relationships occasionally extend into the real world. Users often admit that the website is their 'online family' which they visited regularly, often many times in a day. The website became an exaggerated mirror of real-world social networks – a social community and online family.

The discussions – three case studies

In order to facilitate narrative analysis, three specific case studies are explored in which users discussed specific areas of their Sufi practice and understanding. Two of the case studies include in-depth discussion about specific subject areas and in one case also includes elements of Western philosophical thinking. The third case study looks at mechanisms on the website to include participation of female users.

Case study 1: Discussion topic – logic or love?

In this discussion, participants debated the relationship between logical thinking and faith. The participant who initiated the discussion wondered whether this was the difference between Sufi practice and *Wahhabi* practice which was perhaps more 'logically derived' because of its literary approach to interpreting Islamic foundational texts and also in its rejection of the more esoteric practices of Islam. While the conversation was perhaps initially aimed at critiquing *Wahhabi* practice, it quite quickly moved into a more philosophical discussion about the possibility to rationally and logically arrive at a religious standpoint of deep belief in God and then sustain this belief. Some participants contrasted a logical approach to God with an approach that focussed on love. As one participant asked – 'Does love for God and the Prophet (pbuh) supersede logic?'

As participants progressed through the discussion, they began to develop and at the same time deconstruct their own conceptual understandings of the term 'love' in the contexts of religious and more specifically Sufi discourse. What did love mean? Was it a universal theme or is love based on self evolution and therefore experienced differently from individual to individual? One discussant offered the opinion that the only route to love was *adab* (respect) and that this *adab* needed to be for God, Prophet Muhammad and also for knowledge. Therefore, in order to achieve love for God, one needed knowledge of God and to achieve this knowledge one needed to respect the processes of knowledge which also included logic and rationality. For this user, love and logic were somewhat interconnected and inseparable. However in contrast, another user wondered, 'Does sentiment and emotionality falsify knowledge?'. Towards the end of the discussion thread, participants concluded that perhaps faith evolved from both logic and love and this relationship between faith, logic and love varied according to individuals' contexts.

Case study 2: Discussion topic – religion and God

This discussion thread, which was initiated by a female user, refers to Friedrich Nietzsche's idea of a 'dead' God. She wondered whether it was perhaps formal and structured religion that was dying and that God was becoming perhaps more personalized and internalized to individuals and their lives. Religious people, she felt, were often hypocritical and self-contradictory. She felt perhaps there was a need in current contexts for an intellectual separation between God and religion, replacing religion with simple morality. Another participant agreed with her that the problem was the structure in religion which 'degenerates [religion] to a mere set of rules and mathematical calculations for good and evil'.

Other participants disagreed and felt that structured religion was important and gave meaning to peoples' relationship with God – how would human beings know God if it was not for religion? Not many users participated in this discussion perhaps because it entered difficult and abstruse waters, which even for an online discussion was too complicated. Perhaps this discussion which questioned and debated the nature and existence of God was perceived as a step too far away from structured religious concepts of God, which even in the 'safe' and 'liberal' world of the internet could take discussants away from their comfort zones. As the conversation began to draw to a conclusion, participants discussed Islamic understandings of a transcendent all-seeing, all-knowing God. Finally a participant suggested that it is possible to know God both from within and outside formal religion. And that whether or not God is known because of religion, understandings of his transcendence impacts on moral values and behaviours – 'our knowledge of God no matter where it comes from shapes our personalities, who we are and who we become'. This was a matter for much more contemplation, however what participants agreed on was that in the process of knowing God, there was no place for religious arrogance – anybody can know God and be impacted by God's mercy. For these Sufi users, faith is about choice, humility, difference of opinion and freedom of expression.

Case study 3: Women's discussions

The forum, like many Islamic sites (both online and offline), had a discussion area that was especially for women and where men were not allowed to participate. Access to this section was regulated by the forum moderators. As a female, I was privileged to have access to this area and in order to protect women's privacy, my analysis in this case study, as in the other two, will be completely anonymised. Women and girls spoke about faith and its relevance to every day life. Discussions ranged from recipes for Ramadan, poetry sharing and general chit-chat. I spoke to women about my work and plans for this paper. I asked about woman and knowledge – Do they agree with French feminist philosopher Michèle Le Doeuff that women have been sidelined from the processes of knowledge?[15] Female users agreed that there were cultural issues in many Muslim communities that prevented women from acquiring and disseminating knowledge. However, they also said that they did not like feminism and felt that it lacked in *adab* or respect that was an essential aspect of their Sufi practice.

I also asked about Sufism and what I should include in a paper about young Muslims' opinions and concerns. Women presented their understandings of Sufism which ranged from 'I am here to learn more about my faith' to 'it is about practising Islam both from the inside and from the outside'. These definitions are discussed more in detail along with others in the following section. These women also said that they were concerned about misconceptions about Sufism in Muslim and non-Muslim communities. 'Too much focus on mysticism' meant that the Islamic basis of Sufi practice was often neither spoken enough about nor understood. For some women, this mean that the essence of Sufism was being lost and that this was also opening the door for *Wahhabi/Salafi* criticisms of Sufism.

Young people's Online Sufism

Sufism was a key aspect of these young people's identities and was constructed in different ways. First, there was these young people's inherent Sufi belief, which in the case of some forum users was neither fully articulated nor formed, but which nevertheless was recognized by these young people as an underpinning aspect of their faith and religious practice. These young people were Sufis without knowing or practising the deep reflective practices that are characteristic of Sufism. They came online to find a safe space where they could 'learn' and 'ask questions' without the fear of being 'converted to' non-Sufi Muslim stances.

For these young people, Sufism was also constructed by their criticisms of Islamic practices and interpretations that were perceived as too literary or dogmatic. The latter often being associated with Saudi inspired *Wahhabi* or *Salafi* Islam. In many cases, Islam as practiced by the *Deobandis* was also included in these criticisms of Muslim practice that focussed on outwardly appearance rather than inward purity. Forum users did not seem to be aware of the Sufi traditions within *Deobandi* practice. Furthermore, since the forum was open-access, and users from *Deobandi*, *Wahabbi* and *Salafi* traditions were able to join the forum and participate in discussions, it was possible for users to engage in debates with people who held viewpoints other than their own. As users defended their specific belief practices from criticism, such debates often become tense.

Other online Sufis were more 'knowledgeable' and were able to articulate their awareness through poetry and prose, sometimes their own and on other occasions through quotations and commentaries on the work of scholars, philosophers and Sufi saints including historical figures such as Ghazali (1058–1111), Ibn Arabi (1165–1240), Rumi (1207–1273) and the Indian Saint Moinuddin Chishti (1141–1230) and more modern figures such as Abdul Hakim Murad (Tim Winter), Muhammad Al-Ninowy and the American Sufi scholar Hamza Yusuf. They had reasonably mature understandings of Sufism that they often stated they had developed for themselves including a few who had learnt about Sufism only after joining the site.

These more *aware* young Sufis had diverse understandings of the meaning of Sufism and had a different focii for their Sufi practice. So, for example, this online Sufi sought to situate his Sufi thought and practice in the teachings of the Turkish Sufi saint Mevlana Rumi. The inclusivity within Sufism towards all of humanity and positioning it as a basic necessity for human well-being was extremely important to this young person

> Sufism is the exercise/practice of the soul, like *shariah/fiqh* is the exercise of our physical body. The essence of Sufism is to search for the roots of a man, which essentially is to believe in God, love God and worship God. Because it is a subject that applies to all humanity, all are welcome, like how Imam Rumi (*rahimullah*) says: come, come whoever you are!

Others rooted their Sufism more strongly in Islamic theology. For these Sufis, their faith practice was a natural extension of divine doctrine as clarified in the

Qur'an and as practised by Prophet Muhammad and recorded in the *Hadith*. *Fiqh* (Islamic Jurisprudence), *Shariah* (Islamic Law) and *Sunnah* (Prophetic example) were consolidated into their Sufi epistemologies. Sufism became an inner struggle or *jihad* to purify oneself and one's Islamic practice:

> Sufism for me is medicine for the heart. Just like *shariah* is needed for the brain so is Sufism. It commences from love and ends in love. It's the daily struggle of your own *jihad* and controlling of the *nafs*.

Conclusions

This exploration of the discussions on this Online Sufism website led to greater clarity of the balances between secularism and religious belief that young Muslims, particularly in the West, have to navigate. In some cases, the discussions simply mirrored offline communities and led to new hypertextual articulations of Islam.[16] This was particularly evident in young peoples' prayer requests around exam time or when someone was ill – which was similar to prayer requests being sent to extended family or being announced in mosques after prayer congregations.

In other cases, discussions were transformational. The young people engaging in such discussions seemed equipped with the appropriate tools: knowledge – both Islamic and Western secular, the ability to reflect, to be self-critical and finally with an openness that allowed them to free their minds – perhaps the ultimate Sufi aspiration? It must also be noted that although not all users were equipped with these tools, these discussions were open-access and most users read these conversations which perhaps may allow them to gradually learn these tools – as was evidenced in some young people's narrations about having known and learnt Sufism only after visiting the website. Clearly, at least with regard to discussions such as those about the nature and existence of God, these forums gave users an opportunity to engage in self-critical philosophical discussions that they may not have the space to have elsewhere. As these young people carry their virtual reality discussions into their real lives, they may be able to engender transformational social change in practice and perceptions of Sufism and Islam.

To conclude I quote Arberry

> The wheel now appears to have turned a full circle. Sufism has run its course; and in the progress of human thought it is illusory to imagine that there can ever

be a return to the point of departure. A new journey lies ahead for humanity to travel.[17]

These young people have indeed initiated a new journey. Rather than let it run its course, these young people have reclaimed and revitalized Sufism. While retaining the mysticism, philosophical roots and theological underpinnings of Sufism, they are also bringing it up-to-date with technology, thereby facilitating its continued relevance to their changed social contexts. Although online relationships and communities may never fully replace real world ones, using the tools of the internet and their own wisdom, common sense and indeed their naivety and curiosity, these online Sufis have reclaimed for themselves both Sufi practice, wisdoms and community, rooting these firmly in the Islamic faith and in (this case) their Western social contexts. And within these online communities are spaces where the transformative potential of Sufism continues to endure in the hearts and minds of the young people who inhabit them. God is their destination, humanity their route and when asked what is Sufism, this young Sufi concludes

> [It is to]attain ultimate truth [. . .] concentrated focus on the fountainhead of all creation, God [. . .] kinship with all humanity.

Notes

1   T. Burckhardt (1995) *Introduction to Sufism*. London: Thorsons.

2   I. Shah (1980) *The Way of the Sufi*. London: Octagon Press.

3   Also F. Haeri (1990) *The Elements of Sufism*. Dorset: Element Books.

4   P. Werbner and H. Basu (Eds) (1998) 'Introduction' in *Embodying Charisma: Modernity, Locality and the Performance of Emotion in Sufi Cults*. London and New York: Routledge.

5   M. Lings (1975) *What is Sufism?* London: George Allen and Unwin Ltd.

6   F. Haeri (1990) *The Elements of Sufism*. Dorset: Element Books.

7   S. Contractor (2010) *De-mystifying the Muslimah: Exploring Selected Perceptions of Young Muslim Women in Britain*. PhD Thesis, University of Gloucestershire; S. Contractor (2012) *Muslim Women in Britain: De-mystifying the Muslimah*. London and New York: Routledge.

8   R. Rao (1968) *Gandhi and Pragmatism – An Intercultural Study*. Bombay: Oxford and IBH Publishing.

9   Examples of research that explored the online or digital practice of various religions
    or online religious communities include G. Bunt (2003) *Islam in the Digital Age:
    E-Jihad, Online Fatwas and Cyber Islamic Environments*. London: Pluto Press;
    G. Bunt (2004) 'Rip.Burn.Pray'.: Islamic Expression Online in *Religion Online:
    Finding Daith on the Internet*. L. Dawson and D. Cowan (Eds), London and
    New York: Routledge, pp. 123–34; G. Bunt (2009) *iMuslims: Rewiring the House
    of Islam*. Chapel Hill: The University of North Carolina Press; A. Piela (2011)
    Muslim Women Online: Faith and Identity in Virtual World. London: Routledge;
    L. Cantonia and S. Zygab (2007) 'The Use of Internet Communication by Catholic
    Congregations: A Quantitative Study', *Journal of Media and Religion*, 6, 4, pp. 291–
    309; and A. Ostrowski (2006) 'Texting Tolerance: Computer-Mediated Interfaith
    Dialogue', *Webology*, 3, 4 http://webology.org/2006/v3n4/a34.html (retrieved
    February 12, 2012).

10   M. El-Nawawy and S. Khamis (2009) *Islam Dot Com: Contemporary Islamic
    Discourses in Cyberspace*. New York: Palgrave Macmillan, p. 3.

11   G. Bunt (2009) *iMuslims: Rewiring the House of Islam*. Chapel Hill: The University
    of North Carolina Press.

12   M. El-Nawawy and S. Khamis (2009) *Islam Dot Com: Contemporary Islamic
    Discourses in Cyberspace*. New York: Palgrave Macmillan, p. viii.

13   G. Bunt (2009) *iMuslims: Rewiring the House of Islam*. Chapel Hill: The University
    of North Carolina Press, p. 119.

14   M. El-Nawawy and S. Khamis (2009) *Islam Dot Com: Contemporary Islamic
    Discourses in Cyberspace*. New York: Palgrave Macmillan, p. 53 and p. viii.

15   M. Le Doeuff (1998). *The Sex of Knowing* (trans. K. Hammer and L. Code (2003).
    London: Routledge.

16   G. Bunt (2004) 'Rip.Burn.Pray'.: Islamic Expression Online in *Religion Online:
    Finding Faith on the Internet*. L. Dawson and D. Cowan (Eds), London and
    New York: Routledge, pp. 123–134, p. 123.

17   A. Arberry (1979) *Sufism: An Account of the Mystics of Islam*. London: Unwin,
    p. 134.

9

The Rise of the 'Traditional Islam' Network(s): Neo-Sufism and British Muslim Youth

Sadek Hamid

Introduction

The popularity of Islamist and Salafi religious perspectives among second-generation British Muslims grew in part, as a protest to the conservative, quietest faith traditions dominant in South Asian Muslim communities. The Barelwi Sufi tradition in particular was in danger of being abandoned by younger Muslims for deculturalized, scripturalist approaches to Islam.[1] In the middle of the 1990s, a small network of influential Western Sufi figures led by American convert scholars-Hamza Yusuf, Nuh Ha-Mim Keller and British academic Abdal Hakim Murad, responded to Salafi polemics against Sufism by tackling their doctrinal critiques head-on, using the same primary textual sources to defend their interpretations and appropriating their organizational techniques. An intellectual demanding, activist form of 'sober Sufism', they provided a counter response to anti-Sufi discourses among existing hegemonic revivalist narratives. This chapter highlights the main features of the 'Traditional Islam' scene, how it differs from existing ethnic/transnational Sufi orders, provides a narrative of how it became established in the United Kingdom, outlines its main ideas, characteristics, profiles some of its leading proponents and concludes by explaining why its message resonated among some young British Muslims.

The mid-1990s proved to be the turning point in the fortunes of Sufism among younger Muslims in Britain due to the influential interventions of groups of convert scholars and the shifting dynamic among rival Islamic trends. As indicated earlier, established Sufi *tariqa*s (orders) had a limited appeal to the second generation who saw them as folkloric legacy of their parent's generation.

In particular, the inability of older traditional South Asian Muslim communities to respond to the needs of young British Muslims, deeply entrenched sectarian divisions and the inadequacies of reformist and Salafi trends left a gap for a new form of Sufism. This vacuum came to be occupied by what is called the Traditional Islam (TI) network. Several inter-related characteristics connect TI activists in Britain. These ideas could be condensed to seven themes; the promotion of classical theology, *tassawuf* (Sufism), adherence to one *madhab-* of the four schools of Sunni law, transmission-based scholarship, traditional teaching pedagogies, implicit critiques of Salafi and Islamist interpretations of Islam and active social engagement. The emphasis on social engagement is the defining feature of this trend as this is the main feature that distinguishes it from followers of established Sufi tariqas. Individuals associated with the TI scene are more likely to be interested in current affairs and involved in activities that are aimed at inviting others to Islam. It is an increasingly popular current among young British Muslims, demonstrated by a growing infrastructure of educational centres, publishing houses, magazines, journals, websites, businesses, charities, campaigning groups, self-help groups and specialists in art, poetry, photography, music, theatre and even stand-up comedy. Within this unity of purpose is a wide diversity of backgrounds, nationalities, ethnicities and levels of scholarly authority, priorities and methods of engagement with other Muslim and non-Muslim groups. This neo-Sufism also distinguishes itself from the more well-known Sufi currents by the way it engages with the experiences and challenges facing Western Muslims. Its emergence and growth reflect a transnational coalescence of peoples and institutions, friendships and networks, virtual and real spaces, scholars and students that agree on a consensus of priorities rather a single formal organizational entity, hence 'ethnicity is transcended to discover common cause in either a universal consciousness of *umma* or the ideological belonging to the '*Ahl as-Sunna wa Jama'at*'[2] Surveying this new Sufi trend in Britain, Geaves notes that

> They are not exponents of folk tradition or the Islam of local traditions but they are often fluent in their understanding and use of *fiqh*. The new Sufis are as scriptural as their old adversaries, able to utilise Qur'an and Hadith to great effect to put across their message on the issues that matter to them.[3]

It can be argued that the Sufism of South Asian elders in the tariqas compared to this new transglobal current is isolationist and often territorial 'in their respective spiritual fiefdoms of Coventry, Birmingham, Bradford or Manchester and have no time for defending hereditary lineages descended from long deceased *awliya* (friends of God)'.[4] The establishment of this trend was catalysed by the private and public work of a group of individuals whose efforts converged in the year 1995. The interventions of three people in particular, initially helped to publicly define the TI scene-American convert scholars Nuh Keller and Hamza Yusuf and British academic Abdal Hakim Murad. Within the United Kingdom, Fuad Nahdi, Ibrahim Osi-Efa, Masud Khan and Aftab Malik were critical in articulating and promoting TI perspectives. In America, Imam Zaid Shakir and Dr. Umar Faruq Abd-Allah are important figures, while Nazim Baksh, Faraz Rabbani and Abdur Rehman Malik were pioneers in Canada. The TI network was also linked early on to some of the most well-known Sunni scholars in the Muslim world such as Dr Sayyid Ramadan al-Buti, Shaykh Muhammad al Yacubi, Shaykh Muhammad an-Ninowy from Syria, Habib Ali-Jifri, Yemen and significantly, Shaykh Abdullah bin Bayyah of Saudi Arabia.

This trend has developed to a point where it has acquired a distinct aesthetic branding and vocabulary. Today the TI scene is populated with dozens of young shaykhs and *ustadhs* (teachers), many of whom are converts. This has led to the development of institutes and centres that hold regular study circles, courses, seminars teaching 'sacred knowledge' in many British cities and towns with significant Muslim populations. Notable among these educational initiatives are the Ibn Abbas Institute and Greensville Trust both in Liverpool, Abu Zahra Trust in Keighly, Shifa Trust in Oxford, Sacred Knowledge Trust in Dewsbury, Habiba Institute in London, Zaytuna Institute and Nawawi Foundation, Ihya Foundation in America, Darul Mustafa, Yemen, Tabah Foundation in Abu Dhabi, and Qasid Institute in Jordan.[5] Magazines promoting TI perspectives include the now defunct *Q-News* and *Islamica*, Seasons and *Illume* journals. The most prolific publishers include Amal Press, Islamic Texts Society, StarLatch Press Wakeel Books and White Thread press and Alhambra Productions.[6] Prominent internet sites include Deenport.com and Masud.co.uk, Sunni Path, Seekers Path, Zhikr.org, Shadilli Teachings.org and Lamppost Productions.[7] Interestingly, these sites tend not to emphasize their sympathy towards Sufism, but instead prefer to claim that they represent traditional Islamic teachings within the parameters of classical orthodoxy. Leading websites such as Deenport are strikingly modern, English language based and combine concerns about the importance of classical Islamic knowledge, spirituality, current affairs and has an active eclectic discussion forum that discusses everything from fatwas to football.[8] Masud Khan's personal website is one the first and richest information points for TI internationally.[9] It contains articles by Abdal Hakim Murad, Nuh Ha Mim Keller, a section on British Muslim Heritage, audio lectures and links to other TI-oriented sites. The Sunni Path website uses cutting edge technology to advertise 'several subject areas such as basic and advanced Arabic language, foundational Islamic sciences and advanced-level Islamic sciences.(. . .) distance courses utilize unique online learning tools, and combine both ancient and modern methods of teaching'.[10] Another popular site, Seeker's Digest, was set up by young Canadian-Pakistani scholar, Faraz Rabanni, and contains opportunties to ask questions on Islamic law and browse articles that address contemporay Muslim concerns which 'function as pedagogical material for young supporters of *tasawwuf* and recruitment devices for the uncommitted'.[11] After examining these sites, one notices the enduring influence of three individual scholars.

'Western Muslim Shaykhs'

Nuh Ha-Mim Keller became a Muslim in 1977, while living in Egypt and since the mid-1990s, has gained a significant number of followers both in the United Kingdom and United States. A philosophy graduate of University of Chicago and the University of California, his journey to Islam began in 1975 after he started to study classical Arabic at Chicago. He then began a prolonged study of the Islamic sciences with prominent scholars in Jordan and Syria. He joined the Shadilli tariqa in 1982 and achieved scholarly seniority and title of Sheikh in 1996.[12] He is best known for his English translation of the classic Shafi manual of jurisprudence *Umdat al-Salik* (The *Reliance of The Traveller*), the first legal work to be endorsed by Al-Azhar University and has also translated *Nawawi's Manual of Islam* and written *Port in a Storm: A Fiqh Solution to the Qibla of North America, Sufism in Islam, The Sunni Path: A Handbook of Islamic Belief, Tariqa Notes* and most recently *Sea Without Shore: A Manual of the Sufi Path*. He was introduced to the UK speaker circuit by Masud Khan in January 1995. His lecture series delivered in London, Birmingham and Nottingham faced a hostile reception from members of the Salafi organization JIMAS, as they followed him around on his tour. The lectures gained wider circulation through publication later that year in *Q-News* magazine. His speeches, entitled *The Concept of Bidah in the Islamic Sharia, Why Muslims follow Madhabs, Literalism and the Attributes of Allah and the Place of Tassawuf in the Traditional Islamic sciences*, became instrumental in foregrounding TI perspectives to British Muslims.[13] What was new about Keller's articles was the deep but accessible scholarship, explored the lighting rod issues among British Muslim activists – theological orthodoxy, normative Prophetic practice and the status of Sufism in Islam. His choice of topics were a deliberate attempt to address contentious issues that were being used by Salafis to define the boundaries of what constituted orthodoxy and could be interpreted as some of the first warning shots of the Sufi fight back against Salafi and Islamist discourses. Over time he has established himself as a popular scholarly reference point for many TI adherents and attracting murids from the United Kingdom, the USA and Middle East. Currently, based in Amman, Jordan, he regularly hosts a large annual *Subha* (spiritual retreat) and frequently returns to Britain for speaking engagements. Nuh Keller's low key, modest public intervention in the mid-1990s can be contrasted with the arrival and emergence of firebrand preacher Hamza Yusuf.

An associate of Keller, Yusuf also converted in 1977 and then spent many years studying the Arabic language and Islamic law in UAE, Algeria and Mauritania. He is a passionate advocate of classical Islamic teaching methodologies, co-founder of the Zaytuna Institute and translator of classical texts such as *The Burda of Al-Busiri* (2002) *Purification of the Heart: Symptoms and Cures of the Spiritual Diseases of the Heart* (2004) and *The Creed of Imam al-Tahawi* (2007). He has become recognized as one of the most influential Muslims in the Western world and is feted by influential organizations and governments.[14] He became famous in the mid-1990s among Muslim communities in Britain and America for being a powerful orator with flawless Arabic, deep Islamic learning and ability to pepper his speeches with references from philosophy, history, science and popular culture. A telegenic figure, often seen wearing traditional Muslim garb, he almost single handedly altered the content of Islamic discourses in British activist circles by popularizing interest in the acquisition of classical Arabic, Islamic learning methodologies and the importance of spirituality. Interestingly, his first public lecture in the United Kingdom was at a large conference organized by the Islamist, Islamic Forum of Europe in London, August 1995. His defining lecture on the signs preceding the appearance of the anti-Christ- *Dajjal and The New World Order*, catapulted him into the Muslim public imagination and made him a favourite among consumers of Islamic audio and video cassettes. Soon his other lectures such as *Education of a Muslim Child* and *Secularism: The Greatest Danger of our Times,* established his profile.[15] He also appealed to young British Muslims because of his status as a convert who had spent most of his early adult life travelling through the Muslim world to seek Islamic knowledge. Though he did not explicitly advocate Sufism, his public talks reiterated the importance of spirituality and linked learning with action, which was a breath of fresh air to many in the activist scene who had grown disillusioned with the narrow rhetoric of existing Islamist and Salafi speakers and struck a chord with those who felt existing Islamic trends lacked a connection to the sacred. Tellingly, people from across the spectrum of rival tendencies started to become drawn to his lectures, and he was soon invited by most of the leading Islamic organizations in the United Kingdom. Hamza Yusuf was initially the most visible figure within this network and helped to pave the way for other TI figures to take a more public role such as his friend, Abdal Hakim Murad.

Abdal Hakim Murad (aka, Tim Winter), is best known as a translator of two volumes of the great Sufi scholar al-Ghazali's *Ihya Ulum al-Din* and as a regular public commentator on British Muslim affairs. A global survey by the Royal Islamic Strategic Studies Centre in 2010, named Murad as the most influential Muslim in Britain and is currently Shaykh Zayed Lecturer in Islamic Studies at the University of Cambridge. After accepting Islam, interestingly, also in 1977, Murad began his studies in Arabic at Cambridge University and graduated in 1983. This was followed by three years in Al-Azhar University and further private study with individual scholars in Saudi Arabia and Yemen. He first started to become known in the mid-1990s through his regular articles in *Q-News*, which were renowned for both erudition and frequently polemical tone towards Salafis and Islamists. Some of his most famous articles include *Islamic Spirituality: the Forgotten Revolution, Understanding the Four Madhabs* and *Recapturing Islam from the Terrorists,* which helped to establish his position as a leading English Muslim scholar.[16] A formidable critic, he pulled no punches in arguing what he saw as the corrosive effect of Saudi-funded Salafism and held the doctrinal excesses of Wahabbi thought responsible for Al-Qaeda terrorism. Winter has been a consistent critique of Salafi and Islamists discourse since his articles started appearing in *Q-News* and also singled out ideologues from the Muslim Brotherhood and the Jaamaat-i-Islami for hyper politicizing Islam and emptying it of its transcendent message. His counter narratives suggested a return to medieval theological Islamic consensus, buttressed by madhab allegiance and active practice of Sufism, and found expression in a short book entitled *Understanding the Four Madhabs.* His prolific writings and engagement with the mainstream media and government have made him an important voice that commands respect among educated Muslims across the United Kingdom and abroad. The combined output effect of these three figures altered the terms of reference in activist circles and introduced a whole new discourse in issues that until then had not been addressed by existing Islamic organizations. In effect, they had re-established Sufism as a legitimate and necessary part of mainstream Islam and inspired young people to deepen their knowledge of tradition. As Geaves observed

Such figures are able to articulate the narratives of *tassawuf* and traditional Islamic sciences in an intellectual environment, addressing both Muslims and non-Muslims, able to communicate fluently in English and are sometimes members of academia themselves. They by-pass the world of the mosque and do not demonstrate their loyalty to *tariqa* and *shaykh* even when they are themselves *murids* but nevertheless Sufism influences their world view.[17]

However, these scholars were only able to enter the public consciousness by utilizing an existing activist infrastructure. Until they created their own, they worked with the main Islamist organizational networks such as the Islamic Forum of Europe Young Muslims UK (YM), Islamic Society of Britain and others within the activist scene.[18]

Building the foundations

Before the leading figures of the network became known to the wider British Muslim communities, a number of individuals had quietly built its foundations. People such as journalist and former publisher of *Q-News* magazine, Fuad Nahdi also believes that TI is normative Islam, and tried to promote this by co-founding the Quilliam Press publishing house in 1989.[19] One of the other most important people behind the scenes in the 1990s was Liverpool-based Ibrahim Osi-Efa, founder of several Islamic initiatives including the Ibn Abbas Institute, Badr Language Institute, Greensville Trust, and co-founder of StarLatch Press. Of Nigerian Muslim heritage, Osi-Efa initially became a Black activist in his teens in the early 1980s.[20] Identifying with the African-American racial pride movement, his interest in Malcolm X eventually led him to rediscover the religious dimension of his identity. Between 1991 and 1992, he became interested in Islamic approaches to social activism and started to attend the activities of the local Young Muslims UK branch. At first, he was attracted by their religious education work and political activism but soon became dissatisfied with what he considered their watered down, superficial teachings. He started searching elsewhere for more spirituality and realism and then encountered the JIMAS organization. After spending time with them and getting to know their senior leadership, he found them to also lack spirituality and Islamic manners. At this point, he sought advice from the influential African-American Muslim preacher, Imam Siraj Wahhaj, who was frequently invited by YM to the UK at the time. Wahhaj encouraged Osi-Efa to 'do his own thing' and encouraged to him to initiate a number of actions that would be instrumental in laying the ground work for the TI network in the UK. First, he set up Al-Muslimoon organization in 1992, which was envisioned as a holistic organization that would provide Islamic, Arabic, health and martial arts education and training. This later became known as the Ibn Abbas Institute for Human Development. By 1994, Osi-Efa felt that he had reached the limit of his own capacity to educate people in the Islamic studies. Realizing that the command of Arabic was the key to furthering his own development, he initially travelled to Sudan for a few months. Upon returning, he organized two month long Arabic classes in liaison with Dr Mawil Izziden, who at the time was working with L'Institut Europeen des Sciences Humaines, in Chateau Chinon Saint, France and John Moores University in Liverpool. It was during this period that he was introduced to Hamza Yusuf, whom he then invited to Britain to teach for month in Liverpool. This was also around the time Hamza Yusuf's profile was increasing in the United Statea, particularly after his lectures at the annual Islamic Society of North America (ISNA) conference. Osi-Efa felt that people in the United Kingdom could benefit from Yusuf, and arranged for him to speak at the Islamic Forum of Europe event of August 1995. After this, Osi-Efa and Masud Khan discussed the possibility of organizing a regular study programme that would provide an introduction to the Islamic sciences and help introduce other TI scholars to the UK scene.

This decision led to the creation of three signature TI education programmes – The 'Light Study' programmes, 'Deen Intensives' and 'Rihla' courses.[21] Each was intended to be progressively deeper introduction to the Islamic sciences. These Light Study programmes usually lasted one day and provided an introduction into a particular topic or text by an instructor. The three day Deen Intensives were held over a weekend and were designed to reconnect participants with the Islamic intellectual heritage and provide an introductory knowledge of the major disciplines. Committed participants could then enrol on the summer month long Rihla knowledge retreats, which were an opportunity for a longer immersion in Islamic studies, worship and historical visits, created to provide an intense intellectual and spiritually transformative experience. Osi-Efa then also became active on the other side of the Atlantic by developing networks with other like-minded American Muslim activists such as Imam Zaid Shakir, Dawud Fricke and Jihad Totten. Zaid Shakir, along with Hamza Yusuf, became the key components of the emerging transatlantic TI network. Shakir is also a very popular figure within the TI network and is regarded as one of the most influential Muslims in America.[22] He also converted to Islam in 1977, while serving as member of American Air Force. A former Lecturer in International

Relations and Arabic at Southern Connecticut State University, he has translated a number of classical texts such as *Heirs of the Prophets, Treatise for the Seekers of Guidance* and authored *Scattered Pictures: Reflections of an American Muslim.* Shakir was encouraged by Osi-Efa to pursue higher Islamic studies in Syria, which he did and spent a total of seven years there and is the first American graduate of Abu Noor University.

Continuing his own personal quest for knowledge, Osi-Efa went on to study for three years in Syria and Mauritania and a further six years in Yemen, while in between helping to develop the growing demand for Deen Intensive and Light Study programmes in the United Kingdom. The first Rihla programme in Britain was held in September 1996 in Nottingham, this was followed by others hosted in Morocco, Spain and Saudi Arabia. The year 1999 proved to be another landmark for the establishment of the TI network in the United Kingdom with the Rihla, that year hosted at the Islamic Foundation, Leicester. Its historic importance is due to the strategic planning meeting attended by all the senior figures of the TI scene at the time. Ibrahim Osi-Efa describes it as a 'Pow wow', a Native American word meaning spiritual gathering. This is an apt term to describe the intent of this gathering as it sought to bring together different perspectives and ideas in the emerging international TI network. Crucially in attendance was Dr. Umar Faruq Abd-Allah, a prominent figure from the United States, who authored the first biography of late nineteenth century American convert Alexander Russell Webb and is Resident Scholar at An-Nawawi Foundation in Chicago.[23] In the Leicester meeting, Abd-Allah gave a seminal paper outlining a vision for (traditional) Islam in the West, which was intended to galvanise a broad consensus of priorities, projects and reinforcing of relationships. Among other issues discussed were the differences of opinion on what constituted TI, for example, Nuh Ha-Mim Keller was quite adamant that adherents should choose to align themselves with an established tariqa, while Hamza Yusuf insisted that it was not necessary and should be optional personal choice. An important outcome of the meeting was the commitment to a 'pact of non-aggression' among the different TI personalities and agreeing to revive 'the tradition of tolerance for diversity that has been the strength of the Islamic legacy'. The scholars present declared that they would 'refrain from attacking, slandering or backbiting fellow Muslims even if their opinions differed.' In the end, all the participants concurred that TI perspectives should reflect a distinctive set of conceptual themes: adherence to a minimum set of normative theological beliefs, practices and pedagogical methods that define their outlook. Also adherence to classical orthodoxy, tassawuf (purification), following a madhhab, *adab*-the etiquette of learning and the *Isnad* & *Ijaza* paradigm.

Classical Orthodoxy

Sunni Muslim normative theological consensus established over the centuries is contained in a coherent body of credal and legal positions. This theological orthodoxy is represented by the acceptance of the Asharite and Maturidi *aqeeda(creed)*, the four main schools of jurisprudence. This understanding relies on the accumulated wisdom of the great classical scholars such as al-Nawawi (1234–78), al-Ghazali (1058–1111), Ibn Qadi Abu Bakr b. al-Arabi (1076–1148), Hajr al Asqalani (1372–1448), Imam al-Dhahabi, (1274–1348) and Ibn al-Qayyum al-Jawzi (1292–1350) among others. TI scholars, such as Nuh Ha-Mim Keller, attempt to demonstrate the organic link between orthodoxy and Sufism by employing textual proofs, analogous reasoning and lists famous orthodox Muslim scholars to validate this approach, to quote at length:

> From Umayyad times to Abbasid, to Mamluke, to the end of the six-hundred-year Ottoman period – Sufism has been taught and understood as an Islamic discipline, like Qur'anic exegesis (*tafsir*), hadith, Qur'an recital (*tajwid*), tenets of faith (*ilm al-tawhid*) or any other, each of which preserved some particular aspect of the *din* or religion of Islam (. . .) Similarly *ilm al-tasawwuf*, "the science of Sufism" came into being to preserve and transmit a particular aspect of the *shari'a*, that of *ikhlas* or sincerity (. . .) To illustrate this point, we may note that the Prophet (Allah bless him and give him peace) never in his life prayed in a mosque built of reinforced concrete, with a carpeted floor, glass windows, and so on, yet these are not considered bid'a, because we Muslims have been commanded to come together in mosques to perform the prayer, and large new buildings for this are merely a means to carry out the command (. . .) we find that so many of the Islamic scholars to whom Allah gave *tawfiq* or success in their work were Sufis. Indeed, to throw away every traditional work of the Islamic sciences authored by those educated by Sufis would be to discard 75 percent or more of the books of Islam. These men included such scholars as the Hanafi Imam Muhammad Amin Ibn Abidin, Sheikh al-Islam Zakaria al-Ansari, Imam Ibn Daqiq al-Eid, Imam al-Izz Ibn Abd al-Salam, Abd al-Ghani al-Nabulsi, Sheikh Ahmad al-Sirhindi, Sheikh Ibrahim al-Bajuri, Imam al-Ghazali, Shah Wali Allah al-Dahlawi, and Imam al-Nawawi.[24]

The recurring emphasis on the connection between the producers of orthodox theology and Sufism is not only intended to educate but also acts as a challenge to Salafi and Islamists keen to erase this historical narrative.

Essentialness of Sufism

The necessity and normalcy of the practice of Sufism enables adherents of TI perspectives to claim a continuity and legitimacy. Quoting Nuh Ha-Mim Keller again from his well-known article *The Place of Tasawwuf in Traditional Islamic Sciences*, one can see his defence in relation to the controversy associated with Sufism:

> It is often forgotten that the 'ulama who have criticized Sufis, such as Ibn al-Jawzi in his *Talbis Iblis* [The Devil's deception], or Ibn Taymiya in places in his *Fatawa*, or Ibn al-Qayyim al-Jawziyya, were not criticizing Tasawwuf as an ancillary discipline to the Shari'a. (. . .) Ibn Taymiya considered himself a Sufi of the Qadiri order, and volumes ten and eleven of his thirty-seven-volume *Majmu' al-fatawa* are devoted to Tasawwuf. And Ibn al-Qayyim al-Jawziyya wrote his three-volume *Madarij al-salikin*, a detailed commentary on 'Abdullah al-Ansari al-Harawi's tract on the spiritual stations of the Sufi path, *Manazil al-sa'irin*. These works show that their authors' criticisms were not directed at Tasawwuf as such, but rather at specific groups of their times, and they should be understood for what they are. As in other Islamic sciences, mistakes historically did occur in Tasawwuf, most of them stemming from not recognizing the primacy of Shari'a and 'Aqida above all else. But these mistakes were not different in principle from, for example, the *Isra'iliyyat* (baseless tales of Bani Isra'il) that crept into tafsir literature, or the *mawdu'at* (hadith forgeries) that crept into the hadith. These were not taken as proof that *tafsir* was bad, or hadith was deviance, but rather, in each discipline, the errors were identified and warned against by Imams of the field, because the Umma needed the rest.[25]

The leading figures of the TI network do not seem to support either the immanentism of people like Ibn Arabi (1165–1240) or popular practices associated with esoteric, 'Drunken Sufism'. Hamza Yusuf, keen to distinguish between genuine practitioners and others that have given Sufism a bad name, once said

> It is well known of the people claiming to be Sufis, putting on the garments of Sufis, and tricking simple followers and worshippers; getting them to give them their money, to slavishly serve them, and these types of things. (. . .) happened

historically in the Muslim world. The [pious] Imams have always been the strictest at trying to prevent this deception, because there is nothing worse than deceiving somebody in religion.[26]

This clarification and distinction and others like it helped dispel the reluctance some young British activists had towards Sufism and proved an alluring alternative for those who wanted to escape the dominant Salafi and Islamist readings of Islam, as well as the localized, ethnic Sufism of their South Asian heritage. This is not to say that all the members of the TI scene joined a tariqa as some took the position that '*tassawuf* is possible without *tariqa*'. It is worth noting that Hamza Yusuf avoids telling people to join a particular tariqa though he teaches that it is important to know the principles of *tassawuf*.

Following a Madhab

Adherents of TI, argue that one's daily practice of Islam is best done through the mediation of one of the four Madhabs. These legal schools represent the eponymous accumulated rulings of the most widely followed jurists in early Islam – Abu Hanifa (699–767), Anas ibn Malik (612–709), Al-Shafi (767–820) and Ahmad Ibn Hanbal (780–855). They function as reference points for believers trying to secure religious guidance in ascertaining what is religiously permissible and impermissible in areas of ritual worship, civil and criminal law, by providing a 'legalistic and non-interpretive mode of thinking that looks for precedence and that utilizes analogical and moralistic reasoning to provide answers for modern problems'.[27] Simply put, madhabs are accessed for matters that lie beyond the layperson's competence. Abdal Hakim Murad, reasons that

> We might compare the Quranic verses and the *hadiths* to the stars. With the naked eye, we are unable to see many of them clearly; so we need a telescope. If we are foolish, or proud, we may try to build one ourselves. If we are sensible and modest, however, we will be happy to use one built for us by Imam al-Shafi'i or Ibn Hanbal, and refined, polished and improved by generations of great astronomers. A madhhab is, after all, nothing more than a piece of precision equipment enabling us to see Islam with the maximum clarity possible. If we use our own devices, our amateurish attempts will inevitably distort our vision.[28]

The rationale being argued here is that only people trained in the religious sciences are qualified to interpret the primary texts of the Qur'an and Hadith.

Ordinary people are not trained to be able to go direct to them and are obliged to follow the jurisprudential reasoning of a legal school of thought. This insistence is largely in response to the popular slogan 'go back to the Qur'an and Sunnah', used by Salafis who claim that madhab adherents are following the legal schools blindly. According to Salafis, the correct interpretation of Islam can only be achieved by returning to the Qur'an and relying only on hadith verified by scholars of their choice. In response, highly regarded Sufi scholars such as Said Ramadan al-Buti in his well-known text, *Non-Madhhabism: The Greatest Bida Threatening the Islamic Shari'a*, compares the skills required by a jurist as similar to that of a medical doctor: 'If one's child is seriously ill', he asks, 'does one look for oneself in the medical textbooks for the proper diagnosis and cure, or should one go to a trained medical practitioner?'[29] Furthermore, Hamza Yusuf's teacher Shaykh Murabtal Haaj, in his fatwa on the necessity of madhabs, quotes an anecdote that captures the essence of the argument:

> Surely the following of our [rightly guided] Imams is not abandoning the Qur'anic verses or the sound hadiths; it is the very essence of adhering to them and taking our judgements from them. This is because the Qur'an has not come down to us except by means of these very Imams [who are more worthy of following] by virtue of being more knowledgeable than us in [the sciences of] the abrogating and abrogated, the absolute and the conditional, the equivocal and the clarifying, the probabilistic and the plain, the circumstances surrounding revelation and their various meanings, as well as their possible interpretations and various linguistic and philological considerations, [not to mention] the various other ancillary sciences [involved in understanding the Qur'an] needed.[30]

This explanation of why it is unwise to approach the textual source without the aid of specialists is meant to counter the prevalence of Salafi polemics against the blind following of a madhab argument, which gained popularity among Muslim youth. This analysis suggests the lack of intellectual leadership in contemporary the Muslim societies resulted from the destruction and reforming of traditional centres of learning in Muslim world during the colonial era. The subsequent affect has been the creation of a crisis of authority both in political and scholarly realms. It is argued by some of these TI figures that the gradual loss of traditional modes of learning which were being replaced with modern Western institutions and approaches resulted in a devaluing of religious knowledge and quantitative and qualitative loss of high calibre Muslim scholarship.

Adab: Etiquette of learning

The sense of loss and rupture with the past is a reoccurring theme of TI discourses. The answer it is claimed is to recover and re-link to the golden chain of learning by students at the feet of qualified teachers. TI adherent, Aftab Malik identifies the demise of the Caliphate, the rise of Islamic movements, growth modernism and the impact of the printing press as affecting the social, cultural and political changes which shaped Muslim self-understanding in the modern era. All four factors have in a sense democratized people's ability to attain scholarly levels of Islamic learning. Of great concern to him, is the ways people started to autodidactically educate themselves in specialized fields of religious knowledge. This he argues, endangers the process of learning Islam with *adab*-the correct etiquette, manners and respect one should have for teachers:

> Adab does not simply imply 'manners' but more so to *discipline* – the discipline
> of body, mind and the soul. Adab in the true sense of the word includes the
> discipline that assures the *recognition* and *acknowledgement* of one's proper
> place in relation to ones self, society and community; the *recognition* and
> *acknowledgement* of one's proper place in relation to one's physical, intellectual
> and spiritual capacities and potentials; the *recognition* and *acknowledgement* of
> the fact that knowledge and beings are ordered in degrees, levels and ranks.[31]

In his view, this levelling process caused the devaluing of religious knowledge and respect and emergence of mediocre standards of scholarship, that often bear their imprint of Salafi and Islamist hermeneutics. This can be seen in the modern activist's tendency to claim the right to *ijtihad,* (independent reasoning) and wanting to reinterpret directly from primary text, and ignore the accumulated tradition available in the classical heritage.

The Isnad and Ijazah paradigm

For seekers of traditional Islamic learning, having a trusted *isnad* (chain of transmission) and relevant *ijazah* (licence to teach) is crucial to be able to acquire a scholarly pedigree. According to Graham, the 'isnad paradigm' provides 'a personally guaranteed connection with a model past, and especially with model persons, offers the only sound basis in an Islamic context for forming and re-forming oneself and one's society in any age'.[32] Resembling the argument to follow a madhab, it is said that this approach disregards the prized status of having been taught through a scholarly *silsila* or scholarly genealogy which can be traced back to the Prophet Muhammad. Masud Khan summarizes the isnad pedagogy as:

> [. . .] the transmission of knowledge from a living shaykh who has *ijazas*, or certificates of learning, for the material he is teaching. Students, not only gain the knowledge, but also benefit from the explanation of the subtleties of the text, which a casual reader may miss. Also, they gain the *barakah* or blessing from receiving the transmission of the text and take their place in a long chain back to the source, the Prophet (May Allah bless him and give him peace). Finally, and most importantly, the most beneficial thing they learn is the *adab*, or the etiquette of receiving knowledge. The importance of *adab* cannot be understated or underestimated, since one realises that the more he learns the more he realises he does not know and this is a very humbling experience.[33]

Studying this way with individual teachers also allows for the possibility of *barakah* – 'the spiritual power of charismatic religious figures . . . perpetuated in a line of spiritual descent that links each new generation of adepts and lay followers of an order to the spiritual authority of the Prophet and ultimately to God-through the Companions and the best of their successors'.[34] The scholarly credentials are thus acquired through apprenticeship with individual teachers in the different Islamic sciences guiding them through 'learning, understanding memorization, recitation, exegesis and important works of Muslim piety and learning'.[35] The goal of this *Ijaza* system perpetuated a method of knowledge transmission linking the past to the present through a network of personal rather than institutional certification. This was maintained through:

> [. . .]oral, face-to-face, teacher-to-student transmission of the text by the teacher's ijazah [SIC}, which validates the written text. It was developed early in Hadith scholarship, involved travelling to specific authorities (shaykhs), especially the oldest and most renowned of the day, to hear from their own mouths their hadiths and to obtain their authorization or 'permission' (ijazah) to transmit these in their names.[36]

And as Graham remarked, 'Muslim scholarship has always been and remains international. The lines of connecting *isnads* criss-cross the geographical and political divisions of the Islamic world just as Muslim students and scholars have done for centuries'.[37] This is certainly reflected in the examples of the new generation of scholars and teachers associated with the TI scene, as many have spent time in Syria, Egypt, Yemen and Mauritania to study the various Islamic sciences. Indeed, *isnad* credentials of the upcoming young scholars are usually declared in the publicity materials used for public lectures and teaching courses.

Conclusion

This chapter has attempted to survey the arrival and growth of a modern version of Sufism which has caught the imagination of many religiously observant Muslim youth in Britain. While well-known historical Sufi orders have transmitted into the United Kingdom, South Asian varieties almost became irrelevant to a generation who viewed them as quaint remnants of their parent's immigrant culture. Those young people who opted for, active religious identities during the mid-1980s and early 1990s, tended to be drawn to Islamist and Salafi readings of Islam. This changed dramatically after the emergence of a new form of Sufism, initially articulated by a set of Western Muslim converts. Unlike representatives of traditional tariqas, these Sufi figures spoke in English, could reference Anglo-American popular culture and emphasized a spirituality deemed missing in other Islamic currents. They changed the terms of reference within existing activist circles and inspired many to study the classical Islamic science overseas. The TI network is in a state of growth with growing numbers of institutions and sympathizers in the United Kingdom, the USA and Middle East, who have mastered communications technology and event management. It has managed to attract people from other Islamic orientations by providing an alternative narrative and intellectual challenge. In conclusion, the neo-Sufism of the TI network demonstrates both continuity with history and change in relation to the impact of modernity and with its adherents skillfully re-inventing and distinguishing their religiosity from other older Sufi currents and rival activist Islamic trends.

Notes

1   Here I refer to the growth of national movements and organizations such as the Islamist Young Muslims UK, British branch of Hizb-ut Tahrir and Salafi organization JIMAS in the 1990s. For most of that decade, they attracted religious active British Muslim young people to their work. For further background, see my 'Islamic Political Radical Radicalism in Britain: The Case of Hizb-ut Tahrir' in *Islamic Political Radicalism: A European Comparative*. T. Abbas (Ed.). Edinburgh University Press (2007), pp. 145–59 and 'The Attraction of Authentic Islam: Salafism and British Muslim Youth' in *Global Salafism: Islam's New Religious Movement*. R. Meijer (Ed.). Hurst. London (2009), pp. 352–79.

2   R. Geaves (2009) 'Transglobal Sufism or a Case of Cultural Binary Fission: the
    Transmigration of Sufism to Britain' in *Sufis in Western Society Global Networking
    and locality*. R. Geaves, M. Dressler and G. Klinkhammer (Eds), London:
    Routledge.

3   Ibid.

4   Ibid.

5   All these organizations have current websites that can be viewed on the internet.

6   A 'Traditional Islam' literary canon of sorts is developing with the following
    articles and titles being 'must read': *Who or what is a Salafi, Albani and His Friends,
    The Place of Tasawwuf in Traditional Islam, Islamic Spirituality, Reliance of the
    Traveller, The Forgotten Revolution,* in *the spirit of tradition, What is a Madhab
    and why it is necessary to follow one, Understanding the Four Madhabs, The Broken
    Chain: Reflections on the Neglect of Tradition, The Obligation of Following the Four
    Madhabs, Remembrance of Death and the After-life, Breaking the Two Desires* and
    Unveiling Islam among others.

7   Their websites can be viewed on the internet.

8   Deenport website address: http://deenport.com/.

9   Masud Khan's website: http://masud.co.uk/.

10 Sunnipath website address: http://sunnipath.com/.

11 Seekers Digest website: http://seekersdigest.org. He was given this authorization by
    the late Sheikh Abd al-Rahman al-Shaghouri (1912–2004). For further details, see:
    http://shadhilitariqa.com/site/index.php?option=com_content&task=view&id=3.

12 See his *Q News* articles at: http://masud.co.uk/ISLAM/nuh/. Among the most
    vigorous counter attacks against Salafi polemics have been produced by the
    convert Gabriel F Hadadd. His *Albani and His Friends* was particularly scathing
    of Salafi approaches and inverts their claims to orthodoxy and Hisham Kabbani's
    Encyclopaedia of Islamic Doctrine.

13 Hamza Yusuf's writings on current affairs can be viewed his website: http://sandala.
    org/blog/.

14 Most of these videos can be seen on youtube.

15 See his *Q-News* articles at: http://masud.co.uk/ISLAM/ahm/.

16 Geaves, Op. Cit., p. 108.

17 The organization websites for the Islamic Forum Europe: http://
    islamicforumeurope.com/live/ife.php YM UK: http://ymuk.net/ ISB: http://isb.org.
    uk/pages06/home.asp#.

18 Along with Abdal Hakim Murad, interview with author July 2009.

19 Interview with author July 2009.

20 'Deen Intensive' and 'Rihla' courses can viewed at the websites: http://deen-
    intensive.com/index.php.

21 They have worked together for over a decade producing some the key documents of
    the TI network-the booklet *Agenda to Change our Condition,* which is a manifesto

for islamically inspired individual and community change. Collaborating together they expanded the work of the Zaytuna Institute and most recently launched the Zaytuna College. Shakir is also frequently invited to the United Kingdom, both by traditionalist and non-traditionalist organizations. His writings can be viewed at: http://newislamicdirections.com/.

22   U. F. Abd-Allah (2006) *A Muslim in Victorian America: The Life of Alexander Russell Webb*. Oxford University Press. He has also authored a number of influential papers such as *Islam and the Cultural Imperative* which can be viewed at the An-Nawawi Foundation website: http://nawawi.org/index.html.

23   Cited in *How would you respond to the Claim that Sufism is Bid'a?* Nuh Ha Mim Keller (1995). http://masud.co.uk/ISLAM/nuh/sufism.htm.

24   Cited in *The Place of Tasawwuf in Traditional Islamic Sciences*. Nuh Keller. http://masud.co.uk/ISLAM/nuh/sufitlk.htm.

25   Imam Hamza Yusuf Tasawwuf/Sufism in Islam by Shaykh Hamza Yusuf. http://sunnah.org/events/hamza/hamza.htm (accessed March 1, 2001).

26   M. Hashem (2006) 'Contemporary Islamic Activism: The Shades of Praxis', *Sociology of Religion*, 67, pp. 23–41.

27   A. Hakim *Understanding the Four Madhabs: The Problem with Anti-Madhhabism.* Murad: http://masud.co.uk/islam/ahm/newmadhh.htm

28   Ibid.

29   Shaykh Murabtal Hajji's Fatwa *on Following One of the Four Accepted Madhabs* (trans.Hamza Yusuf Hanson) http://masud.co.uk/ISLAM/misc/mhfatwa.htm.

30   A. Malik (2002) *The Broken Chain: Reflections on the Neglect of Tradition.* Amal Press, p. 8.

31   Graham, Op. Cit., p. 522

32   Masud Khan, Forward in *Broken Chain*, p. VI.

33   Graham, Op .Cit., p. 515.

34   Ibid.

35   Ibid.

36   Ibid.

37   Ibid.

Bibliography

Ahlberg, N. (1990) *New Challenges, Old Strategies: Themes of Variation and Conflict among Pakistani Muslims in Norway,* Helsinki: Finnish Anthropological Society.

Abbas, T. (Ed.) (2007) *Islamic Political Radicalism: A European Comparative*, Edinburgh: Edinburgh University Press Ltd.

Abd-Allah, U. F. (2006) *A Muslim in Victorian America: The Life of Alexander Russell Webb*, Oxford: Oxford University Press.

Al-Ghazali, Abu Hamid (trans. T. J. Winter) (1989) *Remembrance of Death and Afterlife*, Cambridge: Book XL of the Revival of the Religious Sciences Islamic Texts Society.

— (1995) *Al-Ghazali on Disciplining the Soul and on Breaking the Two Desires*, Cambridge: Books XXII and XXIII of the Revival of the Religious Sciences. Islamic Texts Society.

Ansari, Muhammad, Abdul Haq (1986) *Sufism and Shariah: A Study of Shaykh Ahmad Sirhindi's Effort to Reform Sufism*, Leicester: The Islamic Foundation.

Chittack, W. (2000) *Sufism: A Short Introduction*, Oxford: One World Publications.

Geaves, R. (2006) 'Learning the Lessons from the Neo-Revivalist and Wahhabi Movements: The Counterattack of New Sufi Movements in the UK'. In: Jamal Malik & John Hinnells (eds). *Sufism in the West*. London: Routledge.

Geaves, R., Dressler, M. and Klinkhammer, G. (Eds) (2009) *Sufis in Western Society Global Networking and Locality*, London: Routledge.

Graham, W. A. (Winter 1993) Traditionalism in Islam: An Essay in Interpretation, *Journal of Interdisciplinary History*, 23(3), Religion and History. Cambridge, MA USA, 495–522.

Hadadd, G. F. H. (2004) *Albani and His Friends: A Concise Guide to the "Salafi" Movement*, Birmingham: AQSA Publications.

Ibn Rajab Al-Hanbali (2006) *Heirs of the Prophets*, (trans Zaid Shakir), Chicago: Starlach Press.

Kabbani, H. (1998) *The Encyclopaedia of Islamic Doctrine*, Vol. 1–7, Chicago: As-Sunna Foundation of America, Kazi Press.

Keller, Nuh Ha-Mim (1997) *The Reliance of The Traveller: Classic Manual of Islamic Sacred Law*. (translation of 'Umdat al-Salik di Ahmad Ibn Naqib al-Misri), Beltsville, MD: Amana Publications.

— (2001) *Port in a Storm: A Fiqh Solution to the Qibla of North America*, Chicago: Wakeel Books.

— (2002) *Sufism in Islam*, Chicago, Wakeel Books.

— (2003) (Trans) *Manual of Islam (Nawawi's): Al Maqasid*, Beltsville, MD: Amana Publications.

— (2011) *Sea Without Shore: A Manual of the Sufi Path*, Sunna Books.

Lumbard, J. and Nayed, A. A. (Eds) (2010) *The 500 Most Influential Muslims 2010*, Amman: Royal Islamic Strategic Studies Centre.

Malik, A.(2002) *The Broken Chain: Reflections on the Neglect of Tradition*, Bristol: Amal Press.

Mazen, H. (2006) Contemporary Islamic Activism: The Shades of Praxis. *Sociology of Religion*, 67(1), 23–41.

Meijer, R. (Ed.) (2009) *Global Salafism: Islam's New Religious Movement*, London: Hurst & Co Publishers.

Pasquier, R. D. (1993) *Unveiling Islam*. (trans T. J. Winter), Cambridge: Islamic Texts Society.

Shakir, Z. (2005) *Scattered Pictures: Reflections of an American Muslim*, San Francisco: Zaytuna Institute, NID Publishers.

— (2008) *Treatise for the Seekers of Guidance*, San Francisco: NID Publishers.

Yusuf, H. (2002) (Trans.) *The Burda of Al- Busiri*, San Francisco: Sandala. Ltd.

— (2004) (Trans.) *Purification of the Heart Signs: Symptoms and Cures of the Spiritual Diseases of the Heart*, Chicago: StarLatch Press.

— (2008) (Trans.) *The Creed of Imam al-Tahawi*, San Francisco: Zaytuna Institute.

Yusuf, H. and Shakir Z. (2008) *Agenda to Change our Condition*, San Francisco: Zaytuna Institute.

10

What Is the Naqshbandi-Haqqani *tariqa*? Notes on Developments and a Critique of Typologies

Simon Stjernholm

Not so long ago, scientific study of Sufism practically equalled historical studies of philosophical ideas and mystical poetry. Among historians of religion in the middle of the twentieth century, Sufism was seen as a somewhat curious fossil, expected to quietly disappear as people in Muslim societies grew more enlightened and modern. Sufism in the form of twentieth-century *turuq* was viewed with scepticism as a superstitious, irrational 'folk' religion with little if any resemblance to proper, serious Islam; not to mention the proper, serious Sufism of historical masters of past centuries.[1] A similar view was held by Muslim reformers who wanted to purify Islamic religiosity from what they regarded as unlawful 'innovations' (*bidaʿ*) that had been added to the allegedly pure religion of the first generations of Muslims.[2]

Evidently, Sufism did not disappear. Instead, it developed and adapted to changing circumstances through the workings of individuals and groups in various societies. Scholarship on Sufism in recent decades has also been increasingly attentive to contemporary Sufis as living, historically situated actors. Moreover, a new field of research concerned with contemporary Sufism in traditionally non-Muslim societies has developed.[3] As a result, there has been a tendency within this new field to establish typologies in order to categorize differing forms of Sufism. This article appraises a few such typologies by relating them to one particular transnational *tariqa*, the Naqshbandi-Haqqani, led by Shaykh Muhammad Nazim Adil al-Haqqani (b. 1922; henceforth Shaykh Nazim). This *tariqa*, especially as manifested in one of its centres in London, was studied as the author's doctoral dissertation project.[4] It is suitable to discuss in relation to typologies of Sufism because it has been subject to academic study previously; it represents a relatively well-known case and can therefore illustrate what we 'know' about a particular contemporary *tariqa*.

Learning from the Naqshbandi-Haqqani case

The Naqshbandi-Haqqani *tariqa* has been given more scholarly attention than most other Sufi communities active in non-Muslim societies.[5] This interest can be explained by its high profile in public communications, success in promoting its message in various local contexts, and social accessibility. Below, some key findings of the study carried out by this author are presented.[6]

Publications

A large body of publicized communications by *tariqa* participants was dealt with, including books, mailing lists, video clips and websites. The publicized *sohbets* of the *tariqa's* living leader, Shaykh Nazim, were given attention, as were several books authored by his deputy, Shaykh Hisham Kabbani. The way Kabbani narrates the lives of Shaykh Nazim and his master Shaykh Abdullah al-Daghestani (d. 1973) in his book *Classical Islam and the Naqshbandi Sufi Tradition* (2004) was analysed, as these narratives have informed adherents to the *tariqa* and influenced their understanding of Islamic tradition. Moreover, Kabbani's defence of traditional Sufi practices and polemics against contemporary Salafism in the seven-volume *Encyclopedia of Islamic Doctrine* (1998) was emphasized as important for understanding the claims of Islamic authenticity made by the two shaykhs (and many of their *murids*).

Much has changed in the area of communication techniques and distribution channels since the early 1980s when *murids* first publicized edited versions of Shaykh Nazim's *sohbets* in books. These books have previously mostly been read by scholars in order to understand and summarize the shaykh's message. This study rather looked at the publications themselves as media for the dissemination of his teachings. The books are thus not simply vessels containing the shaykh's words. Because they are edited, distributed and discussed by his *murids* in various contexts, the *murids* are also responsible for the meaning and significance they acquire within the community. Focus was put on a specific early book that was described as particularly important by many *murids*. When the much-appreciated *Mercy Oceans (Book Two)* was first published in 1980 (it was reissued in 2008), knowledge of the shaykh and his message was mainly passed on through personal contacts. Several *murids* related how they were given a book or invited to a talk by an acquaintance and were attracted to the shaykh's person, appearance and spiritual communications. This still happens, but given that it is virtually impossible to avoid Naqshbandi-Haqqani material if one searches the internet using Sufi-related terms, the web has in later years provided additional ways of expanding these networks. Broadcasts and forums on the web connect *murids* worldwide, but they also disseminate the shaykhs' messages to a potentially much wider global audience. Access to the shaykhs' teachings is therefore not at all exclusive or limited anymore. Possibly as a result of this, the early publications, being based on talks that were only heard by a small gathering of early *murids*, have come to enjoy a certain elevated status. *Mercy Oceans (Book Two)* is still recommended reading for new adepts; reportedly, Shaykh Nazim himself has said that this is the best introductory book for new *murids*. Many have told me that it is their personal favourite.

The teachings are thus decontextualized in a double sense: both because they are viewed by *murids* as resulting from the shaykh's direct contact with a non-material spiritual realm of deceased *awliya*, and because the books (and, in recent years, the webcasts) are distributed globally regardless of the context. The books are decontextualized even more than the webcasts, since the latter show a context where teaching is carried out, while in the former references to time and place are scarce. Sometimes a place is mentioned – mostly London, Damascus or Cyprus, at times Munich or Germany – but there is no description of the environment. Moreover, most of the books do not mention the name(s) of its editor(s). It is, however, clear that the shaykh has not written the lectures contained in them; they must have been recorded, selected, named and edited into book format.

Both Shaykh Nazim's *sohbets* and the books authored by Shaykh Kabbani position the shaykhs in representative and hereditary roles as carriers of truth and authenticity. They rely on an inherited practice of building legitimacy on one's predecessor through a *silsila*, a chain of sacred individual authorities through which divine knowledge has allegedly been transmitted. It is therefore crucial that the books convey this authority, this connection to tradition. The early publications of Shaykh Nazim's *sohbets*, including *Mercy Oceans (Book Two)*, explicitly claim to be the teachings of Shaykh Abdullah al-Daghestani, Shaykh Nazim's own teacher, as expounded upon by Shaykh Nazim. In fact, on the covers of the two earliest publications in my collection, Shaykh Nazim is not even mentioned, whereas later there is no mention of Shaykh Abdullah on the covers. Apparently, Shaykh Nazim's own authority and reputation grew as a result of the first publications.

In a similar way, when Kabbani writes the life stories of his predecessors, it is vital for him to establish their authority; they are the source of his own claim to spiritual authority. Kabbani's works have sometimes been read as historiography, theology and polemics; another significant dimension of his corpus is hagiography. His narration of saintly lives (ending with Shaykh Abdullah's and Shaykh Nazim's) can be seen as an attempt to work in the classical tradition of Sufi hagiographies. Moreover, as he is able to include key episodes where he himself was present as an eyewitness or active agent, he simultaneously constructs his own spiritual persona as an heir to the last two shaykhs. The narratives are full of miraculous events through which the shaykhs assert their spiritual power. Both the shaykhs allegedly experienced significant dreams and visions in which the prophet appeared; a prominent trope in Sufi hagiography and a classical way of claiming spiritual authority. In one passage, the young Abdullah has a vision where the prophet tells him to migrate immediately with his family from Daghestan to Turkey. About the same vision, Kabbani quotes Abdullah as saying

> I saw the Prophet embracing me and I saw myself disappearing in him. [. . .] I received the realities that the Prophet poured into my heart in words of light, which began as green and changed into purple, and the understandings were poured into my heart in a quantity that is immeasurable.[7]

This pouring of knowledge by the prophet into the heart of Shaykh Abdullah was followed by a later vision in which the shaykh claimed to speak directly to God: 'I saw that I was speaking with the Divine Presence. I received answers to questions that saints had never been able to reach before.'[8]

A key event is the passing away of Shaykh Abdullah (allegedly, he predicted the exact date), in which Kabbani is a central participant, feeling the pulse of the dying shaykh and being called 'my son' by him. As Kabbani narrates the events of that day, after the pulse and blood pressure were no longer detectable, a present doctor (Kabbani's brother) wanted to inject 'medicine' and try to revive the dead shaykh although 'over seven minutes' had passed.

> Then Grandshaykh opened his eyes, put his hand up and said in Turkish, '*Burak*', which means, 'Stop!'[9]

> Everyone was shocked. They had never heard the dead speak before. I will never forget this in all my life. All those present, professors and doctors, will never forget either. We stood there in shock, not knowing what to say.[10]

This is indeed a dramatic narrative of the shaykh's miraculous power. Meanwhile, Shaykh Nazim is remarkably absent from the scene, although he soon arrives from Cyprus miraculously fast, buries the body with his own hands, prays the funeral prayers and returns to Cyprus.

Kabbani's hagiographical narration of Shaykh Nazim's life also includes dreams and visions, but is at its most engaging when the author himself enters the story. The prophet allegedly intervened directly in the affairs of the shaykh, both in his own dreams and in the dreams of those he was about to visit. During his first night spent together with Shaykh Abdullah, he is said to have experienced a vision in which they both prayed on the right hand side of Abu Bakr al-Siddiq, while the prophet led them together with prophets and *awliya* in prayer.

A key scene is once again that of a death bed: this time it is Kabbani's own father who died in 1971. One day, Shaykh Nazim came unexpectedly to Beirut and said the prophet had told him that Kabbani's father (who seemed to be in good health) was going to die and that Shaykh Nazim was 'to wash him, shroud him and bury him, and then go back to Cyprus'.[11] Surprised, the Kabbanis summoned the family in preparation – some family members did not believe them and did not come. At quarter to seven in the evening, Shaykh Nazim went up to the father and read the Qur'anic sura Ya Sin (as is traditionally done at Muslim deathbeds). Immediately after, when the clock struck seven, the father cried out: 'My heart! My heart!' Within minutes he was dead. As Kabbani relates this miraculous appearance of Shaykh Nazim in his intimate family affairs, which had his family wondering what kind of man this was, he comments

> He is like all saints of the Naqshbandi Order before him, like all saints of other orders before him, like his ancestors, [. . .] who followed and preserved the tradition for 1,400 years. [. . .] The pen cannot express these feelings. We can only say one thing: this is the Truth.[12]

Kabbani thus inscribes his two shaykhs into a hereditary *silsila*, the idea of which is a central aspect of Sufi historical consciousness. Robert Rozehnal uses the term 'hagiographical habitus' to capture the way contemporary shaykhs' lives are narrated to reflect the wondrous examples of past masters: they establish a '*model of* and a *model for* moral and ethical behaviour'.[13] These narratives can provide a sense of connection, identification and edification to its audience; this aspect is perhaps even more central for *tariqa* participants than determining 'what actually happened'. As Rozehnal's vocabulary suggests, the portraits of the shaykhs are expected to have a real impact on the audience's lives.

Observations

The bulk of material analysed in the study came from fieldwork, where weekly *dhikr* sessions, *jum'a* prayer and other gatherings were regularly attended at the Haqqani Islamic Priory in North London. Conversations and interviews with individual *tariqa* participants were also vital. The initiative by Naqshbandi-Haqqani representatives to create a broader voice for Sufi Muslims in Britain, the Sufi Muslim Council, and its public activities came to be a significant aspect during the studied period.[14] In addition, two visits were made to Shaykh Nazim's home in Lefke, Northern Cyprus, where his *murids* come from all over the world to be near him. These visits by *murids* are important not least because the shaykh, since the early 2000s, no longer travels abroad. Shaykh Hisham Kabbani has largely taken the role of travelling shaykh in the *tariqa*.

The many encounters with Naqshbandi-Haqqani Sufis meant that an understanding gradually developed of how *tariqa* activities and narratives provide meaning and identity for participants. Earlier studies have emphasized different characteristics when it comes to ethnicity and converts, especially in the British context: Tayfun Atay (1994) distinguished between *murids* of Turkish, Western and South Asian background and showed antagonisms between these groups; Mustafa Draper (2002) focused on 'postmodern' aspects of *tariqa* activities, including the playing down of specifically Islamic vocabulary. My own fieldwork gave the impression of a multi-ethnic and distinctly Islamic *tariqa*. Although some *murids* talked about ethnic divisions among *murids*, for example, with particular ethnic groups arranging separate *dhikr*, multi-ethnic presence in the Haqqani Islamic Priory (a Naqshbandi-Haqqani centre in London) was striking. People with family backgrounds in, for example, Turkey, Cyprus, Pakistan, several Arab countries, Britain, Malaysia, Singapore, India, the United States and Jamaica were encountered in London. When visiting Shaykh Nazim's home in Cyprus, this impression was strengthened. Both aspects of the *tariqa* evidently exist simultaneously; a degree of ethnic division does not exclude ethnic mixing within the same *tariqa* structure. It is not always a question of either–or. Previous studies emphasize the unifying impact of Shaykh Nazim's visits. Shaykh Hisham Kabbani has now taken over the role of travelling shaykh. There are divisions and controversies, but these appear to have more to do with approval or disapproval of Kabbani as a person rather than with ethnicity.

For many participants, Sufism was not thought of as a category of practices that could be separated from other parts of one's life; rather, it was envisioned as encompassing all aspects of an individual's life. How Sufism permeated everyday life was the topic of a small weekly study group in the Haqqani Islamic Priory calling itself the 'Institute of Advanced Practical Sufism'. The group gathered under the leadership of an elderly man who held lectures based on verses from the Qur'an and his own writings about the connection between Sufism and practical life matters. Current news items and the participants' own narratives about their experiences were woven into the teaching; 'Sufism' thus became a concept that touched upon every aspect of life. For some *murids* in the priory, another dimension that was tied to their commitment to Sufism was physical exercise. The Southeast Asian martial art Silat has for some years been integrated in Naqshbandi-Haqqani activities in London. Individuals have been socialized into the *tariqa* as a result of training in Silat, while for some participation in Silat has rather been an effect of being part of the *tariqa*. All aspects of a person's life have the potential to be purified and understood as crucial to the individual's spiritual journey. A notable feature is also the supposedly 'Ottoman' style of dress worn by many Naqshbandi-Haqqanis, in emulation of the shaykh. This was explained as bringing divine blessings on its wearer and serving as a reminder to act according to Islamic morals and Sufi etiquette (*adab*).

One of the central activities of the *tariqa* is individual and communal *dhikr*. During the time of fieldwork, approximately 100 attendees generally frequented Thursday evening *dhikr*; sometimes fewer, sometimes more. When Shaykh Kabbani was visiting, the priory would be filled to the brim with several hundred people listening to his *sohbet* and participating in rituals. *Dhikr* developed during the period of field research: at the beginning it was a loud variant of the classical *khatm al-khwajagan* that characterizes the Naqshbandi tradition (although silent *dhikr* has been emphasized historically).[15] It later changed into a hybridized *dhikr* consisting of a shortened *khatm* followed by a *hadra*, which is otherwise usually practiced in North African Sufism. This may reveal the historical and contemporary significance of North African Sufism in the British context, as well as influences from Shaykh Nazim's followers in this region. When I first visited the priory in late 2004, whirling in the style of the Mevlevi *tariqa* by a few *murids* had already been included in the weekly *dhikr*. The incorporation of *hadra* in Naqshbandi-Haqqani *dhikr*, a clear change in regular ritual habits, was reportedly started at Shaykh Nazim's home in Cyprus at his orders. It was practiced there at the time of both my visits.

The hybrid *dhikr* can be understood as resulting from a desire to present a set of ideas and practices as part of a generalized, unified 'Sufism' in order to counter anti-Sufi sentiments that characterize much global Islamic discourse. To the shaykhs, it was apparently more important to present Sufism as inclusive and adaptive than to uphold strict separation between various *turuq* and particular ritual practices as exclusively 'belonging' to different spiritual paths. I therefore regard this ritual development as related to perceived social pressures of formulating a broad, generalized global Sufism, as well as the shaykhs' adaptive response to expectations of their *murids* with varying cultural backgrounds, rather than a development of 'postmodern' relativity and eclecticism. In my view, relativity regarding truth claims and correct Islamic practice is not the primary issue here, but rather attempts to respond to changing circumstances and evolving perceptions of the religious Other. The significant Muslim Other against whom identity is shaped is currently not primarily other Sufi *turuq*; it is Muslims of anti-Sufi orientation.

An important aspect of conversations with participants in Naqshbandi-Haqqani activities was their self-narratives of being and becoming Sufi (and, for some, becoming Muslim). Individual narratives are in one way very personal, as they include specific details about when and where a person was affected and attracted by the shaykh, including that person's pre-history. At the same time, the narratives display remarkably similar traits, such as: a hidden life purpose known by God but at first unknown to the narrator; a life-changing turn of events and insights following contact with the shaykh; and dreams or visions bearing messages of guidance from another realm. These narrative traits connect the self-narratives of individual *murids* to tropes in Sufi hagiography, since this repertoire of narrative models, in Jerome Bruner's words, become 'available for describing the course of a life'.[16] Thus, the lives of contemporary individuals are connected to a purposeful past, present and future. The great saints throughout history (including the recent shaykhs of the Naqshbandi-Haqqani, as told by Shaykh Kabbani) experienced extraordinary moments of insight and miracles, often through dreams and visions with spiritual masters. So too the common *murids* described moments they thought of as life changing; this included dreams and visions in the style of hagiographies, although more modest. The feeling of recognizing the shaykh without having physically met him before was common. These narratives offer a chance to connect to a sacred history and a sense of purpose, which in turn can provide meaning and identity. Focus is on the shaykh: he is the key figure connecting individual narratives to ideas of a purposeful existence. In creating personal narratives that include diverse topics and cultural items (such as films, books, cultural experiences), individual actors establish a connection between their own lifeworld and 'Sufism'.

At the same time, there is great diversity regarding who seeks the shaykh's guidance: this was evident not least at the shaykh's home in Cyprus, where people from all parts of the world gathered. During my visits I encountered *murids* from, for example, Spain, Britain, Russia, North America, China, Italy, Germany, Australia, Turkey and Somalia. They came from very different backgrounds and their paths to contact with the shaykh varied. Many had been raised as Muslims and had been attracted to Sufism as adults; some had converted to Islam either before or as a result of contact with Shaykh Nazim; and some did not express a consistent commitment to Islam as a religious tradition but felt personally connected to the shaykh and participated in the Islamic rituals in his home. The factor binding all the visitors together was their strong bond to the shaykh. This diversity makes it difficult to talk about the Naqshbandi-Haqqani *tariqa* or the 'group of Shaykh Nazim' as an entity that can be easily defined, typologized and fixed in time. It is an integral part of the *tariqa* to be 'travelling', that is, unbound by a particular place and definition: it is continuously evolving because the people of whom it consists change due to time and social processes.

Examples of typologies of contemporary Sufism

In a series of informative articles, Marcia Hermansen has discussed various types of American Sufi movements.[17] She has placed the Naqshbandi-Haqqani in the 'hybrid' category, those who 'identify more closely with an Islamic source and content' as opposed to those with a perennialist outlook.[18] Neither of these categories include what is sometimes called 'transplanted' Sufism, that is, communities defined by their ethnic and cultural background. Hermansen writes

> Sufi movements that are essentially 'transplants' of orders active in Muslim countries and retain the same clientele and language among immigrants in the United States or Europe might not be thought of as significantly 'Western' at all. However, other Sufi movements that have made substantial adjustments to a new context and attract larger numbers of Europeans or North Americans are more likely to be seen as generically 'Western'. Once one starts to consider these Western Sufi movements more closely, a category of 'American' Sufi movements emerges as both informative and inadequate. It is informative in the sense that movements with significant activities based in the United States do adapt styles and practices resonant with American ways of doing things. It is inadequate with respect to the impossibility of drawing a line between the United States and Europe and imagining no cross-fertilisation and circulation of leaders, members

and publications of particular groups, even more so in an age of electronic communication and Internet linkages.[19]

A crucial question then emerges: what are the 'American ways of doing things'? Hermansen mentions promotion and advertising one's message through media, lectures and conferences, networking and cooperation between orders, global travelling, 'psychological models of transformation and healing', and a tendency towards female leadership and participation.[20] Shaykh Hisham Kabbani of the Naqshbandi-Haqqani *tariqa* is used by Hermansen to exemplify a more strictly Islamic Sufi movement.

In a more recent article, Hermansen has suggested a different typology of Sufism, namely, 'theirs' and 'ours'. The former denotes 'Sufi movements originally based in Muslim societies' but whose missionary and organizational scope is global, while the latter refers to 'any mode of Sufism that is primarily centred in the West'.[21] The category 'ours' is divided into three: '1) eclectic Sufi movements; 2) those with a Western convert shaykh; and finally, 3) movements headed by charismatic shaykhs from the Muslim world'.[22] The Naqshbandi-Haqqani is placed in the third category of 'ours' and juxtaposed with other groups more oriented towards issues of Islamic jurisprudence (*fiqh*) or personal transformation and psychology, though these elements are also found among Naqshbandi-Haqqanis. Because traditional Sufi modes of organization are difficult to maintain in the new settings, Hermansen observes, 'new forms of networks include multi-tariqa conferences, post-tariqa Sufi movements and many individual articulations of Sufi practice and identity'.[23]

In addition, Markus Dressler in a recent article discusses the heterogeneousness of New York's Sufi Muslim scene in 'doctrinal and ritual matters as well as with regard to how different Sufi groups position themselves towards American society and culture'.[24] He uses an offshoot of the Naqshbandi-Haqqani with one centre in Manhattan and one in upstate New York to exemplify an ideal-type that criticizes American society and culture and secludes from it. Moreover, Dressler identifies some characteristics of 'Western Sufism': 1) the unquestioned legitimacy of Sufism (in state regulation); 2) the possibility of advertisement and outreach activities; 3) the commodification of Sufism; 4) Sufi travelling and intra-Sufi competition; 5) the regularity of multiple affiliations and intra-Sufi networking.[25] There are thus clear similarities in how Hermansen and Dressler characterizes 'Western' or 'our' Sufism.

It should be observed that 'Western' here does not simply refer to a geographical space, since Sufis residing in, for example, Western Europe and North America are not by default considered 'Western Sufis'. Hermansen talks of 'transplants' while Dressler mentions those who 'gather along ethnic lines': both of these are not defined as 'Western'. Rather, the quality of being 'Western' refers to *a way of doing things* that relates to religious pluralism, commodification, consumption, and non-static patterns of authority and belonging. But it is questionable whether this way of doing things is unique to 'the West' or 'us'; it is also not clear who 'we' and 'they' are.[26] It is therefore reasonable to ask how analytically useful typologies such as these are. Even a relatively well-known Sufi movement such as Naqshbandi-Haqqani cannot be unambiguously categorized. It is more complex, fluid, transnational and multi-faceted than the typologies admit.

An objection to this critique is that a particular *tariqa* can represent various types of Sufism in different localities: for example, that it can be 'Western' in one context (though not necessarily in Europe or North America) and a 'transplant' in another. But the typology does not explain why this would be the case. An analysis of activities and narratives that permeates the *tariqa* locally as well as the social context of the *tariqa* in a particular setting is needed. Reference to a geographic place or ethnicity does not in itself explain what type of Sufism a *tariqa* would manifest itself as in a given locality. Another framework for discussing contemporary Sufism is needed.

An alternative framework

The main criticism of typologies above is that they offer limited analytical and explanatory potential in the further study of contemporary Sufism, although the empirical descriptions they build on are relevant. The Naqshbandi-Haqqani could, for example, be categorized in several different ways, while not revealing that much about what it actually means for the people involved in the *tariqa*. Contemporary religious movements are often transnational and undergo processual changes in response to various social contexts – they can be many things at once. It may be more useful to closely analyse the actual activities and narratives conceptualized as 'Sufi' in these social contexts, as well as how this conceptualization is made, than attempting to determine which type of Sufism we are dealing with. These activities and narratives need not be determined by what geographical place they are located in (for example, 'Western', 'ours'); probably a more determining factor is what larger historical narratives the religious agents in a given setting experience and express a degree of resonance with.

In an article discussing the question 'what is a Sufi order?' where the Egyptian Khalwatiyya is used as an example, Rachida Chih suggests that

> [T]he *tariqa* is based first on the person of the spiritual master (the shaykh), and more precisely on the idea of his role as heir of the Prophet and representative (*khalifa*) of God on earth on the esoteric level, and on the interpersonal relationships that the shaykh establishes with his disciples. [. . .] The malleable and elastic structure of the *tariqa* allows it to adapt to very different social environments. The longevity of the Sufi path – and implicitly its relevance in modernity – owes most to the fact that the *tariqa* is an individualized and humanized way of establishing contact with the Divine.[27]

Chih thus emphasizes the personal connection between the spiritual searcher for contact with the divine and the mediating power of the shaykh. The individual's effort to establish such contact through Sufi shaykhs is a central nexus for the study of contemporary Sufism. These efforts take different forms: participation in ritual prayers, desire for physical nearness to the shaykh and emulation of his person and character traits, just to mention a few. These efforts are at once intensely personal and generic, related to a multi-faceted yet distinguishable historical tradition. Participating in certain activities and relating oneself to certain narratives, for example, by drawing on hagiographical styles of narration in constructing self-narratives, are ways of linking the personal to the tradition. Throughout Sufi history, and no less in modern times, these processes have been diverse and locally varied. It should only be expected that varieties regarding organization and social profile are present in Europe and North America as well as in other parts of the world.

In sum, it seems appropriate to use a perspective for the study of contemporary Sufism that focuses on *activities* and *narratives* of socially situated Sufis, relating these in turn to competing conceptualizations of Islamic tradition, to transnational flows of people and information, and to the politics of belonging and identity on both individual and collective levels. Such a perspective accommodates the complexity and malleability of contemporary religious formations and makes no decisive distinction between studies of Sufis in Muslim and non-Muslim societies.

The question in the title still needs an answer: what is the Naqshbandi-Haqqani *tariqa*? A possible answer is: a multi-ethnic and locally malleable transnational Sufi movement whose shaykhs stress their Islamic Sufi heritage in communications of various kinds, and whose adherents, related through their personal bond to Shaykh Nazim, range from strict observers of Islamic normativity in faith and practice to those whose ties to the *tariqa* (i.e. their personal connection to the shaykh) does not necessarily imply a consistent commitment to Islam. In order to understand how and why the *tariqa* manifests itself differently in various times and places, one must study the activities and narratives of participants in relation to their social context. Varieties like those mentioned can co-exist within the same country, even within the same building. This co-existence can be calm and unquestioned; it can also entail conflict and division. Being complex and multi-faceted in this way, the Naqshbandi-Haqqani *tariqa* mirrors general processes in contemporary religiosity. Analysing it as an example of contemporary religiosity can lead to a deeper understanding of its workings than reducing it to a particular type of Sufism. The observations of Naqshbandi-Haqqani settings in London and Cyprus reported in this chapter are therefore not interpreted as representing a certain type of Sufism. Rather, they illustrate multiple ways of being Sufi co-existing within the same *tariqa*, indeed within the same building. These are expressed in the activities and narratives of individual Naqshbandi-Haqqani participants in Britain and elsewhere who claim a spiritual connection to the shaykh. The examples brought forward in this article, together with this volume's other contributions, show the malleable, complex and continuously evolving presence of Sufism in contemporary Britain. The developments of Sufism in Britain relate both to opportunities and constraints in the local context of British Sufis, and to transnational flows of ideas, people and goods.

Notes

1 For discussion of this type of reasoning and later developments, see, for example, J. Malik (2006) 'Introduction', in *Sufism in the West*. J. Malik and J. R. Hinnells (Eds), New York: Routledge, pp. 1–27; M. van Bruinessen and J. D. Howell (2007) 'Sufism and the "Modern" in Islam' in *Sufism and the 'Modern' in Islam*. M. van Bruinessen and J. D. Howell (Eds), London: IB Tauris, pp. 3–18; M. Dressler, R. Geaves, and G. Klinkhammer (2009) 'Introduction' in *Sufis in Western Society: Global Networking and Locality*. R. Geaves, M. Dressler and G. Klinkhammer, (2009), London: Routledge, 1–12.

2 E. Sirriyeh (1999) *Sufis and Anti-Sufis: The Defence, Rethinking and Rejection of Sufism in the Modern World*. Richmond: Curzon.

3 See, for example, R. Geaves (2000) *The Sufis of Britain: An Exploration of Muslim Identity*. Cardiff: Cardiff Academic Press; C. Raudvere and L. Stenberg (Eds) (2009) *Sufism Today: Heritage and Tradition in the Global Community*. London: IB Tauris; R. Geaves, M. Dressler and G. Klinkhammer (Eds) (2009) *Sufis in Western Society: Global Networking and Locality*. London: Routledge.

4   The resulting dissertation is Simon Stjernholm 2011, Lovers of Muhammad: A
    Study of Naqshbandi-Haqqani Sufis in the Twenty-First Century. PhD thesis,
    Centre for Theology and Religious Studies, Lund University.

5   For previous studies of the *tariqa* in various localities, see D. Habibis (1985) *A
    Comparative Study of Workings of a Branch of the Naqshbandi Sufi Order in Lebanon
    and the UK*. PhD thesis, University of London; Tayfun Atay, *Naqshbandi Sufis
    in a Western Setting*. PhD thesis, University of London; M. L. Laughlin (1999)
    Eating Poison: A Tale of Women and Discipleship in a Naqshbandi Sufi Community.
    MA, University of Washington; M. Draper (2002) *Towards a Postmodern Sufism:
    Eclecticism, Appropriation and Adaptation in a Naqshbandiyya and a Qadiriyya
    Tariqa in the UK*. PhD thesis, University of Birmingham; L. Schlessmann
    (2003) *Sufismus in Deutschland: Deutsche auf dem Weg des mystischen Islam*
    (Köln: Böhlau). These dissertations have also resulted in journal articles and
    book chapters. In addition, there are academic publications by a number of
    scholars that have contributed to research about the Naqshbandi-Haqqani and
    its shaykhs, among them are Geaves, *The Sufis of Britain*; A. Böttcher (2006)
    'Religious Authority in Transnational Networks: Shaykh Nazim al-Qubrusi al-
    Haqqani al-Naqshbandi' in *Speaking for Islam: Religious Authorities in Muslim
    Societies*. Gudrun Krämer and Sabine Schmidtke (Eds), Leiden: Brill, pp. 241–68;
    J. S. Nielsen M. Draper and G. Yemelianova (2006) 'Transnational Sufism: The
    Haqqaniyya' in *Sufism in the West*. J. Malik and J. R. Hinnells (Eds), Abingdon:
    Routledge, pp. 103–14; D. Damrel (2006) 'Aspects of the Naqshbandi-Haqqani
    Order in America' in *Sufism in the West*, J. Malik and J. R. Hinnells (Eds),
    Abingdon: Routledge, pp. 115–26.

6   International publications resulting from the same project are S. Stjernholm
    (2009) 'A Translocal Sufi Movement: Developments among Naqshbandi-Haqqani
    in London' in *Sufism Today: Heritage and Tradition in the Global Community*. C.
    Raudvere and L. Stenberg (Eds), London: IB Tauris; S. Stjernholm (2010) 'Sufi
    Politics in Britain: the Sufi Muslim Council and the "silent majority" of Muslims',
    Journal of Islamic Law and Culture, 12, 3, pp. 215–26.

7   Shaykh Muhammad Hisham Kabbani, *Classical Islam and the Naqshbandi Sufi
    Tradition*. Fenton, MI: Islamic Supreme Council of America, 2004, 425f.

8   Ibid., p. 431.

9   The Turkish word meant is probably *bırak*.

10 Kabbani, *Classical Islam and the Naqshbandi Sufi Tradition*, 452f.

11 Ibid., p. 478.

12 Ibid., p. 478f.

13 R. Rozehnal (2007) *Islamic Sufism Unbound: Politics and Piety in Twenty-First
    Century Pakistan*. New York: Palgrave Macmillan, p. 41.

14 The Sufi Muslim Council is analysed in Stjernholm, 'Sufi Politics in Britain'.

15 See I. Weismann (2007) *The Naqshbandiyya: Orthodoxy and Activism in a Worldwide Sufi Tradition*. Abingdon: Routledge for a history of the Naqshbandi tradition.

16 J. Bruner (1987) 'Life as Narrative', *Social Research*, 54, 1, p. 15.

17 M. Hermansen (1997) 'In the Garden of American Sufi Movements: Hybrids and Perennials' in *New Trends and Developments in the World of Islam*. P. B. Clarke (Ed.), London: Luzac Oriental, pp. 155–78; M. Hermansen (2000) 'Hybrid Identity Formations in Muslim America: The Case of American Sufi Movements', *The Muslim World*, 90, pp. 158–97; M. Hermansen (2004) 'What's American about American Sufi Movements?' in *Sufism in Europe and North America*. D. Westerlund (Ed.), London: Routledge, pp. 36–63; M. Hermansen (2009) 'Global Sufism: "Theirs and Ours"' in *Sufis in Western Society: Global Networking and Locality*. R. Geaves, M. Dressler, and G. Klinkhammer (Eds), London: Routledge, pp. 26–45.

18 Hermansen, 'In the Garden of American Sufi Movements: Hybrids and Perennials', p. 155.

19 Hermansen, 'What's American about American Sufi Movements?', p. 36.

20 Hermansen, 'What's American about American Sufi Movements?'.

21 Hermansen, 'Global Sufism: "Theirs and Ours"', p. 26.

22 Ibid., p. 33.

23 Ibid., p. 39.

24 M. Dressler (2009) 'Pluralism and Authenticity: Sufi Paths in Post-9/11 New York' in *Sufis in Western Society: Global Networking and Locality*. R. Geaves, M. Dressler and G. Klinkhammer (Eds), London: Routledge, p. 91.

25 Ibid., p. 85.

26 For discussions of various forms of modern Sufism in Indonesia, see J. D. Howell (2001) 'Sufism and the Indonesian Islamic Revival', *The Journal of Asian Studies*, 60, 3, pp. 701–29; J. D. Howell (2007) 'Modernity and Islamic Spirituality in Indonesia's New Sufi Networks' in *Sufism and the 'Modern' in Islam*. M. van Bruinessen and J. D. Howell (Eds) London: IB Tauris, pp. 217–40. For a discussion of related issues in Morocco, see P. Haenni and R. Voix (2007) 'God by All Means . . . Eclectic Faith and Sufi Resurgence among the Moroccan Bourgeoisie' in *Sufism and the 'Modern' in Islam*. M. van Bruinessen and J. D. Howell (Eds) London: IB Tauris, pp. 24156.

27 R. Chih 'What is a Sufi Order? Revisiting the Concept through a Case Study of the Khalwatiyya in Contemporary Egypt' in *Sufism and the 'Modern' in Islam*, M. van Bruinessen and J. D. Howell (Eds) London: IB Tauris, p. 22.

11

Reliving the 'Classical Islam': Emergence and Working of the Minhajul Quran Movement in the UK

Amer Morgahi

There is increasing research on the Muslim experiences in Europe to see how Muslims are negotiating their lives within liberal democracies, often referred to as 'European Islam'.[1] A prominent theme emerging out of these studies speaks of a 'break' as a result of migration that led Muslims to reflect on the religious practices as performed in the country of origin.[2] These changes involved, as the argument goes, a 'secularization process', which repositions 'Islam into the private sphere'. Cesari observed that the transformations in Europe 'demonstrate the capacity of this culture to reconcile its religious traditions with issues of social and political modernization'.[3] Thus as a result of the 'democratic societies in the West' the process of social adaptation of Muslim minority groups has placed Islam within the three inter-related paradigms of secularization, individualization and privatization' thus making it compatible with the Western liberal democracy.[4] However, these studies were criticized for various reasons.[5] The process of individual choice does not necessarily mean privatization of religion as the personal forms of religiosity can become public through religious mobilization.[6]

Another approach to 'European Islam', used in this chapter, sees Muslims as subjects and their religious organizational life as an extension of their migration process. These studies argue that the transnational Islamic communities based in Muslim-majority countries have a significant impact on the individual religiosity of immigrant populations to Europe.[7] Some of these studies, for example, assume that the 'tradition-rooted categories of social and religious authority' are part of a process whereby 'forms of authority are transformed' through social powers.

Salvatore and Moazzami think of a longer process of 'internal reforms' within the 'Muslim traditions' in view of modernity and as a part of the historical process of 'reform of tradition' as these 'traditions' are under 'permanent internal interventions, since their inception'.[8] Following these inspirations my study, by focusing on the Minhajul Qur'an (henceforth MQ), will show the changes as a result of Muslim experiences in European countries and the nature of choices that the movement's followers have made that led to transformations within the tradition. Though these transformations are of local, thus European, origin, they occurred in an atmosphere where the religious inspiration was provided through transnational religious groups. In this sense the emerging localization of the Muslim experiences occurred under a constant interaction between the 'universal' elements of religious texts or authorities that embodies such sacred forms, and the particular context of the practices of the followers.[9]

On the basis of an intensive study of the MQ from 2002 to 2005 in the Netherlands, United Kingdom, Denmark and Pakistan this chapter deals with specific transformations that the movement caused within the existing Barelvi groups within the United Kingdom. It shows the emergence and foundation of the MQ as a transnational religious movement that shapes the collective identity of the followers. It demonstrates how such a transnational movement emerging from the Muslim-majority country influences the local religious formations within Western societies. In doing this, it contributes to widely published material about such movements and how they function among Muslim groups across different regions. Thus some studies focus, for example, on transnational networks of Sufi groups as examples of such interactions on Sufi orders, while others have studied the effects of political religious networks among Muslim groups.[10] These movements work within the context of flow of 'ideas and goods' and are also theorized under the phenomenon of 'glocalization' by Appadurai to show how these affect the local conditions of the people.[11]

Although the MQ emerged within the Barelvi tradition, that although ulama-led is able to accommodate folk Islam in South Asia, it caused transformations within it. The transformations occurred in an atmosphere where the Barelvi institutions in the United Kingdom were criticized by their local followers for their sectarian politics and for their inability to cope with the demands of the local society. Interestingly these presumed inefficiencies of the Barelvis were also reflected in some academic studies of the Barelvis in the past decades. Thus writing on the Pakistani religious groups in Norway, Ahlberg found an 'escape' strategy or 'ghettoization' among the followers of folk Islam.[12] Other observers have explained the relative success of the Islamists and the reformists compared to the traditionalists and the popular Islam in the diaspora context due to the former's emphasis on institution building. They see that in their outreach to the youth the reformists and, the Islamists are more successful compared to the Barelvis. The Barelvis feared to lose their children to the reformist or Islamist groups.[13] Some studies that specifically focus on more ideological groups among the second-generation Muslims observed that the 'village Islam' of their parents hold little solutions for the day-to-day problems that young Muslims in Europe faced; thus the youth turned away from the traditional sources of religious leadership and authority.[14] Owing to their specific focus on reform and activist Islam, these studies however ignore development and emergence of neo-traditional groups and they describe tradition only in rigid terms.

Beside the nature of the self-reflection among the Barelvis in the United Kingdom that led to the emergence of the MQ, some accounts see its rise as a process of learning 'lessons from the Salafis and Reformists' leading to new initiatives among the Barelvis.[15] In his study of British Islam in the 1990s, Lewis checks different South Asian based religious groups along a 'localization' map through their use of local language, establishing religious institutions and their use of modern media for religious dissemination.[16] He found shortcomings among all the sectarian groups in these fields and thought it necessary that these Muslim groups should find answers to questions like how they were dealing with the question of their tradition and how to bridge the sectarian differences prevalent among them.[17] In their approach, the MQ transcends the prevalent sectarianism of the Barelvis as it defines the Muslim tradition following the concept of Muslim umma. By introducing modern techniques of mobilization and the new media, the movement succeeded in mobilizing a sector of the Muslim youth for its activism. In a recent study of Sufi groups in the United Kingdom, Geaves sees new developments among the neo-traditional groups that are meant to 'win loyalty of British-born generations'; however, they have to develop a systematic doctrine of Sufism in Europe and 'an educational system' in the European context.[18] As I considered elsewhere the MQ was less successful in developing educational institutions in the United Kingdom,[19] however under its leadership the MQ is working to provide a Sufi-cum-intellectual authority for the neo-traditional Islam in the United Kingdom. Through its doctrines and institutional activism it has challenged the political Islam-based activism within the European context by providing alternative forms of religious activism based on devotional practices and new ways to relate with the Muslim tradition that can appeal to the locally born generations.

The Pakistani migration

The Barelvi religious thinking dominates among the British Pakistanis that form a substantial number of Muslims in the United Kingdom. The major flow of migrants from South Asia including Pakistan, which are focus of this study, was after the Second World War when as a result of the devastation caused by the War, manpower was needed to run different industries and to operate the transport system. Among the Pakistani migrants, the Kashmiris form a substantial number (more than 70%), the majority of whom came in the 1950s and 1960s to the United Kingdom. Being a generation away from the agrarian culture,[20] they did not have any former experience of working under an organized religious network. In addition to this, their earlier poor living conditions in the United Kingdom did not allow them to develop a mosque. The result was that the earlier mosques, created on non-sectarian base, were largely dominated by more educated Deobandi leadership with an overwhelming Barelvi following. Similarly their affiliation with the Barelvi stream of Sunni Islam, which is associated with Sufism and the popular practices associated with shrines, enticed them to invite ulama and *Pir* – a title given to the spiritual Sheikh, from Pakistan. The latter were more interested in building their networks in Pakistan through the resources of the migrants, thus they oriented them to the country of origin. These matters hampered the earlier institutional building of the Barelvis in the United Kingdom.

With the family migrations in the 1970s, the need for the religious education of children and family socialization increased. As a result, we see an increase in mosque buildings in the United Kingdom in the 1970s and 1980s, which often accompanied an increase in sectarian conflicts on mosque issues resulting in an increase in the number of mosques along sectarian lines. An accompanied development saw a parallel growth of the Barelvi umbrella groups, which spread their networks within the United Kingdom and other European countries. The prominent among them were the World Islamic Mission (WIM), founded in 1972 in Makkah and based in Bradford.[21] They had their influences as far as in Norway, the Netherlands, South Africa and so on. In the United Kingdom, another group, *World Jama'at-e Ahl-e Sunnat* (WJAS) was founded which is based in London, but its network stretches across the United Kingdom and the Netherlands.

The Barelvis

The Barelvi stream owes its name to the ulama who follow the school associated with Ahmad Raza Khan Barelvi (1854–1921). Barelvis call themselves *ahl-i sunnat wa'l jama'at* in South Asia. The Barelvi ulama profess belief in miracles and the intercessionary powers of saints and the dispensing of amulets and charms.[22] Usha Sanyal, the author of an important study of the Barelvi movement, makes a distinction between the shrine-visitors and the Barelvi ulama and argues that not every visitor to Sufi shrines is a Barelvi and vice versa (Sanyal, 1996: 11).[23] Some Barelvi practices however are criticized as un-Islamic by the ulama associated with the reformist Deobandi movement, established in 1867, named after the reformist madrasa in Deoband in India.[24] One of the most important religious events of the year, for Barelvis, is the *milad* or commemoration of the birth of the Prophet Muhammad. Deobandis strongly object to the Barelvis' belief that the Prophet is spiritually present at *milad* celebrations and that he will personally intercede on behalf of his devotees on the Day of Judgement. The *Ahl-i Hadith* (followers of hadith), an even more radically puritan reformist movement in South Asia, are more fiercely critical of traditional practices and reject all that smacks of local culture. These intra-sectarian debates and rivalries were carried to the overseas Pakistani communities and have an effect on the organizational development of the South Asian religious organization bodies.

The MQ emerged within the Barelvi stream of Islam and accepts all Barelvi premises. The early intellectual life of Tahirul Qadri, the founder of the MQ, shows his intensive engagement with the Barelvi positions on sectarian issues.[25] He was not always in full agreement with all of his Barelvi colleagues, and soon differences between the MQ and other Barelvi ulama came to the surface. Qadri criticized these ulama for their continuous sectarian rhetoric and castigated their madrasas for spreading archaic religious knowledge that cannot cope with the problems of modern society. Similarly on the question of *diyat* or compensation for injuries for women, Qadri, as member of the Federal Shariat Court, declared that *diyat* of women should be equal to that of men, thus deviating from the 'consensus' of traditional ulama. This led to a broader social debate on this issue and Qadri received the wrath of traditional *ulama* who called his position as '*gumrah*' or 'deviation' and declared him a '*munkir-e ijma*' on this position, while more forceful opponents called him ' *la-din*' or 'secularist', a 'socialist' who caused a disruption in umma and *ijma-e ummat*' and positioned him along with Maulana Maududi, thus declaring him a *non-muqalid*.[26]

Qadri developed a new program under the platform of the MQ movement that he established in 1980 in Lahore. Criticizing the Barelvi ulama for creating an inertia or *jamood* of the Muslim tradition he calls for creating '*mustafvi* revolution' through Islamic activism in order to establish an 'Islamic system'. In using such language, he is influenced by the Islamists like Maududi and modernists like Burhanuddin Farouqi.[27] The modernist influence on the MQ was visible in the organization and mobilization structures that the MQ established: through the MQ Institute he started publishing lectures and books and producing audio and video recordings of his lectures. These materials covered different aspects of daily life and through it Qadri dealt with everyday problems according to the teachings of Qur'an and sunna (sayings and doings of the Prophet). These publications and his regular interaction with the state institutions and media – depicting him as a tele-ulama in the 1980s – helped him to create a network of religious teaching at an informal level. In using audiovisual materials and print media for his movement, he opted for a different technique and appealed to a modern class of the Barelvis in Pakistan and among the overseas communities. Later, Qadri established the Minhajul Qur'an University in Lahore in 1986. In this university, modern subjects are taught alongside the traditional *dars-i-nizami* syllabus, thus differing from traditional Barelvi ulama, and its selected graduates were sent to the MQ centres abroad.

Qadri approached the state institutes and the social classes affiliated with the structures of modernity: he visited the Lawyers' forums, teachers' associations, the military and bureaucratic institutes to spread his religious message. Similarly at organizational level, the MQ also developed a much more elaborate organizational structure than is common among the Barelvis, and the mosques it controlled became more than just houses of worship but also centres for various social and cultural activities, notably including activities for and by the youth and women, two categories that hardly find a place in traditional Barelvi mosques. Traditional Barelvi ulama looked upon these changes, especially the greater participation of women, with suspicion. In their view, even women's participation in congregational prayer is not advisable because it may lead to moral degeneration.

Among the overseas communities

From mid-1980s, Qadri started visiting the overseas Pakistani communities where he called upon the existing mosque-based organizations for his organizational activities. These visits were meant to make people familiar with the MQ message, and these were aimed at developing networks of the MQ in future. During these voyages his key message to the ulama and the mosque bodies in the United Kingdom was that 'constructing mosques and madrasas is not enough, we have to re-vitalize the message of the Prophet for the next generation in this society. We have to do this in revolutionary terms.'[28] It is obvious now that these mosque bodies were aware of the controversial position of Qadri and some like those affiliated with the WJAS never invited him into their mosques.[29] However, anticipating the support of younger generations among the *Ahl-e Sunnat* ulama Qadri was less blatant in his criticism of these ulama. Similarly he relied on the services of the traditional authorities to bring the message of the MQ for the *Ahl-e Sunnat* public in the United Kingdom. For example, young Tahirul Qadri accompanied his sheikh, *Pir* Tahir Allauddin – a descendent of Abdul Qadir Jilani Baghdadi, during the *kunzul iman* or Hijaz Conference that the *Ahl-e Sunnat* umbrella organizations across the United Kingdom held in order to protest against the Saudi government.[30] Qadri also made a speech at the Conference where he introduced the MQ to the broader *Ahl-e Sunnat* public in the United Kingdom.[31]

Qadri's exposure to the *Ahl-e Sunnat* mosque bodies and *Ahl-e Sunnat* followers led him to develop a niche within the UK Muslims. As a result, a mega event was organized by the MQ at the Wembley Conference Centre in London in 1988 in order to initiate its religious manifesto in Europe. The MQ organized the 'International Islamic Conference' on June 18, 1988, where a diverse gathering including various ulama, *Pir* and intellectuals from the sub-continent, some Arab and African scholars were invited. Presided over by Tahir Allauddin the prominent speakers included Yousaf Ahmad Al-Rifa'i, a Kuwaiti religious minister, Ahmad Deedat, a South Africa based Muslim scholar known for his religious polemics and French scholar Maurice Bucaille, known for his 'Islam and science' project where he 'proves Qur'anic truth on the basis of modern science while Bible fails this test'. Thus the event reflected a mobilization for a 'dialogue of global umma?' where the prominence of Islam should be manifested for an overwhelmingly *Ahl-e Sunnat* constituency. The different issues for this two day event included, 1) unity of global umma, 2) revival of spiritual values among Muslims, 3) re-organization of Islamic *dawa* and *tabligh*, 4) rehabilitation of Islamic educational system and 5) faith in the seal of the Prophets – the base of Islamic system (din-e Islam). Qadri presented the message of the MQ in 'revolutionary terms'. Claiming that this message is based on 'the Quranic philosophy of revolution', he said that

> the base of it would be three points a(*ilmi* and *fikri inqilaab* (educational and ideological revolution, its practical picture is the Minhaj University that combines the religious and worldly education to prepare young Muslims who can face the challenges of the present time. In foreign countries its implementation would be to prepare new syllabus in the MQ *idara* according to the local needs; B) moral and spiritual revolution, the MQ will organize locally and at its foreign centers the events of spiritual training on the lines of Islamic *tassawuf* (spiritualism); and C) economic and social revolution to create a just and equal society on the lines of idea of *mo'akhat'e* medina, brotherhood of Medina. All these objectives of the movement will work for the creation of an 'Islamic Common Wealth'.[32]

The Wembley conference led to the formation of 'majlis al-ittihad al-'alemiyya al-islamiyya' – International Council for the Unity of Muslims. Yousaf Al-Rifa'i became its head with Qadri as its Secretary General. The terms like 'International' and 'Muslim unity' refer to the 're-vivalist' message that the MQ projected during the Conference and was meant for all 'Muslim umma', thus it transcended itself above the sectarian terms of the traditional *Ahl-e Sunnat* groups. Similarly the choice of the location for such a message showed that the MQ took the footsteps of the Jamaat-i Islam-(JI) or other politically active Islamic groups in bringing its message outside the mosque premises into the public arena. Moreover, it presented a public manifestation of Muslim identity that appealed to a new generation of the Barelvi followers. These aspects led to further enhancing the authority of the MQ and its stature within the *Ahl-e Sunnat* in United Kingdom. The MQ introduced a vocabulary and modes of mobilization that enabled it to create certain niches for itself within the overseas communities. In describing the emergence of these networks among European countries, the transnational character of the movement is revealed.

Transnational aspect

In the last couple of decades much has been written on transnationalism and globalization. I will build the transnational aspect of the MQ following the observations of Piscatori who sees the role of religion in shaping the language of politics, creating new communities and generating self-awareness of one's tradition as crucial aspects of transnational politics'.[33] The MQ is part of a range of religious organizations working among the South Asian Muslim communities in the United Kingdom. A significant point about these movements is that they influence each other in their workings and the methods of organizations both in South Asia as well as among overseas communities. Thus Werbner noted that 'most reformist movements in South Asia, while disapproving of some Sufi practices and rejecting notions of divine intercession in favour of sacredness of the Qur'an and Hadith, replicate Sufi forms of regional and transnational social organization focused around exemplary charismatic leaders.[34] Similarly the influence of more 'fundamentalist' movements upon the Sufi-based groups from South Asia in United Kingdom is observed by some authors.[35] Following these observations, the workings of the MQ in United Kingdom are seen to be in a competition with other political and reformist movements when the MQ adjusts its activism following these influences.[36]

Writing on the transnational networks of a Sufi group, Ghamkol Sharif, Werbner described how different centres of the group were developed after the *Pir* sent his *khalifa* or deputy who developed lodges among the overseas communities.[37] These *khalifas* or deputies were thus central in introducing and maintaining the transnational links of the Sufi movement. Similar processes could be observed within the MQ where the founder of the movement himself visited different European countries to establish earlier contacts of the movement with the local Pakistani communities. The emergence of the local networks of the MQ occurred as a result of following factors: the personal predicaments of the MQ initiators, the message of the movement and the charisma of the movement founder. These local mobilizations were built in tension with the existing Barelvi groups in the United Kingdom, and it worked on feelings of disillusionment that the local Barelvis felt towards the existing Barelvi networks. In the following section, I describe the emergence of the local networks of the MQ in the United Kingdom and show, by focusing on the MQ Centre in London, that organizational innovations and specific socialization practices contributed to the strengthening of the movement.

New institutional and organizational structures

The MQ introduced certain novelties at its grass root network to enhance its activism. It introduced the concept of *idara* or centre, to replace the mosque, as the former provided more space for religious, social and communal gatherings. The *idara* was organized along modern bureaucratic lines, introducing the

concepts of directors, executives, secretaries, councils and UK councils, that
were further organized through committees and sub-committees. The mosque
imams, called director, were the MQ 'scholars' or graduates of the MQ University
in Lahore. They were appointed as the directors of the *idara*, and they act as the
lynchpin of the organizational and ideological patterns of the MQ. Educated in
both *dars-e nizami* and secular education the Minhaj 'scholars' normally have a
good command of English thus fulfilling the needs of local circumstances more
effectively. It is important to note that the 1990s saw an upsurge of the MQ centres
in the United Kingdom along with the wider mobilization of the movement
during this period in the United Kingdom. This interestingly coincided with the
graduation of the first batch of MQ University scholars in the early 1990s. Many
promising graduates of the University, 'sons of Tahir', as they call themselves,
thus showing a total loyalty to the founder, were posted at the new centres in
various European countries.

Another innovative idea in religious mobilization is the adoption of a family-
based approach. The MQ introduced the idea of 'being born within the MQ',
which means that MQ is a lifelong project that involves the whole family for its
religious activism. Through this concept, MQ introduced new spaces for the
involvement of the youth and women into its network. Thus the idara hosts the
youth, or Muslim Youth League, and Minhaj Women's League into its perimeter.
These platforms were developed to involve youth into its works, while within
the traditional Barelvi mosques the youth are not always welcome in the mosque
affairs. The MQ provided a ladder for youth through its networks to enter into
the administrative hierarchy of the movement. In the case of the MQ centre in
London, for example, the present administration emerged out of the MQ Youth
League in the 1990s.

Similarly the traditional Barelvi are reluctant to involve women in mosque
activities. The lack of women's religious participation among the Barelvis led to
concerns of 'masculinization of religion among the followers of the folk Islam'
based Muslim groups.[38] However, within the MQ, women, through its Women
League, participate in different spheres like the organization of events,and are
invited to different religion and training courses and participation in different
religious rituals. The *idara* became a major centre of religious training of children,
youth and women. Specific programs were developed following the needs of these
sub-categories. Thus there were spiritual gatherings for the youth and elders on
the weekends. Similarly the MQ directors gave specific classes, separately for the
young men and women, on the weekend to transfer religious knowledge and to
discuss the social issues following the needs of the society. These interactions

occurred in local languages thus providing religious knowledge on issues like the justification for organizing *milad*, visiting shrines and the spiritual positions of the Sheikhs and shrines and so on. Such knowledge was provided to youth in order to enable them to confront other youth groups like the *Salafi* and *Hizbul Tehrir* who challenged the religious positions of these devotional events and organizations of these ceremonies.

Significant to note here is that the MQ brought the organization of certain traditional rituals like organizing the *milad* into the broader public level. Thus it held the major *milad* event outside the mosque perimeters into the broader public space like the local City Councils, or it hired the public hall for this purpose. Its youth organized these events at the local Islamic Societies in colleges to create a broader awareness for these rituals; however, these were also meant to compete for intra-Muslim rivalries where the political Islam and *Salafi*-Reformist based groups were defining the public forms of Islam within the UK context. It invited, moreover, people from neo-traditional thinking into its gatherings like the *milad* program. Through these gatherings and platforms it created a neo-traditional consensus to counter the *Salafi* and the Reformists. The MQ formalized these events through the establishment of *Al-Hidaya* and the annual *Al-Hidaya* Camps. Initiated in 2005 these gatherings were meant to present a 'peaceful and integration' message of Islam.

The *Al-Hidaya* initiative

Before detailing the *Al-Hidaya* event, I want to make a note to explain a shift in the approach of the MQ in 2004. In that year, the MQ shifted its focus towards the overseas community, mostly in Europe and North America. In the summer, Qadri visited different centres of traditional Islam in the Middle Eastern countries like Turkey, Syria and Lebanon and met certain traditional ulama and sheikhs. Following these visits in 2004 and 2005, Qadri gradually adopted a different outlook and chose the title of 'Sheikhul Islam' for himself. In October 2004, Qadri resigned from the membership of the Pakistani Parliament to which he was elected as the only member of his party in 2002. More significantly from this year onwards Qadri started to spend more time among the overseas communities and based himself in Canada. As part of these changes Qadri stopped visiting different centers of the MQ across European countries as he annually did during his European tours. Instead the MQ launched a new initiative of *Al-Hidaya*, guidance, in the United Kingdom in which its affiliates from all European countries were encouraged to participate.

In such a shifting of focus of the movement, *Al-Hidaya* becomes an effort to further institutionalize the MQ into British society and within the European Muslim debate. Under this name different ulama of the MQ from the United Kingdom visited the MQ networks in different European countries. The major organizational and educational activism event was the annual gathering of 'Al-Hidaya – a spiritual and educational retreat' where different networks of the MQ in Europe were mobilized to participate. The focus of the *Al-Hidaya* was on Muslim youth to bring them to a 'spiritual journey of quest for thirst of knowledge. And in search of classical and authentic teachings of our beloved Rasul'.[39] Muslim youth were specifically invited on these occasions depicted as 'being in the company of a living Sheikh'. These annual events were held in the UK countryside like in Heythrop Park in Oxfordhsire or in Shropshire counties of the British Midlands. The speakers invited for the gatherings were traditional scholars from the Middle East and South Asia and certain local speakers from neo-traditional thinking. Efforts were made to invite the local academics, media and social actors in an atmosphere of 'dialogue between the communities'. The subjects dealt during these speeches were on issues like 'tassawuf', and 'aqeeda', ideology and philosophy of MQ' and 'dawa'.

A shift occurred within the themes and venues of annual *Al-Hidaya* gatherings in later years. It was no more held in the countryside but the new venues were major cities: thus in 2009 the 'Al-Hidaya retreat' was held at Warwick University. For 2011, the MQ planned a 'Peace conference' in the Wembley Hall in London. The changes in venues accompanied alterations in focus of the Conference. While the themes in earlier *Al-Hidaya* gatherings dealt with the issues like *aqeeda* or beliefs, Sufism and 'knowledge of traditional Islam' with emphasis on classical Islamic education, hadith, and Rumi etc, in later years issues like 'fighting extremism', 'plight of the Muslim youth in Europe' and 'Islam and war against extremism' entered into the program. The 2009 event was converted into the 'International Conference on Peace, integration and human rights', which resonated with the emerging debate about Islam in the United Kingdom.

These shifts in the issues of the *Al-Hidaya* gatherings emerged following changes in Muslim debates in the United Kingdom in the aftermath of the London bombings in 2005. Although the *Al-Hidaya* initiative emerged before the events of the London bombings, in the emerging debates, the MQ sought to rearrange its activism and focused on extremism among the youth. Moreover it presented its centre as a service for government officials to contact Muslim communities. Just after the London bombings the head of Scotland Yard chose the MQ Centre to speak to Muslim congregations on Friday. Similarly the MQ did its best to be part of the emerging government initiatives directed at Muslims. However, the MQ regretted that it was not approached for the initial meetings of the government with Muslim organizations and individuals invited by Tony Blair to the 10, Downing Street. It approached the media to communicate a 'missed chance' for the British government as MQ represented the 'voice of the Muslim youth'.[40]

In the following years, the MQ initiated programs that echoed the government initiatives of 'de-radicalization policies' for Muslim youth. Thus a recurring theme in the *Al-Hidaya* event was 'to combat radical Islam' through 'counteracting the root of Islamic radicalism' and 'promoting peace and mutual understanding' within Britain.[41] The MQ started to engage with the public debate on Muslim issues, and in doing this it became a sustained critic of the existing Muslim organizations with 'extremist' views. For example, in January 2010 in a meeting at the parliament offices on 'poverty, radicalism and religion' MQ officials supported a ban on groups like the Hizb ut-Tahrir (HT), and it supported the efforts of the government 'to fight the Muslim radicalism in the Universities'. In fact such an advocacy meant an implied support of the government initiative of the 'Campus Control', which had been criticized by the Civil Liberty and Muslim groups and also criticized by British academics. In that year it also organized programmes in different universities under 'Muslim Perspective' to 'discuss the roots of extremist behaviour among British Muslims and invited young people to listen to an alternative moderate view'. In early 2010, the MQ founder Tahirul Qadri published a 'comprehensive fatwa against terrorism' through the platform of the Quilliam Foundation, which is supported by the government, and emerged as part of its de-radicalization policy.[42] The fatwa got praise from many circles for its 'comprehensiveness', however it was also criticized for 'adding nothing new to the debate on terrorism'. Some critics referred to its sectarian bias when it says that 'every Salafi or Deobandi is not terrorist, but among them one finds a well-wisher of terrorism'.[43] Similarly some accused the MQ for its sectarianism when it took exception to the London Mosque project initiated by the Tablighi Jama'at, and opposed it saying that 'it should not be an individual initiative but from the Muslim communities'.[44]

Thus we see a shift in the MQ message within the European context when it started to focus on some critical issues of Muslims in Europe. This shift was signified through a new institutional and organizational form of the *Al-Hidaya*. The focus of *Al-Hidaya* shifted from, religious education and spiritual training of Muslims in Europe, to the issues of 'extremism' and 'Muslim youth' in the aftermath of the London bombing. A related shift in the MQ was the decision of its founder to base himself in Europe thus involving himself directly with the Muslim debate in Europe and North America.

Qadri and the making of the Sheikhul Islam

The MQ poses itself as a movement that works for 'the spiritual and intellectual nourishment' of its followers. Under this slogan, the MQ introduced different activities for its followers as we considered in the previous section. Here I specifically deal with the position of Qadri as a spiritual and intellectual figure and how such a position was created within the movement. The MQ founder, Tahirul Qadri, is a disciple of the Qādiriyya spiritual lineage in Pakistan that links it with Abdul Qadir Jilani of Baghdad. Thus the link with the Qadiriyya order goes through his personality, however, these links were not established along formal patterns, like *bayat*, or oath of allegiance or other *pir-muridi* structures to link his followers with the Qadiriyya Sufi order: 'I do not do *bait*; I am not a *Pir*', Qadri used to say. The MQ developed a modern structure to qualify its spiritual link with this order: 'filling a form of the MQ membership puts one within the lineage of the Qadiriyya'. However, some forms of traditional patterns of Sufism or its attributes were maintained, as following my talks with the secretary of the MQ United Kingdom, Ishtiaq, mentioned

> 'For the followers joining MQ brings one under the umbrella of Qadiriyya order: 'the members of the MQ will be raised in the company of Qadir Jilani on the day of judgment . . . on this matter Qaid-e inqlab once had a dream where all his followers will automatically be under the guidance of Abdul Qadir Jilani'.

Appropriating dreams for justification and operation of an action is a traditional practice among Sufi groups. Dreams appeared in different interviews that I conducted. Many followers told me stories of how they got guidance from Qadri on certain questions, and how his appearance during their dreams helped them to pass through some testing times in their lives. Many followers, mostly MQ graduates, during their interview described Qadri of possessing 'ilm-e laduni' or 'special knowledge' that is bestowed upon some selected people of Allah through 'His blessings'. Similarly such reverence is also seen through material objects. For example, during his visits to Europe, his followers often brought him a bottle of water and requested Qadri to blow on it for *baraka*. The water was later used for healing practices. Some acts of devotion appeared in some other interviews as a criticism of the followers of the MQ: some people mentioned how the followers of the MQ kept handkerchiefs or other articles touched by Qadri as a form of blessings in their homes, and how they decorate their homes and sitting rooms with his portraits and other articles of devotion of the MQ. Significant also are different devotional songs developed for Qadri like 'Qadri *Pira* way' – 'Qadri Oh! Our *Pir*', which praise Qadri as a spiritual guide and these were sung during 'spiritual gatherings' in his presence. Out of these observations, it is clear that though he may not formally use the title of a *Pir* or spiritual sheikh, he had all functions or attributes of a *Pir* for his followers.

In many MQ fora and with individual discussions with the youth Tahirul Qadri was presented as an 'all-rounder'[45]: He is seen as a teacher, guide, reformer and a popular star whose image should be decorated in drawing rooms. The term 'all-rounder' thus best gives the various features how the followers of the movement want to see 'their leader'. Within the movement's structure, Qadri adopted the name 'patron-in-chief', that indicates a modern classification referring to relationships as in 'patron client', where patron's role is more of guidance, thus helping others out. From the very beginning of the MQ, Qadri denied for himself any title, like *molvi* etc. that brings him into the category of the traditional Barelvi ulama. He and the MQ followers rejected the term 'Barelvi' used to refer to themselves: 'I am not a Barelvi', he has declared. Instead he chooses more modern titles like 'Professor', 'Doctor'. Many times such an adoption of a title went hand in hand with adoption of an appropriate cap on different occasions by his followers. The most significant example in this regard is his adoption of Al-Azhar style cap that went parallel with his adoption of the title 'Sheikhul Islam'.

In the summer of 2004, Tahirul Qadri went to Turkey, Syria and Lebanon to visit some shrines of the classical scholars and Sufis and to meet some traditional scholars. On the journey, he was mostly accompanied by his family and some selected followers from the Middle East and Europe. During this journey he visited the centres of traditional Islamic learning and visited Sufi shrines and lodges in Turkey, Damascus and Beirut. During his visit to Beirut he met an aged Sheikh Al-Useeran – a descendent of the Prophet, and one who was student of Sheikh Yusuf an-Nabhani.[46] From the former Qadri received *ijaza* for a *hadith almusalsal bil-musafa*. Qadri also got an *ijaza* or credential to 'transmit' this and other *hadith* or traditions of the Prophet – an act that gave him, as said by his followers, the status of *sheikhul hadith*. The significance of the *hadith bilmusalsal* was, as one follower told me, that it should be transmitted through the *musafa*, or shaking of hands, and there were only four links between Qadri and the Prophet as the first persona in the chain was a *jinn*, a *sahabi* or friend of the Prophet, with a long age.[47] The transmission of this *hadith*, is considered to guarantee the Prophetic blessing on the Day of Judgement. On his return to Pakistan Qadri, who was now wearing a *jalaba* with an Al-Azhar-style headgear, transmitted this *hadith* to his fellow ulama, the MQ graduates and his students. A MQ scholar remembers the occasion and described it in emotional words: 'the sphere of this gathering was very spiritual and *Qaide-mohtaram* or respected leader was sitting for the first time in his new dress of *alimana waqar* or an honourable sheikh'.[48]

The transmission of the *hadith*, as Qadri always told in subsequent gatherings, 'should not be seen as a *ba'it*, or oath of allegiance, as I do not take *ba'it* from any person', neither the hadith should be taken as something that makes you 'a reporter' of hadith. He described it as 'just a blessing or *baraka*' and which should be transmitted to other people in this form. However, the MQ developed certain protocol to transmit it during the gatherings that were specifically called for this purpose. Before his visit to the United Kingdom, the MQ network in London an Arabic version of the text prepared mentioning the names of different scholars of the Middle East through which the lineage reached Tahirul Qadri and thus created a chain. During his following visit to the United Kingdom in August 2004, the MQ created a setting to 'transfer' the hadith in certain ritualized fashion, first during the annual Minhaj Camp held in Glasgow, and later for general Barelvi ulama at the Ghamkol Sharif mosque in Birmingham.

On the second day of the Camp held in Glasgow, Qadri delivered the second speech of the Camp in which he first detailed his recent visits to Turkey and Lebanon and his meetings with certain local scholars of the traditional Islam and how he received the specific *hadith almusalsal bil-musafa*. As the hadith is meant for 'baraka' to link oneself with the Prophet, Qadri asked the people to make two chains, on his right hand for the men and on his left for the women, 'thus linking with the Prophet through me'. He next asked everybody to close their eyes and think themselves to be in *Gunbad-e Khidra* – the Green mosque in Medina. He then started reading the 'ijaza' in Arabic, mentioning the name of the Prophet and all other figures who 'transfer' this hadith to the next generation, ending on his own name. In such way a continuous chain of scholars were linked leading to the name of Qadri. In the beginning, he spoke in soft voice but his tone overflowed with passion as he recited the text. With his raised voice people became emotional and broke into tears until the ritualized reading was completed. Qadri asked the participants to embrace each other and congratulate each other for achieving this *sa'adat* or blessing. People were clearly moved by the incident, as one participant told me afterwards: 'I feel it like a power upon myself; I think a link is created between me and the Prophet.'

There are certain points where a juxtaposition of the spiritual and intellectual authority of Qadri occurs for his followers: he is already considered an intellectual authority, but through ritualized events like the above his spiritual authority is emphasized by presenting and centralizing himself in a chain that goes back to the Prophet. Furthermore, the event added to the newly created Middle-Eastern links to add to the spiritual and intellectual reputation of Qadri for his followers. His adoption of a new outfit during the ceremony of 'ijaza' of hadith when he wore a long Arabic robe with an Al-Azhar headgear placed him apart from the traditional South Asian ulama and brought himself closer to the Middle Eastern scholars of traditional Islam. All this is also linked to a certain Arabization within the MQ emphasized through adopting Arabic semantics of greetings and calling each other 'akhi' or brother . Interesting here is to note that the MQ followers, mostly the MQ scholars, traditionally copied a cap or any other dress that Qadri took to wear 'as a matter of devotion and respect for the Qaid [leader]'. Interestingly, an official order was issued this time to all branches of the MQ to discourage people from copying the new outfit of their leader. The adoption of the new outfit was accompanied by the adoption of the title 'Sheikhul Islam' and, was officially adopted through the media of the MQ.[49]

The appropriation of the terms like 'transmission of hadith', ' ijaza', 'isnad' are traditional methods through which different religious scholars linked themselves with their predecessors. Sunni Islamic tradition focuses on the importance of chains and legitimization. Similarly in Sufism, sheikhs are connected by a continuous spiritual chain (isnad, sanad, silsila). These chains link every previous Sufi shaykh, and eventually can be traced back to the Successors, and to the Prophet himself.[50] Thus the founder MQ Tahirul Qadri appropriates his newly established links with Middle Eastern scholars and sources of knowledge to build upon his image as a Sheikh, even though he would not permit using of the South Asian based ideas of piri-muridi. It is further reflected in his choice of title of Sheikhul Islam and adopting the Middle Eastern outfit through which Qadri looks for the legitimacy of his religious credentials from the Middle Eastern institutes. It is an effort on part of the MQ leadership to transcend its religious credentials beyond the religio-sectarian politics of South Asia. In the UK context, these adoptions get extra meanings as many locally born youth consider the South Asian ulama inferior to the Middle Eastern scholars due to their lack of Arabic language and scholarship that goes with it.

Conclusion

In this chapter, I have shown a transformation in the Barelvis, the traditional religious group in the United Kingdom through the workings of a transnational religious movement, the MQ. The MQ emerged within the Barelvis, and it shared its worldview with the Barelvis. It appealed to those sections of the Barelvis that were dissatisfied with the sectarianism of the traditional Barelvi institutes in the United Kingdom and the latter's inability to appeal to the generations born and brought up in the United Kingdom. These groups feared that they were losing their next generations to the reformist, *Salafi* and activist groups with apparent extreme views. The MQ appealed to these groups and it introduced a new message that translated the Muslim identity beyond such sectarian politics, and initiated new forms of activism. It converted its mosques into *idaras*, places of social, religious and communal gatherings and developed an approach that involved the whole family for the MQ project. As a result the *idara* or centre of the movement became an active place of family socialization and activism, which was later utilized into the broader society.

The MQ brought its neo-traditionalism based activism outside the mosque premises into the broader public sphere that was traditionally defined by the reformist, *Salafist* and more politically engaged groups. Its disciplinary techniques and active religious engagement led to the formation of a new group that, equipped with the traditional Islamic and Sufi intellectual and experiential teachings, wants to have a claim on the broader public level along with other neo-traditional groups. The youth and women cadres of the MQ are most specifically mobilized to provide an Islamic activism that gets its inspiration from the traditional Islamic education and that challenges the views of those groups that define their religious identity in political or narrow religious terms. The most prominent institutional structure that the MQ developed is that of *Al-Hidaya*, that offers to 'educate in classical knowledge and enhance spirituality'. However, following societal developments in United Kingdom, mostly after the London bombing, the *Al-Hidaya* turned into a venue to present a nursery to move the youth away from 'extremist paths'. In doing this, the MQ moulded its message to develop an image of 'peaceful and tolerant' Islam. In this regard 'fighting extremism among youth' dominates the agenda of the *Al-Hidaya* – an aspect of its religious activism that was criticized for being too close to the official policies of the UK government.

In realizing the changes among the Barelvis through the working of the MQ, the charismatic role of its founder was significant. He acts as a reformer, a leader, a guide, a spiritual sheikh and a popular figure for the movement's followers. His teachings, behaviour and modes of outlook are ritually followed by his followers. Although he did not define himself as a *pir* in traditional sense of the word, his reverence, appeal and spiritual links all act to present him as a spiritual figure. I have demomstrated that in recent years a shift within the MQ happened as a result of which Qadri spent more time in Europe and North America and he made the predicament of the European Muslims as part of his central message. By developing links with Arab scholars and sites of devotion in the Middle East, he introduced a certain innovative idea into the movement that can be depicted as Arabization happening within the MQ. At the same time, he is a welcome guest among the policy-making institutes in his new found places of residence where his outspoken position against terrorism is warmly received.

Notes

1   O. Roy (1998) 'Naissance d'un Islam European'. *Esprit*, 239, pp. 10–35.
2   J. Cesari (2003) 'Muslim Minorities in Europe: The Silent Revolution' in *Modernizing Islam: Religion in the Public Sphere in the Middle East and in Europe.* J. L. Esposito and F. Burgat (Eds), London: Hurst, p. 251–69.
3   Cesari, p. 253.
4   Cesari, p. 260.
5   F. Peter (2006) 'Individualization and Religious Authority in Western European Islam', *Islam and Christian–Muslim Relations*, 17, 1, pp. 105–18.
6   See J. Casanova José (1994) *Public Religions in the Modern World.* Chicago: University of Chicago Press.
7   See S. Allievi and J. S. Nielsen (Eds) (2003) *Muslim Networks and Transnational Communities in and across Europe.* Leiden: Brill.
8   S. Amir-Moazami and A. Salvatore (2003) 'Gender, Generation and the Reform of Traditio': From Muslim Majority Societies to Western Europe' in *Muslim Networks and Transnational Communities in and across Europe.* Stefano Allievi and Jørgen S. Nielsen (Eds), Leiden: Brill, p. 55.
9   J. R. Bowen (1998) 'What is 'Universal' and 'Local' in Islam?' *Ethos*, 26, 2, pp. 258–61.
10 For Sufi groups see J. Malik and J. Hinnells (Eds) (2006) *Sufism in the West.* London: Routledge and P. Werbner (2003) *Pilgrims of Love: The Anthropology of a Global Sufi Cult.* Bloomington: Indiana University Press, and for the political

groups see P. Mandaville (2007) 'Globalization and the Politics of religious Knowledge', *Theory, Culture and Society*, 24, 2, pp. 101–15.

11 See A. Appadurai (1996) *Modernity at Large: Cultural Dimensions of Globalization*. Minneapolis, Minn.: University of Minnesota Press.

12 N. Ahlberg (1990) *New Challenges, Old Strategies: Themes of Variation and Conflict among Pakistani Muslims in Norway*. Helsinki: Finnish Anthropological Society, p. 244.

13 R. Geaves (2000) *The Sufis of Britain: An Exploration of Muslim Identity*. Cardiff: Cardiff Academic Press, p. 220.

14 P. Mandaville (2003) 'Towards a Critical Islam: European Muslims and the Changing Boundaries of the Transnational Religious Discourse' in *Muslim Networks and Transnational Communities in and across Europe*. S. Allievi and J. S. Nielsen (Eds), Leiden: Brill, p. 136.

15 See R. Geaves (2007) 'Learning the Lessons from the Neo-Revivalists and Wahhabi Movements: The Counterattack of the New Sufi Movements in the UK' in *Sufism in the West*. J. Malik and J. Hinnells (Eds), London: Routledge.

16 Geaves, 2007, pp. 80–1.

17 Ibid., p. 112.

18 Ibid., 2007.

19 A. Morgahi Amer (in press) *Religion, Recreation, and Devotion: A Comparative Study of the Minhajul Qur'an Movement among the South Asian Youth in Europe*.

20 T. Modood (1990) 'British Asian Muslims and the Rushdie Affair', *Political Quarterly*, 61/2.

21 Its founders included Maulana Shah Ahmad Noorani, *Pir* Maroof Hussain Naushahi and Allama Arshadul Qadri from India.

22 H. Alavi (1987) 'Pakistan and Islam: Ethnicity and Ideology' in *State and Ideology in the Middle East and Pakistan*. F. Halliday and H. Alavi (Eds), London: MacMillan, p. 84.

23 U. Sanyal (1996) *Devotional Islam and Politics in British India: Ahmed Raza Khan Barelwi and his movement, 1870–1920*. Delhi: Oxford University Press, p. 11.

24 See B. Metcalf (1982) *Islamic Revival in British India: Deoband, 1860–1900*. Princeton: Princeton University Press.

25 M. Rafiq (1996) *Nabigha-i 'Asr (The Sage of Our Time)*. Lahore: Minhajul Quran Publications, pp.231–3.

26 M. M. Sadiq *Khatrey ki ghanti*, [the warning bells]. Gujranwala: Maktaba-e Raza-e Mustafa Publication, pp. 24–9.

27 B. Farouqi (1988) *Minhajul Quran*. Lahore: Institute of Islamic Culture.

28 T. Qadri. Speech, London, August 1985.

29 It was only on the eve of 'International Peace Conference' in London on September 24, 2011, that the two groups came together after 1984.

30 For a report of this Conference see Lewis, 1994.

31 K. Ather (1998) *birtania ke ulma-e ahl-e sunnat aur mashaikh*, [*Ahl-e Sunnat* ulama and Sufi sheikhs in Britain]. Islamabad: PPA Publications. Part 3. p. 86.

32 Speech in Wembley Hall to be found in the book of Tahirul Qadri, (1999) *qurani falsifa-e inqilab* [Quran's philosophy of revolution]. Lahore: MQ Publications. pp. 474–81.

33 J. P. Piscatori (1992) *Islam in a World of Nation-States*. Cambridge: Cambridge University Press, p. 7.

34 Werbner, p. 10.

35 See Roy, 1998.

36 Geaves, 2007, p. 112.

37 Werbner, 2003.

38 Ahlberg, 1990.

39 www.alhidaya.co.uk (accessed June 2005).

40 *Times*. July 19, 2005, 'Example of Blair's failure'.

41 See *Al-Hidaya* Press Release August 17, 2006 and also *BBC* Online, August 25, 2006.

42 *Guardian* online. March 2, 2010, 'Fatwa Wars are not the Solution'.

43 http://blogistan.co.uk/blog/mt.php/2010/02/27/qadris_fatwa_breaks_no_new_ground.

44 *BBC* online, January 7, 2010.

45 The term 'all-rounder' came from cricket, and it is attributed to someone who is equally good in different aspects of the game like bowling, batting, etc.

46 Yusuf an-Nabhani was 'a Sunni, Sufi, Ottoman Palestinian Islamic scholar, judge and poet'. http://en.wikipedia.org/wiki/Yusuf_an-Nabhani (accessed March 12, 2008).

47 The *Minhajul Quran Magazine*, September 2004.

48 Ibid.

49 In March 2005, on the occasion of Imam Azam Conference in Lahore 'Sheikhul Islam was firstly used for Qadri; it was in April 2006 that 'sheikhul Islam' was added to Qadri's name on the website of the MQ after its major reload. Minhaj.org accessed on April 12, 2006. See also the Department of Foreign Affairs, Notice, date 15–04–2008.

50 A. Buehler (1998) *Sufi Heirs of the Prophet: The Indian Naqshbandiyya and the Rise of the Mediating Sufi Shaykh*. Columbia: University of South California Press. pp. 1–2.

Bibliography

Ahlberg, N. (1990) *New Challenges, Old Strategies: Themes of Variation and Conflict among Pakistani Muslims in Norway,* Helsinki: Finnish Anthropological Society.

Alavi, H. (1987) 'Pakistan and Islam: Ethnicity and Ideology'. In: Fred Halliday and Hamza Alavi, (Eds). *State and Ideology in the Middle East and Pakistan*. London: MacMillan.

Allievi, Stefano and Nielsen, Jørgen S. (Eds) (2003) *Muslim Networks and Transnational Communities in and across Europe*, Leiden: Brill.

Amir-Moazami, S. and Salvatore, A. (2003) 'Gender, Generation and the Reform of Tradition: From Muslim Majority Societies to Western Europe'. In: Stefano Allievi and Jørgen S. Nielsen (Eds). *Muslim Networks and Transnational Communities in and across Europe*. Leiden: Brill.

Appadurai, A. (1996) *Modernity at Large: Cultural Dimensions of Globalization*, Minneapolis, Minn.: University of Minnesota Press.

Athar, K. (1998) *birtania ke ulma-e ahl-e sunnat aur mashaikh*, [*Ahl-e Sunnat* ulama and Sufi sheikhs in Britain], Islamabad: PPA Publications.

Bowen, J. R. (1998) What is 'Universal' and 'Local' in Islam? *Ethos*, 26(2), 258–61.

Buehler, A. (1998) *Sufi Heirs of the Prophet: The Indian Naqshbandiyya and the Rise of the Mediating Sufi Shaykh*, Columbia: University of South California Press.

Casanova, J. (1994) *Public Religions in the Modern World*, Chicago: University of Chicago Press.

Cesari, J. (2003) 'Muslim Minorities in Europe: The Silent Revolution'. In: John L. Esposito and Francois Burgat (Eds). *Modernizing Islam: Religion in the Public Sphere in the Middle East and in Europe*. London: Hurst.

Farouqi, B. (1988) *Minhajul Quran*, Lahore: Institute of Islamic Culture.

Geaves, R. (2000) *The Sufis of Britain: An Exploration of Muslim Identity*, Cardiff: Cardiff Academic Press.

— 'Learning the Lessons from the Neo-Revivalists and Wahhabi Movements: The Counterattack of the New Sufi Movements in the UK'. In: Malik, Jamal and Hinnells, John. (Eds). *Sufism in the West*. London: Routledge.

Lewis, P. (1994) *Islamic Britain, Religion Politics and Identity among British Muslims*, London: IB Tauris.

Malik, J. and Hinnells, J. (Eds) (2006) *Sufism in the West*, London: Routledge.

Mandaville, P. (2003). 'Towards a Critical Islam: European Muslims and the Changing Boundaries of the Transnational Religious Discourse'. In: Stefano Allievi and Jørgen S. Nielsen (Eds). *Muslim Networks and Transnational Communities in and across Europe*. Leiden: Brill.

— (2007) 'Globalization and the Politics of Religious Knowledge', *Theory, Culture and Society*.

Metcalf, B. D. (1982) *Islamic Revival in British India: Deoband, 1860–1900*, Princeton: Princeton University Press.

Modood, T. (1992) 'British Asian Muslims and the Rushdie Affair', *Political Quarterly*.

Morgahi, A. (in press) *Religion, Recreation, and Devotion: A Comparative Study of the Minhajul Qur'an Movement among the South Asian Youth in Europe*.

Peter, F. (2006) 'Individualization and Religious Authority in Western European Islam', *Islam and Christian–Muslim Relations*.

Piscatori, J. P. (1992) *Islam in a World of Nation-States*, Cambridge: Cambridge University Press.

Qadri, T. (1999) *Qurani falsifa-e inqilab* [Quran's philosophy of revolution], Lahore: MQ Publications.

Rafiq, M. (1996) *Nabigha-i `Asr (The Sage of Our Time)*, Lahore: Minhajul Quran Publications.

Roy, O. (1998) 'Naissance d'un Islam European', *Esprit*.

Sadiq, M. M. (nd) *Khatrey ki ghanti*, [the warning bells], Gujranwala: Maktaba-e Raza-e Mustafa Publication.

Sanyal, U. (1996) *Devotional Islam and Politics in British India: Ahmed Raza Khan Barelwi and His Movement, 1870–1920*, Delhi: Oxford University Press.

Werbner, P. (2003) *Pilgrims of Love: The Anthropology of a Global Sufi Cult*, Bloomington: Indiana University Press.

12

'Ours is not a caravan of despair': The Influence and Presence of the Turkish Sunni Nurcu Movement of Hojaeffendi Fethullah Gülen in the UK

Ian G. Williams

Introduction

In his novel, *Greenmantle*, first published in 1916, the English statesman and writer John Buchan (1875–1940) speculated on the possibility of a mass-mobilization of Islamic sentiment directed against Britain, France and Russia, which would assist Germany and Austria to defeat the Allied forces in the 1914–18 European and Middle Eastern conflict. The generalizations of Islam made by the characters in *Greenmantle*, as cited above, reduce Muslims to an undifferentiated whole that strides across fundamental clefts in political, social and religious terrain.

> 'But in the provinces, where Islam is strong, there would be trouble . . . The Syrian army is as fanatical as the hordes of the Mahdi. The Senussi have taken a hand in the game. The Persian Moslems are threatening trouble. There is a dry wind blowing through the East and the parched grasses wait the spark. And the wind is blowing towards the Indian border . . ' 'It looks as if Islam had a bigger hand in the thing that we thought', I said 'I fancy religion is the only thing to knit up such a scattered empire'.

> (Buchan, 1957: 165)

A century later similar such sentiments are to be heard in European and Western estimates of the contemporary vitality of Muslim communities and traditions.

Far from the militaristic portrayals of energies within Islam, however, are equally vigorous movements which focus upon inter-religious dialogue, educational initiatives and social cohesion. One such community is associated with the Turkish Muslim scholar and teacher, Hojaeffendi Fethullah Gülen (b. 1941).

Emerging from the Islamic-Turkish synthesis with its global network of schools and universities, inter-religious dialogue activities, media and a relief organization, this movement has an established school in England – the Wisdom Schools, Haringey, London, as well as active Dialogue Centres in London, Birmingham, Manchester, Leicester and Oxford. Education, dialogue, peace and tolerance between religions, cultures and civilizations have become more and more Gülen's personal emphases. This significant contemporary *hizmet* (service) movement combines traditional Muslim Sufi sourced spirituality and modern Western values and ideals which may explain part of the attraction of the Gülen movement for many socially and economically prominent persons not only in Turkish but also in European and specifically British societies compared to other renewalist Muslim movements from the Middle East and South Asia. As an innovative religio-social movement whose network of relationships is based on common faith ideals, it differs from both classical *tariqa* models and parallel *nurculler* groups with a diffused leadership and the priority being on personal and group initiatives (Della Porta and Diani, 2006: 16). Both these aspects of this pro-social religiously inspired movement are pertinent for the UK context, as it represents a distinct model of a European Islam which contrasts with the more familiar South Asian heritage expressions.

Operational breadth; spiritual depth

Many descriptions have been applied to the Gülen inspired initiatives, civil, cultural, political, confrontational, conflictual, reactionary, regressive, exclusivist, sectarian, alienating, competitive, Islamist, mediating, reconciliatory, pluralist, democratic, altruistic and peaceful (White, 2002: 112). In using social movement theories how may one define this association? Is it a civil society movement; a reaction to a crisis, a Sufi *tariqa* or order, a political movement; or an altruistic collective action?

There is clear evidence from both the writer's own fieldwork that the Gülen Movement is notable for its unrelenting contribution to the potential of students and people in positions of influence to pursue and implement new goals and life changing decisions. It has encouraged voluntary participation and service in a network of global schools and universities, developed trusting relationships between faith leaders and communities though inter-faith dialogue, creating shared objectives for their respective societies (Gülen, 2000a: 21).

A 'civil society' type of group covers a spectrum of organizations that are essentially outside the institutional structures of government. They are also distinct from business organizations and therefore are not primarily commercial ventures set up principally to distribute profits to their directors or owners. They are self-governing and people are free to join or support them voluntarily (Zald and McCarthy, 1998: 226). Hefner offers a definition that a civil society is a '. . . voluntary association beyond the household but outside the state . . . and providing citizens with opportunities to learn the democratic habits of free assembly, non-coercive dialogue, and socioeconomic initiative.' (Hefner, 2004: 10). I will argue that the Gulen Movement can be defined as a civil society group as the approach of the movement especially through its educational 'agencies' is from the grass roots upwards. It is the transformation of individuals through education to facilitate the establishment of a harmonious and inclusive society based on a liberal public sphere. This is the rationale for Gülen's emphasis on the primacy of 'education' among the Movement's commitments regardless of whether it is a paralyzed social and political system or one that operates like clockwork (Gulen, 2004: 199).

While critics such as secularist groups in Turkish society may wish to cast the 'movement' as threatening to a status quo within Turkey itself, there is evidence that whether within the borders of the republic or globally the Gülen Movement promotes an apolitical, highly tolerant and open regeneration of individuals and thus of societies. The 'movement' draws upon the Islamic creedal statement and the example of the Prophet Muhammad as mediated through the traditions of Anatolian Sufism. It is also modernist in tone and in the sphere of education emphatic on achievement within the empirical sciences as they are an international language. If implicit then the heritage of the Prophet and the Qur'an are the streams of inspiration for the place of the schools, universities, medical provision and inter-religious dialogue initiatives of the 'movement'.

Education is the Movement's priority. In Gülen's view it is not only the establishment of justice that is hindered by the lack of well-rounded education, but also the recognition of human rights and attitudes of acceptance and tolerance towards others. He writes

> . . . If you wish to keep the masses under control, simply starve them in the area of knowledge. They can escape such tyranny only through education. The

road to social justice is paved with adequate, universal education, for only this
will give people sufficient understanding and tolerance to respect the rights of
others. (Unal and Williams, 2000: 22–3)

As I have observed in four national contexts, the schools are focussed on
creating literate, independent thinkers who will be agents of change for equality,
inclusiveness and social justice.

The 'spirituality' evident in Gülen's writings as observed by Michel (2006:
110) include not only directly Qur'anic and Sunnah-based teachings, but also
ethics, logic, psychological and emotional health. Key terms are 'compassion' and
'tolerance'. Gülen believes that 'non-quantifiable' qualities need to be instilled in
students alongside training in the 'exact' disciplines. Equally, there is no one
conformist curriculum for the schools as they adopt the prescribed curriculum of
the state within which they are placed. This leads towards an inclusive openness
that is an attribute of the many expressions of the movement if coupled with an
optimistic idealism about the future of humanity and the construction of a new
social order. Unal and Williams (2000: 277) cite Gülen

> Gigantic developments in transportation and telecommunication technology
> have made the world into a big village. In these circumstances, all the peoples
> of the world must learn to share this village among them and live together in
> peace and mutual helping. We believe that peoples, no matter of what faith,
> culture, civilization, race, colour and country, have more to compel them to
> come together than what separates them. If we encourage those elements which
> oblige them to live together in peace and awaken them to the lethal dangers of
> warring and conflicts, the world may be better than it is today.

The movement is not so easy to categorize as a *tariqa*. It is only so to the extent
in which the volunteers adopt and follow their *din* and fulfil their *dawah* in a
manner that is universally Qur'anic, based on the *sunnah* of the Prophet and
centred upon seeking the state of *insan i-kamil* with the ideal as the faith model
of the Prophet Muhammad.

Gülen and the key sources of his theology and spirituality

Gülen is explicit about the fact that he has found the basis for his ideas for
contemporary forms of Islam in the sources of the Islamic tradition, albeit
these sources are used in different ways in the phases of Gülen's discourse.

All biographical materials concerning Gülen mention that the Qur'an and the example of Prophet Muhammad were of paramount importance in the domestic context in which he grew up. Therefore, it makes sense to consider the Qur'an and the *hadith* literature as the most important source of Gülen's later theological thought, even though references to these sources tend to diminish in his later works.

The same biographical materials relate the importance of the mystical tradition in Islam in Gülen's foundational religious education and nurture. This influence is mostly connected with the name of Muhammad Lütfi Effendi, the honorary imam of Alvar where Gülen lived at the time. A few years later, Gülen came to know the *Risale-i Nur*, the commentary on the Qur'an by Bediuzzaman Said Nursi (1878–1960), a text which influenced many Turkish Muslims in the early days of the secular republic in defending a rational form of Islam open to the empirical sciences and modernity. Although Gülen never met Nursi, and although he denies to be a follower of Nursi in the strict sense of the word, it is clear that Nursi's writings have influenced Gülen and his followers to such an extent that the Gülen movement is sometimes called the neo-Nur movement (Yavuz, 2003: 179–205). In its formative period, the Gülen movement developed as a separate subgroup of the Nur movement, as for example when Gülen used the methodology of reading Scriptures together in Nursi's *dershanes* but at the same time giving it an interpretation of his own in the *ışık evler* or 'lighthouses'.

These three main sources are evident in Gülen's works in diverse ways. The influence of the Qur'an and the *hadith* literature can be seen in the sheer quantity of Qur'anic references from the Qur'an and the *sahih* ('sound') collections of *hadith* literature in Gülen's works. At a more theoretical level, the importance of the Qur'an is highlighted in Gülen's most explicitly theological works, for example, his study of the Prophet Muhammad and his work *Essentials of the Islamic Faith* (Gülen, 2000a: 257–94; 2005) and his work *Fatiha Üzerine Mülahazalar* ('Considerations on chapter *al-fatiha*') which is his only explicit commentary on the Qur'an.

On exegeting the Qur'an

In *Fatiha Üzerine Mülahazalar*, Gülen comments

The Qur'an is a translation of this universe as a book. Yes, the universe is a book. It is needed for a reader to read this book, which is well organized with all of its verses and pages. The reader is human and the interpretation of the book is Qur'an. Allah has sent Qur'an as a translation of the universe to the human beings who cannot grasp the universe's immense, deep meaning and its huge vision. This meaning that we cannot easily understand by looking at the big pages and phrases of the universe, we can see at a first glance in the Qur'an, the Miraculous. This is a favour for the human beings. Allah is the one to make the universe book speak. As the others' thoughts upon the universe would be wrong, it is also the same with humans. The Universe is the universe of Allah, Qur'an is the speech of Allah and humans are the slaves of Allah. Allah is the one to establish the interrelation between these three. (Gulen, 1997: 25)

Here Gülen is referring to a tradition found within both Christian and Muslim theological discourse viz., the concept of the 'two books' that display the Creator of heaven and earth: the book of the universe and the book of the revelation. In Islam, this tradition is particularly associated with the word *āya* that can have the meaning of a verse in the Qur'an, and of a sign of God's presence and of God's works in nature. The Qur'an regularly refers to such signs of God in nature, for example, Surah 2. 164 (Ünal, 2006: 79).

The idea that a rational observation of nature leads us to consider God as its origin is one of the main themes in Said Nursi's *Risale-i Nur*. For Gülen, whom as we shall see draws upon Nursi, it leads to the conclusion that there is a harmony of religion and science in Islam. Just like the tradition of 'natural theology' in Christian theology, this convention states that it is possible to find signs of God's existence in the whole of creation. But at the same time as in orthodox Christianity the consideration of nature is not enough; since our human understanding and knowledge are deficient, additional guidance is required in a more conspicuous sign of God – namely, through revelation. While Islam points to the Qur'an as God's Word *inlibrate* revealed to Prophet Muhammad, Christianity sees the Word of God embodied *incarnate* in the person of Jesus Christ. It is significant that the two of the Abrahamic faiths demonstrate parallel theological constructions in that the Transcendent can be recognized in nature and more clearly through revelation albeit with the crucial difference that the revelatory process is either in a text or a historical person.

In the citation *supra,* however, Gülen adds a third element to this tradition of the 'two books' of nature and Qur'an: the human being itself is also related to God as Creator. And it is God as the universal Creator who inter-relates the three: universe, text and humankind. The same idea returns in the second significant quotation given by Tuncer in his article, from Gülen's treatment of the Qur'an in *Essentials of the Islamic Faith*

> The Qur'an also unveils the mystery of humanity, creation, and the universe. The Qur'an, humanity and the universe are the three "books" that make the Creator known to us, and are three expressions of the same truth. Therefore, the One Who created humanity and the universe also revealed the Qur'an. (Gülen, 2000a: 262)

Gülen uses this image of the universe, human beings and the Qur'an as three books to make clear that Islam teaches the harmony of sciences and humanities on the one hand and revelation on the other. Yet there is a difference, since faith in God's revelation is the only knowledge that will lead to the afterlife. Again, this concept of revelation as necessary for human beings to reach their ultimate goal has a clear parallel in Christianity, where Thomas Aquinas (1225–74), for example, states that humankind can gain some knowledge of God by using the insights of the philosophers, but needs the specific knowledge of God's revelation to reach our ultimate and eternal destiny in God. This affirmation in the first article of Aquinas's *Summa Theologiae* is then developed in discussion of God as creator of the universe; followed by an argument that human beings and their moral lives are a way towards God; and thirdly a discussion that in Christ and the sacraments there is further guidance to ultimate salvation. (Valkenberg, 2000). There are therefore parallels between Aquinas and Gulen in the model of the three 'books' the universe, human beings and the Historical Christ/Qur'an that guide us to knowledge not only of the present world but also to eternity.

In this respect, it is significant that the Qur'an in the first *āya* after the opening prayer and the bismillah introduces itself as a book of guidance;

> This is the (most honoured, matchless) Book: there is no doubt about it (its Divine authorship and that it is a collection of pure truths throughout); a perfect guidance for the God-revering, pious, who keep their duty to God. (Surah 2:2; Ünal, 2006: 10)

This is one of the four verses (the others are 1:7, 2:10, and 2:17) explained by Gülen in the small collection of 'reflections on the Qur'an' available on his English website (.en.fgulen.com/). This explanation of the verse is technical since it discusses the infinitive form of the Arabic word *hudan* ('a guidance') to point out the difference between an indefinite form which in Arabic grammar indicates a perfect meaning, and a definite form ('the guidance') that is more specific. Gülen uses this insight to say that the Qur'an is a perfect and transcending divine guide for believers who 'are ready to comply with both the injunctions of faith (*sharīʿa al-garra*) and the principles that are in effect in nature (*sharīʿa al-fitriyya*).

This demonstrates some major characteristics of Gülen's thinking as a hermeneutist of the Qur'an. This interpretation is entirely in line with the mainstream Muslim tradition in both its intellectual aspects with the problem of God's omnipotence and human free will and its spiritual aspects of the role of faith and knowledge as first stage on a path (*tarīqa*) with God's pleasure as goal. While Said Nursi is a representative source for the intellectual interpretation of the Qur'an in Gülen's works, Jalaluddin Rumi is a representative source for its spiritual interpretation. But the entire explanation of the word 'guidance' in Gülen matches with the other Abrahamic traditions as well, since it interprets what Burrell has pointed out as a basic idea in the three Abrahamic religions: the notion of 'created freedom' (Burrell, 2004).

Such a 'balanced' and reflective reading of the Qur'an that Gülen offers and commends forms a contrast to the more rigid interpretations of literalist and fundamentalist Muslims. In parallel, the same tension is visible in Christianity where the belief in the Bible as God's Word also may lead to the idea that 'the Bible contains all truths' and 'the Bible is always right'. Gülen would concur that the Qur'an contains all truth and that the Qur'an, being the Word of God, is always right. But he would also say that in our interpretation of the Qur'an we would have to make a distinction between the main reason for which the Qur'an has been revealed to us, namely, to function as our guidance on our way to God, and everything else that might be interesting but of secondary importance. As Gülen says at the end of his *Essentials of the Islamic Faith*: what ultimately counts is our faith (iman), not the amount of our knowledge.

> After we have understood as much as we can about the objective and subjective evidence we have gathered, we must break our dependence on the outer circumstances, qualities, and conditions of such evidence. Only by doing this will we be able to make any spiritual progress. When we abandon this dependance and follow our heart and conscience within the Qur'an's light and guidance, then, if God wills, we will find the enlightenment for which we are looking. As the German philosopher Immanuel Kant once said: 'I felt the need to leave behind all the books I have read in order to believe in God'.

Undoubtedly, the grand Book of the Universe and the book of humanity's true nature, as well as their commentaries, have their proper place and significance. But after we use them, we should put them aside and live with our iman, as it were, face to face. This might sound rather abstract to those who have not gone deep into the experience of faith and conscience. But for those whose nights are bright with devotion, and who acquire wings through their longing to aspire to their Lord, the meaning is clear (Gülen, 2000a: 290–1).

Essentially, Gulen stresses the core value of personal faith in God in his interpretative methodology of the Qur'an, which also serves as an introduction to the influence of Sufism in general and of Jalaluddin Rumi in particular on his theology.

Mevlana Jalal ud din Rumi (1207–73 CE) as a source of Gülen's Theology

It is evident that the writings of the Mevlana Jalaladdin Rumi is another significant source in Gülen's theological construction. One of Gulen's main works and, according to Celik (2008: 15) the most systematic fruit of his authorship, are the three volumes of *Emerald Hills of the Heart: Key Concepts in the Practice of Sufism*, translated from the Turkish Kalbin Zümrüt Tepeleri. In these three volumes, Gülen (2004b; 2004c; 2008) discusses a number of key terms in the teachings and the practice of the Sufi *tariqa*. Although Rumi is certainly not the only author quoted in these volumes, he is the Sufi poet quoted most often throughout Gülen's works.

Arguably there are two reasons for this connection between Gülen and the Movement and Rumi and his specific interpretation of the Sufi path. First, it is a priority in Rumi's as much as in Gülen's thought to be focused upon the personal relationship of the believer and the Transcendent God. The quotation given *supra* demonstrates that iman or personal faith in God is the core of Islam for Gülen, and in fact the sole ultimate concern. The same is the case for Rumi: the core of the Mevlana movement that is named after 'Our Master' (maulana) Jalaluddin Rumi is the liturgy of the Sema in which the dancers perform a dhikr (continuous mindfulness of God). Many people go to see the 'whirling dervishes' as a cultural phenomenon, but in fact their performance is a liturgy, a public service to or worship of God. Public meetings of the Societies of Dialogue in the United Kingdom (London and Birmingham), the Islam and Dialogue Foundation in the Netherlands and of the Rumi Forum in Washington DC have included such liturgical performances, which show the close association between the Gülen movement and the Sufi tariqa in the tradition of Mevlana Rumi. The second characteristic that unites both teachers is the central place of the notion of love. Rumi is known as the founder of the 'Sufi Path of Love' (Chittick, 1983), and 'love' is also one of the central notions in Gülen's writings. In his introduction to Can's book about Rumi, Gülen defends this notion as follows:

> Some people do not consider it proper to use the phrase "love of God" in the Islamic tradition. Like many of God's lovers, Rumi, in a way that is appropriate to the holiness and exaltedness of God, courageously defended that the concept of love of God should be above all human concepts of love and relationships. He left a legacy of ambiguous divine love which was open for interpretation to the generations that followed him. (Gülen in Can, 2004: xvii)

In the same text, Gülen adds a note that is of importance to properly understand both Rumi and Gülen, namely, the 'love of God' is deeply shaped by the Islamic tradition and therefore it goes together with a deep love for God's messenger, Prophet Muhammad. The same is the case with Gülen, as study of the Prophet Muhammad (Gülen, 2005) shows. It is important to notice this, since the popularity of Rumi in the Western world leads many people to disregard the roots of Sufism within Islam; while there are obviously non-Sufi ways to be a Muslim as, for example, in the traditions of Salafism and Wahhabism it is arguably not possible to be a Sufi outside Islam. Gülen's thinking is deeply rooted in the classical Muslim tradition.

While the notion of 'love' is central in the writings of both Rumi and Gülen, there is an obvious difference as well in that Gülen concentrates more on 'love' as a universal dimension of humankind's life and he tries to find ways to let this love be operative not only in religious and interpersonal relations but also in social and political relations. This is one of the major themes in Gülen's books on inter-cultural and inter-faith dialogues, such as *Love and the Essence of Being Human* (Gülen, 2004d) and *Toward a Global Civilization of Love and Tolerance* (Gülen, 2004a).

The stress on love, tolerance and openness that unites Gülen with Mevlana Jalaluddin Rumi is phrased by Gülen as a specific kind of Islam. At times, he refers to 'Turkish Islam' or 'Anatolian Islam' in contrast with Iranian or Arab Islam. Sufism is certainly one of the most important dimensions of this expression as Gülen reveals in an interview with Nevval Sevindi (Sevindi, 2008: 68).

Islam is one, but interpretations and practices are different. There is something called the Turkish Islamic conception. This is a conception that was formed by the thousand-year old Turkish culture and understanding, and reached its highest point with Yunus Emre and Mawlāna Jalāl al-Dīn Rūmī. Mawlāna describes Sufism by saying, 'They asked a divine what Sufism is; he said, finding space in the age of hardships'. The Turkish Islamic conception is entwined with Sufism.

Gulen goes on to comment 'Arab Islam is based on fear of Allah, Turkish Islam is an Islamic understanding based on love of Allah' (Sevindi, 2008: 73). At other places, Gülen connects this idea of an 'Anatolian Islam' with greater openness to modernity, to democracy, to an equal place of women and openness to other cultures and religions.

Bediuzzaman Said Nursi (1878–1960) as a source of Gülen's Theology

When Fethullah Gülen introduces Jalaluddin Rumi, he does so in terms that could be taken to refer to Said Nursi as well.

> In addition to his ascetic life, his fear of God, his chastity, his divine protection from sinfulness, his self-sufficiency, and his pure life that was directed toward the world of the unseen, Rumi's knowledge of God, his love of God, and his utmost longing for God kept him, throughout his life, rising as one of the moons that illuminate the sky of sainthood. His love for God was one that surpassed the normal bounds of love – it was a transcendental love. (Gülen in Can, 2004: xv)

Again, it is clear that the influence of Bediüzzaman Said Nursi and his *Risale-i Nur* collection has been considerable upon Fethullah Gülen and his followers. First, in many of his works Gülen follows the style of reasoning by Nursi, so much, so that one does not immediately notice when he adopts a number of arguments for Divine Unity from Nursi's *Words* at the beginning of his *Essentials of the Islamic Faith* (Nursi, 1992: 299–317; Gülen, 2000a: 9–18). The careful observation of nature leads Nursi (and Gülen) to conclude that there is but One Creator of the universe. While Rumi is the greatest poet of love in the Islamic tradition, Nursi is for Gülen the greatest interpreter of the signs of God in the Universe and the Qur'an. And yet the two approaches, namely, knowledge of the Creator through the creation and awareness of divine love cohere.

Gülen's acquaintance with Nursi began with reading the *Risale-i Nur* when he was appointed to preach and teach in Edirne in 1963; according to Agai, being a member of the *Nurcu* community helped Gülen to gain certain fame, although it excluded him from other Muslim communities. Gülen's ideas about religious education, and his first practical steps towards establishing summer camps, student dorms and later schools were obviously inspired by ideas in the *Nurcu* movement (Agai, 2004: 140–5).

Although Gülen has always denied his belonging to the *Nurcu* movement in the strict sense of the word, some scholars see so many similarities that they write about Gülen's followers as the neo-Nur movement (Yavuz, 2003: 179). Indeed, at places where Gülen's faith-based service communities come together works by both authors are marketed.

There are differences, however, between Gülen and Nursi in their thought. First, Nursi is more straightforwardly an intellectual who at least in the second period of his life, the so-called 'New Said' in contrast with the 'Old Said' (Vahide, 2005: 15) wished to concentrate on Qur'anic study. Gülen is an intellectual as well, but he is more interested in exploring the possibilities of translating intellectual ideas into practice. Yavuz describes Gülen's ideas as a 'theology of action', characterized by three traditional Islamic principles: '*hizmet* (rendering service to religion and state), *himmet* (giving donations and protecting good work) and *ihlas* (seeking God's appreciation for every action)'.

There is a second difference between Nursi and Gülen in that Said Nursi wrote about the West and its intellectual traditions in a negative way. While the 'Old Said' was interested in philosophy and sciences, and involved in politics, the 'New Said' decided to concentrate on the religious sciences of the Qur'an alone. Although he sometimes wrote about the possibility for collaboration between Muslims and Christians, this collaboration was mainly a defence against the powers of atheism. Consequently, most of the followers of Said Nursi tend to focus on other Islamic countries when they want to spread his writings, although they may be interested in the West as well. In the case of Gülen, it is quite clear that he and his network are interested in spreading into the Western world with less emphasis on Arabic-speaking Islamic nations.

There are therefore both similarities and differences between Said Nursi and Fethullah Gülen in their thought, influence and activities. In his lifetime, Nursi proposed both to the Ottoman government and its secular republican successor state the need for a university in Anatolia that would combine traditional and modern teaching methods, the teaching of the religious sciences and modern sciences. Such a project Nursi suggested (who was born in Nurs, a small village in the province of Bitlis in eastern Anatolia) should be established in the nearby city of Van (Vahide, 2005: 8). Nursi proposed this idea as a means of providing new opportunities to this impoverished Anatolian and largely Kurdish region of Turkey, and he even secured some funding for this university (the *Medresetü z-Zehrā*) on the shores of Lake Van, but the First World War initially prevented its building (Vahide, 2005: 10). Gülen is said to have proposed a similar idea for a university where scholars and students from the three Abrahamic religions would come together, in Urfa or in Harran, two places in Anatolia associated with prophet Abraham (Gülen, 2000a: 284 and 294). The most significant aspect of this proposal was probably that it was offered to Pope John Paul II when Gülen visited him in 1998. In addition, therefore, as Gülen was one of the first Muslim leaders to visit the Vatican such openness to dialogue marks another difference between him and Nursi.

Jalaluddin Rumi, Said Nursi and Fethullah Gülen

By focusing again on the similarities between Jalaluddin Rumi, Said Nursi and Fethullah Gülen, there are parallels between them in their respective socio-historical contexts.

First, the three thinkers represent the model of Islam described by Gülen in his interviews with Nevval Sevindi (2008) as an 'Anatolian style of Islam': an open, tolerant style of Islam with the love of God as central characteristic. Even though Rumi was born in present-day Afghanistan, he settled in Konya and is therefore considered as a representative of the Anatolian Sufi tradition just as Nursi or Gülen, although neither of them has been a Sufi teacher or master (*shaikh*) in the traditional sense of the word.

A second similarity that has been mentioned by Gülen in referring to Rumi, but that may just as well be said about Nursi or about Gülen himself is the insight that love grows through hardships and suffering. For Rumi, this yearning that grows out of suffering is a yearning for the lost participation in God, as expressed in the famous 'Song of the Reed' at the beginning of his *Mathnawi* in which the characteristic wailing sound of the *ney* (reed flute) is interpreted as its lamentation over being severed from the reed bed. In his own life, Rumi suffered since he was forcefully separated from two of his spiritual friends, Shams al-dīn Tabrizi and Husām al-dīn Chalabi.

Nursi suffered in a different way, since he spent 25 years from 1925 either in prison or under house arrest because of the perception by the authorities that he opposed the political changes in the transition from the Ottoman Empire to the secular Republic of Turkey. Following the establishment of the secular republic Nursi affirmed that he was no longer interested in politics and that he only wanted to spread the Qur'anic message. Subsequently, Nursi interpreted this lengthy period of isolation as a lesson that God wanted to give him in the 'school of Joseph', referring to Prophet Joseph who 'languished in prison for a number of years' (Surah 12:42).

Gülen was imprisoned in 1971 following accusations that were similar to the allegations that were used against Said Nursi, and he describes his experiences as a 'school of Joseph' as well (Agai, 2004: 144). From within his writings as well as observations of his life, Gulen seems to have adopted a life of frugality and asceticism for himself. In his *Emerald Hills of the Heart* he suggests that the notion of *taqwa* (piety; also: fearing God) on the way of the Sufi does not only imply a strict observance of the *shari'a* by avoiding what is forbidden but also a cautious use of what is permitted.

Conclusion

> Come, come, whoever you are.
> Wanderer, worshipper, lover of living, it doesn't matter
> Ours is not a caravan of despair.
> Come even if you have broken your vow a thousand times,
> Come, yet again, come, come.   (Rumi in Citlak & Bingul, 2007: 81)

For Gülen, the essence of Islam as in the very word 'Islam' involves surrender (to God), peace, contentment and security. He cites a well-known episode from the life of the Prophet. When asked what practice of the faith is most beneficial, Muhammad remarks that feeding the hungry and offering *salaam* (the greeting of peace) to both friend and stranger are the most beneficial (Gulen, 2004a: 56).

Essentially, the pursuit of peace and seeking to establish peace are fundamental to Islam. If 'peace is better' as the Qur'an teaches (Surah 4:128) then the true Muslim will work towards peace. For Gülen, love and empathy are ultimately rooted in the attributes of God. God is All-forgiving, All merciful and All-compassionate.

This expression of a contemporary religio-social movement emanating from Turkey offers an eirenic, socially cohesive, non-confrontational Islam rooted in the Qur'an, which calls all Muslims to engage in tolerance and forgiveness because of the very nature of God (Surah 64:14). This is a uniquely creative platform for a dialogue of civilizations and faiths in modern Britain in the post 9/11 and 7/7 world.

Bibliography

Agai, B. (2003) 'The Gülen Movement's Islamic Ethic of Education'. In: M. Hakan Yavuz, John L. Esposito (Eds). *Turkish Islam and the Secular State: the Gülen Movement.* Syracuse, NY: Syracuse University Press.

Buchan, J. (1957) *Greenmantle,* London: Penguin.

Burrell, David B. C. S. C. (2004) *Faith and Freedom. An Interfaith Perspective,* Malden MA, Oxford: Blackwell Publishing.

Can, Ş. (2004) *Fundamentals of Rumi's Thought: A Mevlevi Perspective.* Forword by M. Fethullah Gülen (trans. Zeki Saritoprak and Cüneyt Eroğlu), Somerset, NJ: The Light.

Çelik, G. (2008) *The Gülen Movement. Building Social Cohesion through Dialogue and Education,* Nieuwegein.

Chittick, W. (1983) *The Sufi Path of Love: The Spiritual Teachings of Rumi,* Albany, NY: State University of New York Press.

Citlak, M. Fatih and Bingul, H. (2007) *Rumi and His Sufi Path of Love,* New Jersey: Light Inc.

De la Porta, D. and Diani, M. (2006 2nd edn) *Social Movements: An Introduction,* Malden, MA: Blackwell Publishing.

Gülen, F. (1997) *Fatiha Üzerine Mülahazalar,* Izmir: Nil.

— (2000a) *Criteria or Lights of the Way,* London: Truestar.

— (2000b) *Essentials of the Islamic Faith.* (trans. Ali Ünal), Fairfax, VA: The Fountain.

— (2004a) *Toward a Global Civilization of Love and Tolerance,* Somerset, NJ: The Light Inc.

— (2004b) *Emerald Hills of the Heart: Key Concepts in the Practice of Sufism,* (trans. Ali Ünal). Vol. 1, Rutherford, NJ: The Light, Inc.

— (2004c) *Emerald Hills of the Heart: Key Concepts in the Practice of Sufism,* (trans. Ali Ünal). Vol. 2, Somerset, NJ: The Light, Inc.

— (2004d) *Love and the Essence of Being Human,* Istanbul: Journalists and Writers Foundation.

— (2005) *Muhammad, the Messenger of God: Aspects of His Life,* (trans. Ali Ünal). Somerset, NJ: The Light, Inc.

— (2008) *Emerald Hills of the Heart: Key Concepts in the Practice of Sufism,* Vol. 3, Somerset, NJ: Tughra Books 2008

Hefner, R. W. (Ed.) (2004) *Democratic Civility: The History and Cross-Cultural Possibility of a Modern Political Ideal,* New Brunswick: Transaction Publishers.

Michel, T. (2006) 'Gülen as Educator and Religious Leader'. In: *The Fountain,* pp. 101–13.

Nursi, S. (1992) *The Words. From the Risale-i Nur Collection,* (trans. from the Turkish by Şükran Vahide), Istanbul: Sözler Neşriyat.

— (1996) *The Damascus Sermon. Translated from the Turkish,* 'Hutbe-I Şâmiye' by Şükran Vahide. Second, revised and expanded edition. Istanbul: Sözler Neşriyat va Sanayi A.Ş.

— (1997) *Letters 1928–1932. From the Risale-i Nur Collection, 2,* (trans. from the Turkish 'Mektûbat' by Şükran Vahide). Second, revised edition. Istanbul: Sözler Neşriyat.

— (2004) *Signs of Miraculousness: The Inimitability of the Qur'an's Conciseness. From the Risale-i Nur Collection, 6,* Original title Ishārāt al-I'jāz fi Mazann al-Ijāz (1918). (trans. Şükran Vahide), Istanbul: Sözler Publications.

Sevindi, N. (2008) *Contemporary Islamic Conversations. M. Fethullah Gülen on Turkey, Islam, and the West,* Edited and with an Introduction by Ibrahim M. Abu-Rabi'. (trans. Abdullah T. Antepli), Albany, NY: State University of New York Press.

Ünal, A. (2006) *The Qur'an: with Annotated Interpretation in Modern English,* Somerset, NJ: The Light.

Ünal, A. and Williams, A. (2000) *Fethullah Gülen: Advocate of Dialogue,* Fairfax, VA: The Fountain.

Vahide, S. (2005) 'Bediuzzaman Said Nursi and the *Risale-i Nur'.* In: Ian Markham, Ibrahim Ozdemir (Eds). *Globalization, Ethics and Islam: the Case of Bediuzzaman Said Nursi,* Aldershot and Burlington, VT: Ashgate.

Valkenberg, P. (2000) 'Confessing One God amidst Muslims and Jews: an ecumenical theological conversation (II)', in: *International Review of Mission,* 89, pp. 105–14.

White, J. B. (2002) *Islamist Mobilization in Turkey: A Study in Vernacular Politics,* Seattle: University of Washington Press.

Yavuz. M. H. (2003) *Islamic Political Identity in Turkey,* Oxford and New York: Oxford University Press.

Zald, M. and McCarthy, J. (1998) 'Religious Groups as Crucibles of Social Movements'. In: Denerath, N. J., Hall, P. D., Schmitt, T. and Williams, R. H. (Eds). *Sacred Companies: Organizational Aspects of Religion and Religious Aspects of Organizations.* Oxford: Oxford University press.

Index